RADICAL
DEMOCRACY

RADICAL DEMOCRACY

C. Douglas Lummis

Cornell University Press : Ithaca and London

First published 1996 by Cornell University Press.

Printed in the United States of America

Library of Congress Cataloging-in-Publication Data
Lummis, C. Douglas, 1936–
    Radical Democracy / C. Douglas Lummis.
        p.   cm.
    Includes index.
    ISBN 0-8014-3169-7 (alk. paper)
    1. Democracy.   2. Radicalism.   3. World politics.   I. Title.
    JC421.L86 1996   95-40119
    321.8—dc20

♾ The paper in this book meets the minimum requirements of the American National Standard for Information Sciences— Permanence of Paper for Printed Library Materials, ANSI Z39.48-1984.

Paperback printing   10 9 8 7 6 5 4 3

contents

acknowledgments

I wrote most of the first draft of this book during a sabbatical leave from Tsuda College during the year 1987–88. The first half of that year I spent as a visiting research fellow at the Third World Studies Center, University of the Philippines, and I thank TWSC and its then director, Randolf S. David, for granting me not only that status but also one of its most precious privileges, a desk in the library. During that period I had fruitful conversations not only with Randy David but also with TWSC Vice-Director Cynthia Bautista, P. B. Abinales, Alexander Magno, and other TWSC researchers. I also had the privilege of coteaching a political-theory course with Salvador Carlos and learned much from conversations with him. TWSC also sponsored three talks in which I presented first drafts of what became the first three chapters of this book, for which I received lively and thoughtful criticism. I am particularly grateful to Reynoldo Racasa y Ty, who rented us a room in his lovely house and provided a rich and lively education in Philippine politics and society at his dinner table.

During the second half of the year I was a visiting scholar at the Institute for the Study of Social Change at the University of California, Berkeley, and for that appointment I thank both the institute and its director, Troy Duster. The institute sponsored a talk at which I was able to present what was by then a second draft of Chapter 2. During that period R. Jeffrey Lustig let us have the cottage in his back yard in Berkeley, read chapter drafts, gave very helpful criticisms, and even let me beat him at pool sometimes. Thanks Jeff!

The next group I must mention is a little hard to identify, as it has no name. This is a rather vaguely defined study group that meets irregularly, originally organized by Ivan Illich. I had the privilege of joining this group in San Juan, Puerto Rico, in 1988, at Pennsylvania State University in 1988 and 1989 and at Houston, Texas (after the anti-G7 TOES [The Other Economic Summit] conference there), in 1990. The outcome of these meetings was *The Development Dictionary: A Guide to Knowledge as Power*, ed. Wolfgang Sachs (London: Zed Books, 1992). My own contribution to that volume ("Equality," pp. 38–52) overlaps considerably with Chapter 2 of this volume, and I owe much to our conversations at those meetings. I am particularly indebted not only to Illich and Sachs but also to Harry Cleaver, Barbara Duden, Gustavo Esteva, Ashis Nandy, Majid Rahnema, Jean Robert, and Teodor Shanin.

Another experience that influenced this book was my participation in the planning for the series of conferences held in Japan in the summer of 1989 and collectively called The People's Plan for the 21st Century, in particular the year-long discussion that led to the text of the Minamata Declaration. I am especially indebted to my colleague at Pacific-Asia Resource Center (PARC) Muto Ichiyo, from whom I have learned that any theory of democracy or liberation which stops at the national boundary is—at least at this moment in history—an impoverished one.

In addition, I have gained many insights at Tsuda College from coteaching, with my colleague Miura Nagamitsu, a course we designed together as a critical history of progress theory.

The manuscript itself has been read carefully and criticized thoughtfully by—in addition to Lustig—Frank Bardacke, Hanna Pitkin, John Schaar, and Mark Selden. The encouragement I get from these people is the spiritual bread I eat. I owe special thanks to Jeffrey Isaac, the outside reader for Cornell University Press, for his helpful and constructive suggestions. I note in the Introduction my debts to Muro Kenji, Tsurumi Shunsuke, and Sheldon Wolin.

Heartfelt thanks go to Narahara Junko and Yamaga Junko of Lingua Guild for their professional typing.

I thank my father, Keith Lummis, who gave me, among many other things, the lines that could stand as the epigraph for this book:

You don't have to be smart.
All you have to do is stop,
And think.

Typically the worst moment in acknowledgments by a male author comes at the very end, when he thanks the Patient Wife. Here, I prefer to thank my wife, Saito Yasuko, not for her patience but for her impatience. She has helped me to keep the project in proper perspective with her occasional, "What? Are you *still* working on that thing?"

You would think that with all this help the manuscript that follows would be a whole lot better than it is. The reader will know whom to blame for the discrepancy.

The seed of this book is my article "The Radicalism of Democracy," which appeared in *democracy* 2, no. 4 (Fall 1982), copyright © 1982 by The Common Good Foundation. This article was also published (in Japanese) in *The Radical Constitution of Japan* (Tokyo: Shobunsha, 1987). Chapter 2 originally appeared as "Development against Democracy" in *Alternatives: Social Transformation and Human Governance* 16, no. 1 (Winter 1991), copyright © 1991 by *Alternatives*; used with permission of Lynn Rienner Publishers, Inc. It also appeared as "Development Is Anti-Democratic" in *Kasarinlan* 6, no. 3 (1st Quarter 1991). Some sections included in this chapter are revisions of passages that also appeared in Wolfgang Sachs, ed., *The Development Dictionary* (London: Zed Books, 1992). Chapter 5 was included in *A Book of Friends*, a *Festschrifft* celebrating the sixty-fifth birthday of Ivan Illich. I thank the editors of these publications for their permission to use these materials.

C. D. L.

Tokyo

RADICAL
DEMOCRACY

extracts

And there she stood, with her eyes fixed on the President and his wife, while the endless stream of humanity passed them, shaking hands. . . . And in all that crowd there was no one besides herself who felt the mockery of this exhibition. . . . They thought it was a democratic institution, this droll aping of monarchical forms. —Henry Adams

. . . the whole body of argument against "democracy," . . . the more consistently and better reasoned it is, will turn into an argument against the essentials of politics. —Hannah Arendt

Democracy arose from men's thinking that if they are equal in any respect, they are equal absolutely. —Aristotle

Democracy means government by discussion, but it is only effective if you can stop people talking. —Clement Attlee

At no time, at no place, in solemn convention assembled, through no chosen agents, had the American people officially proclaimed the United States to be a democracy. The Constitution did not contain the word or any word lending countenance to it, except possibly the mention of "We, the people" in the preamble. . . . When the Constitution was framed no respectable person called himself or herself a democrat. —Mary Ritter Beard

Democracies cannot dispense with hypocrisy any more than dictatorship can with cynicism. —George Bernanos

Judge Boshoff: Democracy, doesn't it pre-suppose a developed community, democracy where you have one man, one vote?
Steve Biko: Yes, it does, it does, and I think it is part of the process of developing the community.

A perfect democracy is the most shameless thing in the world. —Edmund Burke

The devil was the first democrat. —Lord Byron

Democracy is, by the nature of it, a self-canceling business and gives in the long run a net result of zero. —Thomas Carlyle

Democracy is the art of saying "Nice doggie" until you can find a rock. —Wynn Catlin

You can never have a revolution in order to establish a democracy. You must have a democracy in order to have a revolution. —G. K. Chesterton

It has been said that democracy is the worst form of government except all those other forms that have been tried from time to time. —Winston Churchill

Democracy is the healthful life-blood which circulates through the veins and arteries, which supports the system, but which ought never to appear externally, and as the mere blood itself. —S. T. Coleridge

. . . democracy is a raft. You cannot easily overturn it. It is a wet place, but it is a pretty safe one. —Joseph Cook

If the people be governors, who shall be governed? —John Cotton

There is one safeguard known generally to the wise, which is an advantage and security to all, but especially to democracies as against despots. What is it? Distrust. —Demosthenes

It cannot be reconciled with any philosophy of democracy that 50,000,000 white folk of the British Empire should be able to make the destiny of 450,000,000 yellow, brown, and black people a matter of solely their own internal decision. —W. E. B. Du Bois

Democracy has failed because so many fear it. They believe that wealth and happiness are so limited that a world full of intelligent, healthy and free people is impossible, if not undesirable. So, the world stews in blood, hunger, and shame. The fear is false, yet naught can face it but Faith. —W. E. B. Du Bois

An other publique weale was amonge the Atheniensis, where equalitie was of astate amonge the people. . . . This maner of gouernaunce was called in greke *Democratia*, in latine, *Popularis potentia*, and in englisshe the rule of the comminaltie. —Sir Thomas Elyot

The democrat is a young conservative; the conservative is an old democrat. The aristocrat is the democrat ripe and gone to seed. —Emerson

. . . Two cheers for Democracy: one because it admits variety and two because it permits criticism. Two cheers are quite enough: there is no occasion to give three. —E. M. Forster

Democracy is based upon the conviction that there are extraordinary possibilities in ordinary people. —Harry Emerson Fosdick

We are now forming a republican government. Real liberty is neither found in despotism or the extremes of democracy, but in moderate governments. —Alexander Hamilton

They were not summoned aristocratically . . . but invited democratically after a popular manner to Supper. —Philemon Holland

Democracy is like love in this: it cannot be brought to life by others in command. —Sidney Hook

I swear to the Lord
I still can't see
Why Democracy means
Everybody but me.
—Langston Hughes

Democracy is not so much a new form of political life as a dissolution and disorganization of the old forms. It is simply a resolution of government into the hands of the people, a taking down of that which has before existed, and a recommitment of it to its original sources, but is by no means a substitution of anything else in its place. —Henry James, Sr.

. . . it is not possible to derive from the proliferation of spaces and the ultimate indeterminacy of the social the impossibility of a society signifying itself—and thus thinking itself—as a totality, or the incompatibility of this totalizing moment with the project for a radical democracy. —Ernesto Laclau and Chantal Mouffe

. . . surely nothing in ancient alchemy was more irrational than the notion that increased ignorance in the elective body will be converted into increased capacity for good government in the representative body; that the best way to improve the world and secure rational progress is to place government more and more under the control of the least enlightened classes. The day will come when it will appear one of the strangest facts in the history of human folly that such a theory was regarded as liberal and progressive. —William Edward Hartpole Lecky

In Switzerland they had brotherly love, five hundred years of democracy and peace and what did they produce? The cuckoo clock! —Harry Lime, in *The Third Man*

As I would not be a slave, so would I not be a master. This expresses my idea of democracy. Whatever differs from this, to the extent of the difference, is no democracy. —Abraham Lincoln

A democratic society might be defined as one . . . in which the majority is always prepared to put down a revolutionary minority. —Walter Lippmann

Democ'acy gives every man
The right to be his own oppressor.
—James Russell Lowell

[The Pueblo people] had nearly a hundred republics in America centuries before *the* American Republic was conceived; and they have maintained their ancient democracy through all the ages, unshamed by the corruption of a voter, the blot of defalcation or malfeasance in office. —Charles Fletcher Lummis

Go thou, and first establish democracy in thy household. —Lycurgus

I have long been convinced that institutions purely democratic must, sooner or later, destroy liberty or civilization, or both. —Thomas Macaulay

Let any competently instructed person turn over in his mind the great epochs of scientific invention and social change during the last two centuries, and consider what would have occurred if universal suffrage had been established at any one of them. Universal suffrage, which to-day excludes free trade from the United States, would certainly have prohibited the spinning jenny and the power-loom. It would certainly have forbidden the threshing machine. It would have prevented the adoption of the Gregorian Calendar; and it would have restored the Stuarts. —Sir Henry Maine

A proper measure of democracy should be put into effect in the army, chiefly by abolishing the feudal practice of bullying and beating and by having officers and men share weal and woe. Once this is done, unity will be achieved between officers and men, the combat effectiveness of the army will be greatly increased, and there will be no doubt of our ability to sustain the long, cruel war. —Mao Tse-Tung

The general will is always wrong. Wrong inasmuch as it objectively counteracts the possible transformation of society into more humane ways of life. In the dynamic of corporate capitalism, the fight for democracy thus tends to assume anti-democratic forms. —Herbert Marcuse

Democracy is the constitution of the Species. —Karl Marx

Under democracy, one party always devotes its chief energies to trying to prove the other is unfit to rule—and both commonly succeed, and are right. —H. L. Mencken

The only remedy for democrats is soldiers. —Wilhelm von Merchel

Thence to the famous Orators repair,
Those antient, whose resistless eloquence
Wielded at will that fierce democratie,
Shook the Arsenal, and fulmin'd over *Greece*
To *Macedon*, and *Artaxerxes* Throne.
—John Milton

The love of equality in a democracy, limits ambition to the sole desire, to the sole happiness, of doing greater services to our country than the rest of our fellow citizens. —Montesquieu

The problem of democracy is not the problem of getting rid of kings. It is the problem of clothing the whole people with the elements of kingship.

To make kings and queens out of a hundred million people: that is the Problem of American democracy. —F. C. Morehouse

Democracy might therefore almost in a sense be termed that practice of which science is the theory. —Joseph Needham

Man's capacity for justice makes democracy possible, but man's inclination to injustice makes democracy necessary. —Reinhold Niebuhr

Boldly addressing the jury, he [Feargus O'Connor] declared that he stood up in the defense of the working men of England. . . . He avowed himself a Chartist—a democrat if they liked—in the fullest sense of the word, and declared that if his life hung upon the abandonment of his principles he would scorn to hold it on so base a tenure. —Frank Peel

Assassination found no advocate or defender in the old Democrat Baines. His aim was not to shoot the masters, but to rouse the people en masse to assert their rights as citizens to a share in the Government; to overthrow what he called the "bloody rule of kings and aristocrats," and establish democracy in its place. Like the great bulk of his class he was not sufficiently enlightened to appreciate the value of machinery, in fact he regarded it as wholly a curse. —Frank Peel

In every village there will rise some miscreant, to establish the most grinding tyranny by calling himself the people. —Sir Robert Peel

Democracy is a process by which the people are free to choose the man who will get the blame. —Laurence J. Peter

It is a pleasant change to be in a country that isn't ruled by its own people. —Prince Philip (on visiting Paraguay)

Sometimes democracy must be bathed in blood. —Auguste Pinochet

Democracy is clearly most appropriate for countries which enjoy an economic surplus and least appropriate for countries where there is an economic insufficiency. —David Morris Potter

[Tom Paine] was as democratic as nature, as impartial as sun and rain. —Marilla M. Richer

We must be the great arsenal of democracy. —Franklin Delano Roosevelt

If there were a people consisting of gods, they would be governed democratically; so perfect a government is not suitable to men. —Jean Jacques Rousseau

A democratic orientation does not grow from and cannot coexist with the present bureaucratic and "meritorian" ethic. It is an alternative to the present ethic, not an expansion or outgrowth of it. —John Schaar

Does the British Empire rest on universal and equal voting rights for all of its inhabitants? It could not survive for a week on this foundation; with their terrible majority, the coloreds would dominate the whites. In spite of that the British Empire is a democracy. The same applies to France and the other powers. —Carl Schmitt

Democracy . . . is more cruel than wars or tyrants. —Seneca

These reactions of disgust with democracy are natural enough where Capitalism, having first produced a huge majority of proletarians with no training in management, responsibility, or the handling of big money, nor any notion of the existence of such a thing as political science, gives this majority the vote for the sake of gaining party advantages by popular support. —George Bernard Shaw

[The leaders of Trade Unionism] are democrats, not because of their faith in the judgment, knowledge, initiative of the masses, but because of their experience of mass ignorance, gullibility, and sheepishness. —George Bernard Shaw

In a democracy you can be respected though poor, but don't count on it. —Charles Merrill Smith

In wicked men there is a democracy of wild lusts and passions. —J. Smith

. . . in the fierce and eventful democraties of Greece and Rome. —Sydney Smith

Democracy is based in the existence of a strong hierarchy. The oligarchy of gross success seekers must have an eager troop of underlings who never cease to work in the interest of their leaders and who derive little material profit from their activity. It is necessary to keep this type of petty nobility in a state of excitement by lavishing them with tokens of friendship and by arousing them with feelings of honor while speaking to them in idealistic phrases. National glory, the domination of natural forces by science, the march of humanity toward enlightenment—this is the nonsense which is heard constantly in the speeches of democratic orators. —Georges Sorel

People who want to understand democracy should spend less time in the library with Aristotle and more time on the buses and in the subway. —Simeon Strunsky

Democracy, which shuts the past against the poet, opens the future before him. —Alexis de Tocqueville

Democraties do not nourish game and pleasures like unto Monarchies. —Edward Topsell

American democracy is the inalienable right to sit on your own front porch, in your pajamas, drinking a can of beer and shouting out "Where else is this possible?" —Peter Ustinov

Democracy is the recurrent suspicion that more than half the people are right more than half of the time. —Elwyn Brooks White

Thunder on! Stride on! Democracy. Strike with vengeful stroke! —Walt Whitman

It would sometimes be easier to believe in democracy, or to stand for it, if the [19th-century] change had not happened and it were still an unfavorable or factional term. —Raymond Williams

Knowledge—Zzzzzp! Money—Zzzzzp!—Power! That's the cycle democracy is built on! —Tennessee Williams

The world must be made safe for democracy. —Woodrow Wilson

"I want to go to Egypt," said Madeleine, still smiling faintly. "Democracy has shaken my nerves to pieces." —Henry Adams

introduction

Sometime around 1980 my friend Muro Kenji dropped by, bubbling with excitement (as is his wont) after a conversation with his mentor and friend, the philosopher Tsurumi Shunsuke. "We live in an interesting time," he said. "Democracy is radical *everywhere*. It is subversive in every system and in every country: in the United States, in the USSR, in Japan, in China, in the Philippines, in Africa and Latin America—everywhere!" There was something fascinating about this old/new, simple/complex, obvious/obscure idea. And it was curious to see someone so excited about a principle that, according to E. M. Forster, deserves two cheers, but never three.

About the same time a letter arrived from the United States announcing a new journal called *democracy* and asking if there were any radical democrats in Japan whom I could recommend as contributors.[1] "Radical democrats"—the idea began to grow in my mind. It was an experience a little like falling in love with the girl (or boy) next door—this being you had always known suddenly appears so new, so fresh, so . . . unprecedented. I had been some kind of movement activist since the early 1960s, both in the United States and in Japan, one of those people never able to pass over the threshold to becoming a Marxist but always dependent on the power of the Marxist critique of the liberal state and liberal economics. In the movement politics of those times, Marxism was always construed as the position to the "left" of democracy, that is, as more "radical"; democrats, on the other hand, were conceived as standing in an uncomfortable middle ground between Marxism and left liberals (and difficult to distinguish from the latter). This spatial metaphor of left-center-right, dating from the French Revolution, has had extraordinary power over the way we arrange, as it were, our politics. It is difficult for one whose political "position" is conceived as located "between" two others to avoid thinking of that position as a kind of compromise or mongrel, without clear principles of its own. It began to occur to me that the Tsurumi-Muro formula ("Democracy is subversive *everywhere*") could be a basis for rearranging this spatial image. With democracy conceived as *the* radical position, as radicalism itself, all other political positions, and the relationships between them, would appear in a new light. This image might be both a more accurate reflection of political realities and also a way of arming democratic theory with greater critical power.[2]

More than a decade has passed since I first began to conceive the idea for this book. In that time we have seen fierce democratic movements in such various countries as Poland, China, Burma, the Philippines. Regime after regime in eastern Europe, and finally in the Soviet Union itself, has been brought down in the name of democracy. At the same time there has been a new wave of activity in the field of democratic theory. Whereas for years it had been a good bet that any book with "democracy" in the title would be a dreary reiteration of the virtues of the status quo in the northern industrial countries, a new generation of theorists was arising that was calling democracy, yes, "radical."[3] While George Bush was proclaiming that during his regime democracy had "triumphed," others were constructing, or rediscovering, a notion of democracy which could serve as the basis for a critique not only of the politics of Ronald Reagan and George Bush but of the ideological framework that Reagan and Bush shared with their liberal opposition. Since the mid-1980s or so the discourse on democracy has become—for the first time in years—*interesting*. This book is intended as a contribution to this discourse.

Interestingly, when I worked at the Third World Studies Center at the University of the Philippines, I had difficulty explaining my choice of study to friends not only in Japan and the United States but also in the Philippines. It seemed odd to them that I would go to the Philippines not to study the Philippines per se but to prepare a work on democratic theory. A hidden prejudice is at work here. No one finds it odd if a scholar who visits Harvard does not specialize in the politics or culture of Massachusetts. No one even finds it odd for a scholar to travel to Cornell to study Southeast Asia, or to the University of London to study Africa. But the reverse is not true: a scholar who visits a Third World country is presumed to want to study that country.

I deliberately chose the University of the Philippines to violate this fixed idea, in accordance with the general principle that if you violate a fixed idea, *probably* you will learn something unexpected. But my choice of the Philippines was by no means a random one. Only a year had passed since the People's Power Revolution of February 1986. "People's Power" is, after all, only a translation into English of the Greek words *demos* and *kratia*. People's power—radical democracy—had done something seemingly impossible: driven a corrupt, well-armed, and filthy-rich dictator out of power and out of the country, not simply by the people's winning an election but by their putting their lives on the line to see to it that the election result was honored. I wanted to go to a place where democracy was not simply a worn-out slogan but a living idea, a principle that truly mattered and that people spoke about with passion and commitment.

Things did not turn out quite that way. Although in the last years of the Marcos regime the public mood was electric with excitement and radical hope, by the spring of 1987 it was falling into disillusion. Radical hope, which is the essence of a people's movement (I shall have more to say about this in Chapter 5), had created a political situation accurately called revolutionary, but the object of this hope had been a liberal politician, Corazon Aquino, seeking to win an election. Radical democracy had expended its energy in the reestablishment of liberal politics. Land reform bogged down, the civil war continued, and 1987 was a gloomy year.

But in spite of this disillusion, rich and urgent discourse on democracy had not come to an end; it had only shifted to the question of what had gone or was going wrong. Marxists were amazed that democracy had done so much, left liberals that it had done so little. Everyone realized that the notion they had held about democracy had turned out to be a little bit wrong. So it was, after all, an intellectually stimulating—though unhappy—time.

Moreover, I was not mistaken in expecting that I would learn something unexpected. In discussing democratic theory with Philippine intellectuals, and in reading about it in their work, I kept slamming into the same brick wall, the wall called "development." The conflict between democracy and development is something more difficult to see from the perspective of a northern industrial country than from the perspective of the Third World. In fact, most books on democratic theory written in the northern industrial countries have very little to say about the Third World: the latter falls under "area studies" or "development economics," which are different "fields" from political theory. But if democratic theory matters in the world, it matters in the Third World, where some of the great democratic struggles have taken, and are taking, place. In the Philippines I realized that anyone who is going to talk about democracy in the Third World (or for that matter, in any world that has a Third World in it) must deal with the problem of development and its antidemocratic bias. This is the subject of Chapter 2.

This book makes no institutional proposals. When I mention institutions I do so to illustrate a principle, not to make a proposal.[4] I do not consider proposals unimportant—on the contrary, they are the very stuff of political discourse—but here I explore the nature of democracy as a principle in human affairs, as distinct from the various institutions or actions through which people seek to realize this principle in practice. All too often these become fused and confused, and we speak as if democracy were free elections, or legal guarantees of human rights, or workers' control. Yet we do not say, for example, that peace is peace treaties, or that justice is trial by jury. That peace may be brought about by peace treaties or justice by jury trials, are hypotheses that, as we know from experience, prove true in some cases but not in all. We are able to judge the relative truth, or success, of these hypotheses because we have notions of justice and peace independent of our notions of trials and treaties. Similarly (as will be argued below) "elections," "legal guarantees," or "workers' control" are hypotheses. To judge their worth, we need as clear as possible an idea of the principle in human relations which it is alleged they can bring into being. This book is intended as a contribution to *that* aspect of the democratic discourse.

Put differently, this book is not intended as a work in utopian theory. I have no proposals that no one has ever thought of before. On the contrary, many fine democratic proposals are already on the table and have been for years, some even for centuries. There are democratic movements on every continent, in each country, in virtually every type of institution. Each of these movements faces a different situation, which requires a different solution. Democratization of the big-money politics of the North is not the same as the democratization of a military dictatorship in the South, or of a factory, a plantation, a "socialist" bureaucracy, a sexist family, a theocracy. Movements fighting for the democratization of these and other institutions all have their methods and aims and hopes. I have no new set to replace the ones that people are fighting for in their real situations. On the contrary, it is my hope that this book can make a small contribution by lending some theoretical support to "actually existing" democratic movements as well as by offering some criteria by which democrats may evaluate, criticize, and clarify their own aims and methods.

In this sense, this book is not really an argument about why democracy is better than other political forms. Rather, it is addressed to people who already think so, or who think they think so. It is not designed to explain why one ought to think so, but to explore some of the consequences of thinking so. If one takes the radical democratic position, what does that turn out to entail? To try to think this through, I have sometimes used the method of hypothesizing an imaginary, or ideal-type, character, the Radical Democrat. This personage will be one of the subjects of examination, and also one of the participants, in what follows, playing a role rather like that of an expert witness. Concerning this issue, what does the radical democrat think? In this situation, what does the radical democrat do? And in so thinking or doing, what does the radical democrat become? The answers are not binding: one may know them, and choose otherwise. But if the argument here is successful, the person choosing otherwise will at least have difficulty calling that choice "democracy."

1

radical democracy

> In the case of a word like *democracy*, not only is there no
> agreed definition but the attempt to make one is resisted from
> all sides. It is almost universally felt that when we call a coun-
> try democratic we are praising it: consequently the defenders
> of every kind of régime claim that it is a democracy, and fear
> that they might have to stop using the word if it were tied
> down to any one meaning. —George Orwell, "Politics and the
> English Language"

Among political words, surely "democracy" is the most cruelly over-
worked. It has been used to justify revolution, counterrevolution, terror,
compromise, and mediocrity. It has been applied to representative institutions, free-enterprise economies, state-run economies, Leninist party rule,
and dictatorship by plebiscite. Wars have been fought to make the world
safe for it, and atomic bombs have been dropped to establish it on foreign
soil. Counterinsurgency operations are carried out to protect it against
guerrillas who say they are fighting for it. Democracy has been treated as
a whore among political words. And as Orwell points out, most of its regular employers have a vested interest in keeping things that way.

Used in an actual sentence, the word often means nothing. The sentence "I'm for democracy" communicates virtually no information. At
best it shows that the speaker is not a straightforward Nazi or a supporter
of the divine right of kings. The statement is likely to be met with a blank
stare or with a puzzled response like "How nice."

On the other hand there are moments when we want to use it, not as a
kind of brand name but as a real political word live with meaning. This
moment was enacted for me with wonderful symbolism when, after the
February 1986 elections in the Philippines, a friend of mine there, a radical leftist, said to me musingly, "We need to rethink the whole question of
democracy." The radical leftists' line had been to boycott the election, for
the very sensible reason that one can't expect to throw out a military dictator in a democratic election. They had been as astounded as the rest of

the world when the election turned into the People's Power Revolution that drove Ferdinand Marcos out of the country. We don't think of democratic elections as capable of generating that kind of power. This turn of events is certainly food for rethinking. But democracy is hard to rethink, or even to think: which among its many meanings and uses are we to think about? Is it possible to rehabilitate a word that has been so corrupted?

Why We Need a Rectification of Names

In this book I take the position that this rehabilitation is both possible and necessary. "Democracy" was once a word of the people, a critical word, a revolutionary word. It has been stolen by those who would rule over the people, to add legitimacy to their rule. It is time to take it back, to restore to it its critical and radical power. Democracy is not everything, but something. When the word is used in the right place, at the right moment, it is fresh, clear, and true. It is not out of habit or nostalgia that we continue to use it, but because there are times when no other word can say what has to be said. And though the history of its use is a history of hypocrisy and betrayal, democracy is somehow still a virginal political idea. Understood *radically*, it contains a promise yet to be fulfilled.

This is a call, then, for a rectification of names. That means insisting that the word "democracy" be used only to describe democratic things. It means identifying and junking twisted and hypocritical uses. As a first step in this process I shall sketch out what I think have been some of the worst misunderstandings and disfigurements of the word. They follow.

Redefining "the People" (a). Democracy is commonly defined as rule by the people. A classic way to escape the radical implications of this meaning is to narrow what we mean by "the people" by excluding slaves, women, certain races, the poor, or some other group. As a general rule when middle- and upper-class people in whatever country say that they support "people's power," what they mean by "the people" is themselves. When they call for democracy, they are not calling for the class of people which provides them with servants and workers, who produce the surplus on which their wealth and status depends, to take power.

But of course the *demos* of democracy originally meant the poorest and most numerous class of citizens, and democracy in its original sense meant rule by that class. Rule by the middle class—aside from whether such may be good or bad—should be called what it is, not democracy but rule by the middle class.

Redefining "the People" (b). Sometimes a ruling party, or one that seeks to rule, will claim itself democratic by redefining "the people" as "those persons who support the party." "The people" becomes an ideological notion, and those persons who don't accept the ideology fall outside its scope. They may be seen as enemies of the people, or they may become simply invisible nonentities. We see this situation in dictatorships in which the government describes the tiny minority that supports it as "the authentic spokesmen of the people." We also see it in the newspapers of tiny opposition parties where the headline "The People Protest" is followed by an article describing a demonstration of a few dozen or hundred persons.

Redefining "the People" (c). A variation of the above is to represent a party as standing for what the people ought to think, or would think if only they had correct consciousness. There is nothing wrong with this position if it is used to attempt political education. The problem arises when a party represents itself as backed by the authority of the people and as the people's authentic voice, when "the people" represents a theoretical abstraction and not flesh-and-blood persons. For such a party to take power is not the same as for the people to take power.

Democracy Is Caring for the People's Welfare. In his forgetful way, Jimmy Carter once described "the original meaning of democracy" as "government for the people." Many ruling elites would like to strip away the other two-thirds of Abraham Lincoln's famous formula. And I have heard ordinary citizens say the same: a democratic government is one that looks after them. Caring for the people's welfare may be a very good thing, but it is different from democracy. A king may care sincerely for the welfare of his subjects, but the form of government will still be monarchy. A party dictatorship may adopt the policy of serving the people, but it will still be a party dictatorship. Democracy does not mean that the people are blessed with kind or just rulers. It means that they rule themselves.

Democracy Is Having a Ruler Who Is Supported by the People. This situation is easy to confuse with democracy. But the ancient Greeks, who gave us the word "democracy," gave us a different word for this type of rule: "demagogy" (*demagogia: agogos* from *agein,* to lead, to drive). The demagogue is one who gains popular support (= power) by promising to do things for the people or to represent them. Although today the term is usually used for name-calling, its original sense does not necessarily have a negative connotation, especially if the demagogue promises appropriate things and carries out his promises. But it is not democracy. Democracy is not a situation in which the people turn over their power to someone else in exchange for promises.

Democracy Is Development (a). Remarkably, there are still a few people who think of democracy as the government of the future, as the end point in some automatic process of historical development. In reality, democracy is one of the most ancient forms of political rule. The spirit of democracy appears now and then in history, at those moments when people fight for it. If you try to achieve democracy by waiting for it, you will wait forever.

Democracy Is Development (b). It is sometimes argued or implied that economic development itself is democratic. It could be, if "economic development" means that people take control of the centers of economic power—the land, the factories, the trading companies, the economic planning agencies, the banks. But if economic development means only the generation of wealth, then however fine this may be in itself, it is not the same thing as democracy. A wealthy country may be democratic or not, as may a poor one. Democracy is a form of political rule, not a stage of economic development. (For more on this subject see Chapter 4.)

Democracy Is the Free Market. When U.S. government officials and their representatives around the world speak of democracy, very often they mean the capitalist economic system. Now that this notion has been taken up by the governments of Russia and other countries of eastern Europe, it seems to be a candidate for the status of universal truth. The logic is simple: socialist command economy is antidemocratic, therefore the free market is democratic. This view is rather amnesiac, forgetting as it does the problem that socialism was hoped to be the solution to. An analogy is a person suffering from a deadly sickness who takes a medicine that makes him worse and then decides that if he stops taking the medicine he will be well. The original problem persists. The free market divides society into rich and poor, a division that is incompatible with democracy. Its freedom is mainly freedom for the corporation, and the capitalist corporation has itself become an antidemocratic system of rule. The question of how to democratize the main actor in the free market—the corporation—is, for the capitalists and the managers, *the* subversive question.

Democracy Is Anything-but-Communism. This reactive definition is a legacy of the Cold War. One begins by positing something called "communism," which is Evil itself, the very Antidemocracy. Democracy then becomes anything that may be useful in destroying this Evil. It could be dictatorship, martial law, *contra* terrorists, Low Intensity Conflict, death squads, whatever. President Harry S Truman displayed greater honesty when he said of Nicaraguan dictator Anastasio Somoza, "He may be a son-of-a-bitch, but he's our son-of-a-bitch."

Democracy Is Communism. On the other side, at least before the collapse of the socialist states of eastern Europe, some Marxists had tried to convince us that democracy is something subsumed in or transcended by communism. That is, when the private ownership of the means of production is abolished, the question of democracy would automatically wither away, along with the state and politics. On this question, the best rule for democrats is, believe it when you see it. Although there is no reason in principle why the social or communal ownership of property cannot be accompanied by political democracy, historical experience has shown that economic systems guarantee nothing, and the only way to achieve democracy in a socialist state or anywhere else (including now a postsocialist state), is to fight for it.

Democracy Is Democratic Centralism. Central control may be useful or even necessary for a party engaged in struggle, but this utility does not justify calling it democratic. "Democratic centralism" is an expression like "hot ice" or "diverse unity"; just because you can say the words doesn't prove that they mean something. In general, democracy depends on localism: the local areas are where the people live. Democracy doesn't mean putting power some place other than where the people are.

Democracy Is the Name of the U.S. Constitutional System. This definition is what many high school texts give, not only in the United States but around the world. The U.S. constitutional system has worthy aspects, but it should not be taken as the definition of democracy. The people of the United States have not solved the problem of economic democracy—democracy at the workplace. They have not found a way of overcoming their country's antidemocratic imperialism. They have not solved the problem of the massive and growing power concentrated in Washington. They have not rid themselves of their forlorn dream that their problems will be solved by the next in their long line of elective kings. Moreover, they are in great danger of forgetting their own older tradition of radical democracy—the radical democracy that led eighteenth-century American democratic revolutionists to oppose the Constitution of 1789 because it gave too much power to the rich and put too much power at the center.[1]

Democracy Is Free Elections. Free elections are an important democratic method—under some circumstances. In other circumstances elections may be a way for demagogues or rich landowners to take power. In the United States today, where election campaigns have been taken over by the marketing industry, they have little to do with empowerment of the people. The Nicaraguan election of 1990 was a parody of the free election: Vote for A and we will make war on you, vote for B and we won't. When someone sticks a gun in your ribs and says, "Your money or your life!"—that's a "free choice" too.

Democracy Is a Way for the Rich and Poor to Get Along Together Nicely. Liberal democrats argue that there is nothing undemocratic about a big economic gap between rich and poor so long as it is guided by fair rules: equal opportunity, elections, certain guaranteed legal rights, and so forth. But wiser theorists have taught us that extreme economic inequality is not compatible with democracy. Either the poor will use their political power to plunder the rich, or the rich will use their wealth to disempower the poor.[2] Of the two outcomes, the former is the more democratic.

Democracy Is Allowing the People to Have Their Say. This and similar expressions are invented to pull the teeth out of democracy: democracy means giving the people "a voice," "the right to dissent," "a chance to express their views," "their day in court," "an opportunity to stand up and be counted,"—that is, anything but power.

Democratic Power Is Vicarious Power. People are sometimes fooled into believing that they are powerful when they are members of a powerful state or when they are soldiers wielding powerful weapons or when they have real or imaginary connections to people in powerful positions. Powerless boys in uniform feel powerful when they think of the empire they represent; powerless masses imagine themselves powerful when they cheer the dictator who oppresses them; powerless bootlickers feel powerful when they think of the mighty personage whose boots they lick. But democracy doesn't mean "feeling" powerful. It means holding real power.

Democracy Is Not Powerful, but It's Safe. On the other hand, democracy is sometimes portrayed as a kind of drab middle ground, uninteresting but anyway safer than its more adventurous alternatives on the left and right. If democracy meant only the debating and deal-making between occasionally honest elected officials, this image might be apt. But people who have had the good luck to participate in genuinely radical democratic movements, and who have caught a whiff of the real thing, will not see it that way. Radical democracy describes the adventure of human beings creating, with their own hands, the conditions for their freedom. And it is an adventure the main part of which is yet to be undertaken.

Democracy Is Common Sense

If, given its muddled meaning in contemporary discourse, to say that you are for democracy suggests silliness, to say that you are *interested* in it, at least in the so-called democratic countries, may be taken as a sign of bad taste, especially in academic circles. "Democracy" is, of course, a word everyone is willing to use, but to fall in love with it is another matter. As for political philosophies of liberation, we are today in a kind of Hundred

Flowers period. We are surrounded by a profusion of schools of thought, many of which are brilliantly sophisticated and terribly difficult, requiring years of study to understand. In this context to choose democracy as the issue to be interested in is hardly stylish. It is rather like entering a society of gourmet cooks and announcing that you like the taste of plain water.

Yet the possibility is worth considering that human liberation may turn out, after all, to be something as obvious as plain water. We could even hope so. For if it turns out that liberation is so rarefied and complex that even the best minds can only begin to comprehend it at the postgraduate level—that is, after eighteen to twenty years of schooling—then we are faced with a paradox: liberation itself is antidemocratic. Certainly some of our most dedicated theorists of liberation seem sometimes to be bent on perfecting this monstrosity, a theory of popular emancipation incomprehensible to the populace. But from the standpoint of radical democracy, it is a perversion of the idea of liberation to transform it into a means for establishing the authority of a small elite of trained specialists. The truest philosophy of liberation must also be the simplest, if it is to have any liberating effect. And it should not be surprising if such a philosophy, were it found, would prove to be not only as common but as radically essential to human life as plain water.

It is the position of this essay that the right name for this philosophy is radical democracy. Democracy, as Tom Paine taught us, is common sense. This assertion, considered itself at the level of common sense, may seem obvious and untroubling. Considered analytically, however, it raises some questions that require explanation. To say that democracy is common sense does not mean that it is agreed to in the same way by everybody. Though people all over the world may like the word, they do not, as I have argued above, agree about what it means. Moreover, to say that it is common sense does not mean that all people are required, either by the objective structure of the world or by the structure of human perception or cognition, to see it in the same way. It is not like recognizing that the sun gives heat or that the shortest distance between two points is a straight line. Democracy is a form of life which may be chosen, and other choices are possible.

To say that democracy is common sense is to say that its idea is simple—although, one must quickly add, deceptively simple. It is simple in the sense that it can be expressed in ordinary language. But ordinary language is not simple at all. It is generally more complex, in a different way, than the specialized languages of social science and philosophy. Technical terms are supposed to refer only to specific and clearly defined meanings, whereas the words of ordinary language bear all the complexity of the disorderly history of their uses. Be that as it may, ordinary language is the language that we share and that therefore structures our common sense. The democratic discourse, if it is to be itself democratic, must be carried on in this language. It must not be confined to the higher reaches of philosophy and attainable only by those whose professions allow them to spend most of their time studying books. This is not to take an anti-intellectual position or to make a know-nothing refusal to think. It is to say rather that the project of thought itself must be carried forward at the level of common sense, in the language of common sense. It is to say further that the language of common sense is, or can be, an appropriate vehicle for carrying on the project of producing democratic thought. How could one not accept that idea and still be a democrat?

Democracy means that the people rule. To do so, the people must form itself into a body by which power can in principle be held. Democratic theorists have argued that democracy requires consensus, a word very close to common sense. The *Oxford English Dictionary* tells us that "common" comes from the Latin *communis*, which seems to be a combination of *com* (together) and *munis* (bound, under obligation). The latter word is the opposite of *immunis* (not under obligation, exempt). These origins help us to understand what sort of thing the common sense of a democratic community must be. It does not mean an accidental convergence of interests among people who are otherwise morally "immune" to one another. The language of democratic common sense must be the language of moral discourse. Put differently, democratic common sense is something created through moral discourse, choice, and action. It is close to the OED's second definition of the word "common": "Belonging to more than one as a result or sign of cooperation, joint action, or agreement, [as] to *to make common cause with*."

Much of the contempt that often comes with the word "common" (as in calling a person "common" or an idea "commonplace") is sheer antidemocratic prejudice, a common person being one who is not a member of the aristocracy, and a commonplace idea being one that is not part of the language of some elite. The contempt seems to be grounded in a fundamental rejection of the project of finding a language, a mode of discourse, a sense, that binds people together into a community of equals. In contrast to this usage are the positive uses of the word: common right, common cause, the town common, common good or commonwealth (translations of the Latin *res publica*), common law; and the archaic verb "to common," meaning "to talk over in common, confer, b. to come to a common decision, to agree."

There is another way in which democracy is common sense. In political theory, democracy stands as a kind of (often hidden) common denominator out of which all other systems of rule are constructed, and back to which their deconstruction would presumably take us.[3] This point is elaborated in the sections to follow.

Radical Democracy Simply Defined

The basic idea of democracy is simple. To understand what it is we must begin naively, by going back to its root meaning, its *radical* meaning, as a philologist would say. To say that this meaning is simple is not to say that it is simple to implement. But it is simple to put in words.

Democracy is a word that joins *demos*—the people—with *kratia*—power. Here it is wise not to be hasty. Before moving on to interpretations and elaborations we should pause at this first step. Democracy is the name of a political form in which the people have power. But who are the people? What is power? Should the people have the power? How could such a situation be arranged? By what set of institutions could it be guaranteed? Democracy, being only a word and not a proposition, is silent on these questions. That is to say, democracy is not the name of any particular arrangement of political or economic institutions. Rather, it is a situation that political or economic institutions may or may not help to bring about. It describes an ideal, not a method for achieving it.[4] It is not a kind of government, but an end of government; not a historically existing institution, but a historical project.

That is, it is a historical project if people take it up as such and struggle for it. It is impossible to prove that people ought to do so, just as it is impossible to prove that people ought to grow into adulthood. I shall attempt no such proof. But here the near-universal use of the term proves to be an advantage, since it is fair to assume that persons who describe themselves as democrats have committed themselves in some degree to this project. To such people, who use the word as their own, we can speak; and where they have contradicted or betrayed its principle, we can accuse them of contradiction or betrayal.

If the word means what it says, there is democracy where the people have the power. Understood in this way, democracy is one of those beautiful, absolute, clear principles—clear as generalities, like "thou shalt not kill"—that poses a maddening, tantalizing puzzle to humankind. It is because there is no sure, fixed solution to this puzzle—the puzzle of how to realize democracy in our collective life—that our commitment to it can take the form only of a historical project. And however successful institutions may be in coming close to it, democracy itself—like justice, equality, and liberty—remains as a critical standard against which all institutions may be measured.

Standard definitions slip away from this primary idea. The *Oxford English Dictionary* tells us that democracy means "government by the people," the *Columbia Encyclopedia* describes it as "a government in which the people share [we are not told with whom] in directing the activities of the state," and the slide begins. The trouble starts with the ambiguity introduced when "power" is replaced by "government." If "government" means governance—the process of governing—then it means about the same as power, and there is no difficulty. But if it means "a government"—the political institutions existing in a society—then we have moved to an entirely different category of proposition. This move is a possibility in the *Oxford* definition which becomes a certainty in the *Columbia* definition. The latter slides still further by assuming democracy is by definition limited in its concerns to "the activities of the state." What we have now is no longer a definition but a hypothesis. The hypothesis is that the way to get power to the people is to put them in charge of the "the government," that is, the state apparatus. The hypothesis presupposes that the state apparatus is where the power is. This is a good bet, but it is no more a definition than "pressing the accelerator" is a definition of "acceleration." Pressing the accelerator won't work if (for example) your automobile is chained down in the hold of a freighter crossing the Atlantic, and assuring that people control "the government" won't work if (for example) "the government" is only a piece of cargo carried along by the ship of corporate power.

Abraham Lincoln's lawyerlike "government of the people, by the people, and for the people" greatly improves the hypothesis by a plugging up some of these loopholes. But improving a hypothesis does not make it a definition. The difference may seem so slight as to be unimportant for practical purpose. Nevertheless, it matters.

Lincoln's formula in the Gettysburg Address is taken by most people as his (for many, *the*) definition of democracy, despite the fact that he did not say it was: the word does not appear in the speech. And it is clear from the context that what he means by "government" is not governance but institutions, a structure designed to empower the people, not the people empowered. After all, if "government" means governance then the phrase "that government of the people . . . shall not perish from the earth" becomes ludicrous: we should have to believe that Lincoln is exhorting his audience to strive on so that the people can continue to be governed.

It is a piece of bad luck that so much of what we have come to believe about democracy comes from words spoken at cemeteries in wartime.

Both Pericles in his Funeral Oration and Lincoln in his Gettysburg Address aimed to justify the deaths of young men to their friends, relatives, and countrymen and at the same time to explain to other young men why they ought to continue on in the business of killing. Both speeches are brilliant. But however apt and true their words may have been in their respective historical situations, the sight and stench of death makes the wartime memorial service a poor setting in which to fix the meaning and spirit of democracy. (On Pericles' speech I shall have more to say in Chapter 4.)

If we take Lincoln's formula for a definition, then democracy is a certain formation of government institutions. It follows that the struggle for democracy becomes state military action requiring an increasingly powerful central government, a military conscription system, a massive army commanded by the likes of Generals Grant, Sherman, and Hooker, and a firing squad for deserters. Once democracy is defined as an existing political system, it is natural that the task of the democrat becomes the struggle to defend that system, to "save the Union." This is not to raise an argument with Lincoln about whether saving the Union was the best policy amid the agonizing dilemmas of his time. Here we are trying only to define a term. For rejecting this as a definition of democracy we may refer to the authority of Lincoln himself: he did not say it was. For Lincoln the Union was not democracy itself. It was to clarify just this distinction that he made his famous figure: government institutions were not the golden apple of liberty but the silver frame by which the apple was (hopefully) to be protected. The difference may seem small but the consequence is great—namely, whether, as democrats, we are to understand our task as the long historical struggle toward democracy or a merely the struggle to achieve decisive military victory over all enemies of the state.

Why Radical?

In writings on democracy we often find the word modified by some adjective or made into an adjective to modify something else. We hear of liberal democracy, social democracy, democratic socialism, Christian democracy, people's democracy (as flagrant a redundancy as, say, "king's monarchy"), popular democracy, strong democracy, and so on. In answer to the question "Which kind of democracy are you talking about?" it would be best if we could say, "Not any of the modified democracies— the thing itself." Just democracy, which is self-defining: the people's having the power. Although this terminology may be logically correct, in the context of the ongoing discourse on democracy some additional tag is useful to help distinguish the approach taken here from others. Among the possibilities, "radical democracy" seems best. For one thing, the choice is an expression of solidarity with other people in the past and in the present who have called themselves radical democrats, and of the hope that I am talking here about the same thing that they were and are. For another, "radical" is a modifier that does not "modify," strictly speaking, but rather intensifies. Radical democracy means democracy in its essential form, democracy at its root, quite precisely the thing itself.

The word "radical" also has overtones that help clarify what the essence of democracy is. Democracy *is* politically radical. It is a commentary on our time that this has to be said. Democracy is left. This inference is also obvious. "Left" is a political metaphor that comes from the side on which the representatives of the people sat in the French National Assembly of 1789. It means nothing more than "on the side of the people." How could a democrat be on any side but that?* Democracy is a critique of centralized power of every sort—charismatic, bureaucratic, class, military, corporate, party, union, technocratic. By definition it is the antithesis to all such power. Though we may find other reasons—order, efficiency, the necessities of struggle—to justify centralization of power, these give radical democracy no reason to yield in *its* critique: "justifiably" undemocratic power remains undemocratic.

Looking at the governments and economic institutions in the world today, we can make a stronger statement: as I wrote in the Introduction, radical democracy is subversive everywhere. It is subversive not only in military dictatorships but also in the countries that are called democratic, those that are called socialist, and those that are "postsocialist." It is subversive not only inside the big corporations but also inside the big unions. It is the idea that joins the people struggling for liberty in all countries and all situations—if only they could all see in that way.

If radical democracy will be found—in our time—mainly in the opposition, another sense of the word "radical" places democracy directly at the center of the polity. The word suggests motion not lateral to the edge (as with "left") but straight down to the source. The first meaning for "radical" listed in the *Oxford English Dictionary* reads, "Radical humidity, humour, moisture, sap: in mediaeval philosophy, the humour or moisture naturally inherent in all plants and animals, its presence being a necessary condition of their vitality. So *radical heat*." Radical democracy, taken in this sense, is like radical humidity—the vital source of energy at the center of all living politics. But the fact that the people are the source of all political power does not mean that in all regimes the people have

---

* But it is not necessarily true that to be on the left is to be a democrat.

the power, any more than the fact that the workers are the source of all economic value means that in all economies the workers control the wealth. Every political regime is built by the taking of power from all the people and the giving of it to a few, every ideology is an explanation of why this power transfer is justified, and regimes are stable and powerful when the people accept those explanations.

From the standpoint of radical democracy, the justification of every other kind of regime is something like the illusion of the emperor's new clothes. Even a people that has lost its political memory—that has been terrorized or mystified into believing that the power of the government is a personal characteristic of the Prince, a punishment from God, an inheritance from the Founders, the direct command of History, an inescapable scientific law, a commodity one can buy, or something that grows out of the barrel of a gun—may still make the discovery that the real source of power is themselves.

Even an army bristling with the most fearsome weapons is of no use to the general if all the soldiers desert, and mass desertion is always a physical possibility. Any regime at any time has the potential to collapse back into the State of Democracy, though in particular times and places such a thing may be psychologically and socially inconceivable. The fact that mass desertion could dissolve the power of the state signifies little in situations in which the people's beliefs prevent them from so acting. At the same time, differences in belief do not alter the physical fact.

In the sense that its physical possibility is always present, radical democracy neither progresses nor regresses with history. Of course a people struggling for democracy may make cumulative gains (or suffer cumulative losses) over time. But a democratic revolution is not a leap forward into the uncharted future; it is, as John Locke indicated, a going back, a return to the source. Democracy is *the radical*, the square root of all power, the original number out of which all regimes are multiplied, the root term out of which the entire political vocabulary is ramified. Democracy is radical politics in the same way that faith was once called "radical grace," acetic acid "radical vinegar," and granite "the universal radical rock."[5]

Why Radical Democracy Has Had No Great Theorist

Radical democracy is the foundation of all political discourse. As a physical matter, it is the root source of the stuff out of which politics is formed: power. As a normative matter, it is the root source of value, the radical answer to the question "What is justice?"

Given this fact, it is strange to find that radical democracy is a subject largely avoided by political theorists. Who among the classic political philosophers is a defender of radical democracy? Though we can catch glimpses of it in John Locke, in Jean Jacques Rousseau, in Thomas Jefferson, in Tom Paine, or in Karl Marx, the great bulk of even avowedly democratic theory quickly moves away from it to other subjects. Pick up a book on democratic theory written before the 1980s and you will probably find yourself reading a description of the political institutions of the United States, Great Britain, France, and maybe a few other countries. Typically there will be a line or two—no more—explaining that "direct democracy" is not possible. It may have worked in ancient Athens, we are told, but "the principle is neither descriptive of nor feasible in any modern state."[6] The radical democrat is disappointed to find that this statement is not followed by a critique of the modern state. Rather, democracy is redefined to mean the characteristics of those modern states customarily called "democratic": "we seek here only the differentiating features or principles of organization typical of all democracies."[7] A study of the features of those systems teaches us that democracy does not mean "rule by the people": "Democracy is not a way of governing, whether by majority or otherwise, but primarily a way of determining who shall govern."[8] Such a scenario is rather like reading a book on how to get rich and learning that of course *you* can never get rich but that there are ways you can help select those who will.

In works on politics past and present, the subject of radical democracy has been skirted and flirted with, but who has stood up for the thing itself, from beginning to end? Who has written its manifesto? No name comes to mind.[9]

There may be several explanations. For one, perhaps no one has really believed in it. Perhaps everyone has, like James Madison, believed that democracy is only for angels and that the best we flawed human beings can hope for is some compromise, some democratized Leviathan. Perhaps radical democracy is more frightening even than anarchism, for anarchism typically seeks to abolish power at the same moment that it liberates the people, hoping thereby to ensure that they will not do anything very harmful in their liberty. Radical democracy does not abolish power, it says that the people shall have it, that the power will be their freedom. Most anarchists envision the political space abolished, and the people either placed under the invisible rule of "society" or so set apart by radical individualism that they will no longer be a people at all. Radical democracy envisions the people gathered in the public space, with neither the great paternal Leviathan nor the great maternal society standing over them, but only the empty sky—the people making the power of Leviathan their own again, free to speak, to choose, to act. Of course when the power of Leviathan is restored to its rightful owners it changes: it is no longer monstrous. Still, perhaps the scale of freedom here implied is so dizzying that the mind quails before it and quickly turns to the more comfortable business of demonstrating the need for centralized authority, representative officials, rule of law, police, jails, and the like.

Another reason for the absence of a political philosophy of radical democracy may be that it is the one political state that requires no argument for its legitimation. It may be that the need for theory begins only when power is placed somewhere *other* than with the people. Isn't that what "legitimation" is? If we give power to the philosophers, the Prince, the elected, or the Party central committee, we have to explain why. In the case of restoring power to the people, no such argument is required. An explanation may be required of why such a situation will be safe, efficient, lasting, or a source of wise decisions but not of why it is legitimate. Radical democracy is legitimacy itself.

In this sense, even though radical democracy is not often talked about openly in political philosophy, it is always there. To detect it, we sometimes need to use the same method used by physicists to detect the presence of the positron. Where it cannot be observed, its presence can be deduced from its influence on the activity of other things that can be observed. Where there is a magnetic field, there must be a magnet. The magnetic power of radical democracy can be observed in the theories and ideologies that have been built for the purpose of justifying its absence, that is, for the purpose of explaining why it is necessary or better to give power to the few rather than to all. In this sense, all other theories and ideologies point to radical democracy, negatively, as the specific thing they do *not* achieve, the area they carefully avoid, the black hole at dead center in their scheme of rule or management.[10] It exists within them as the eternal "other possibility" that they seek to deny, the fundamental critique that they labor to answer, the specter by which they are haunted.[11]

We may take Hobbes's *Leviathan* as the classic example.[12] It is the passionate intensity with which Hobbes works to erase the very concept of people's power from the vocabulary of political discourse and from human consciousness which gives the book its deadly fascination. Not only does he try to convince us that life unruled by state power is worse than life in a cave of hungry lions. He also defines power as something that cannot in principle be held by the people. In his state of nature the "power after power" sought after by individuals (or more accurately, male family heads) is no more than the power to "use Violence, to make themselves Masters of other men's persons, wives, children [yes, in Hobbes's state of nature, "man" has a wife and children] and cattle" (p.

99) and to defend themselves against being similarly treated. The only joint enterprise he suggests is the temporary alliance of several persons to kill someone bigger than themselves (p. 98). Power becomes political power precisely at the moment it is given to Leviathan. Political power is brought into being only by giving it away. Its nature is to rule *over* the people, to "keep them all in awe" (p. 100). Take it back, and it is nothing. If the people all take back the bricks they contributed to the fortress, each will be surprised to discover he has no fortress but only a brick, which he then presumably will throw at his neighbor's head. The people's power is a fantasy, it is something that simply cannot be. What we have to choose is between two forms of powerlessness, one in a state of chaotic fear, the other in a state of institutionalized fear.

In Locke's *Second Treatise on Government* an image of the people's power does appear, though only briefly and rather late in the book.[13] In his analysis, Locke describes two political changes of state, one in which the people, through a social contract, establish political power and construct the state, and one in which the contract is broken and society returns to a government-free condition. The first transformation is, of course, a myth, designed to prepare us to understand the second, which is for Locke a real historical possibility. Interestingly, the second transformation is not simply the first operating in reverse. In the first, the people make what looks like a single social contract to establish civil government as a fair umpire to judge disputes among them. In the second, however, as the arrangement begins to dissolve, it turns out that there was not one contract, but two: "He that will with any clearness speak of the *Dissolution of Government*, ought, in the first place to distinguish between the *Dissolution of the Society*, and the *Dissolution of the Government*. That which makes the Community, and brings Men out of the loose State of Nature, into *one Politick Society*, is the Agreement which every one has with the rest to incorporate, and act as one Body, and so be one distinct Commonwealth" (p. 454).

These two contracts, which Hannah Arendt called the "horizontal" and "vertical" social contracts,[14] are separable: if the horizontal is broken the vertical is of course shattered, but if the vertical is broken the horizontal may remain, for *"when the Government is dissolved*, the People are at liberty to provide for themselves, by erecting a new Legislature, differing from the other, by the change of Persons, or Form, or both as they shall find it most for their safety and good"* (p. 459). The people are "at liberty"; they can act together as a political body: judging, choosing, assuming the role of Founder. Yet Locke limits the possible actions the people may take to one, the formation of a new government. The description of the political condition with a horizontal but no vertical contract is over in less than half a page. The moment of the people in power slips past like a configuration in mist blown by the wind, gone almost the moment you see it.

Still, the moment is precious: what was possible once is possible again. And how shall we interpret the fact that what seemed to be one social contract at the beginning divides into two? Is it simply that the initial promise proves, on analysis, logically to entail two promises? That a contract to incorporate the people into a community was the inescapable necessary condition for the establishment of government? Or is it that the people are different at the second phase from how they were at the first? Perhaps Locke is taking into account the factor of political education. It is difficult to think of a people just out of a state of nature—whatever that may be—immediately forming themselves into a community capable of making political decisions. It is easier to imagine a people at the second stage as having this capacity—a people that has lived under a government, has watched critically as this government became increasingly corrupted, and is now in the middle of revolutionary action. Locke does not tell us; we must work out the puzzle for ourselves. For the radical democrat the moral of this tale is that it is the actual people's democratic struggle under an oppressive government, and not the imaginary "signing" of a social contract, which provides it with the unity and political education that transforms it into a body capable of taking power.[15]

Civil Society?

Or would it be better to say, a body capable of being a power? Could Locke's "politick society" have been something similar to what political writers in the last couple of decades have been discussing under the old-new name "civil society"?

The notion of "civil society," in its present incarnation, can be traced variously to the struggles of the peoples of eastern Europe against the communist bureaucratic states, to the struggles to bring about a "transition to democracy" in the Latin American dictatorships, to the autonomous self-help organizations that grew up in Mexico City after the September 1985 earthquake, to the writings of Antonio Gramsci, and more generally to the search for a theory and praxis for people's movements in the post-Marxist era.[16] Civil society has about as many definitions as definers, but in general it refers to that sphere of society which organizes itself autonomously, as opposed to the sphere that is established and/or directly controlled by the state. Some theorists have advanced the argument that civil society can and should replace "the most oppressed class" or "the vanguard party" as the agent of historical change. But the difference is that, unlike a class or party, civil society does not rise up and seize the power of the state; rather, in rising up, it empowers itself. It does not take over the state or replace it, but rather stands against it, marginalizes it, controls it. Unlike mass society, civil society is not a herd but a multiplicity of diverse groups and organizations, formal and informal, of people acting together for a variety of purposes, some political, some cultural, some economic. Unlike a mass party, civil society does not suffer from an iron law of oligarchy, or if it does, at worst this oligarchy takes the relatively harmless form of the natural leadership that tends to emerge in small organizations. Because of its small-group organization, civil society is unlikely to fall prey to the danger of "tyranny of the majority"; in fact the idea closely resembles, and is in part based on, the model of society which Alexis de Tocqueville, who invented the expression "tyranny of the majority," believed was the best protection against it. Civil society provides space for public discourse, for the development of public values and public language, for the formation of the public self [the citizen], a space separate from the formal political sphere dominated by state power and political parties that aim to control that power. As Adam Ferguson put it in the eighteenth century, in civil society the citizen has a place to "act in the view of his fellow-creatures, to produce his mind in public,"[17] without necessarily becoming a politician. Civil society does not demand freedom, but generates it.

This, at least, is the radical image of civil society, and it is powerful and persuasive. Moreover it closely resembles, and gives theoretical justification to, the form that people's movements have tended to take since the 1970s: networks of small organizations, each focusing on a particular set of issues rather than aiming to take over state power. If it was civil society that put an end to the communist bureaucracies in the "self-limiting" revolutions of Poland and Czechoslovakia, perhaps in retrospect civil society would be an apt name for the network of "sectoral organizations" which undermined and finally defeated the Marcos dictatorship in the Philippines. And it was to Mexican civil society that the other Marcos, Subcomandante Marcos of EZLN, made his extraordinary appeal from the headquarters of the liberated zone in Chiapas: "We will continue to respect the cease-fire in order to permit civil society to organize itself in whatever forms it considers necessary in order to achieve the transition to democracy in our country."[18]

But a problem with the civil-society notion is that it is not that easy to distinguish from the dreary old model of liberal pluralism. It must be remembered that in the United States such social scientists as Robert Dahl,

Seymour Martin Lipset, and Daniel Bell were developing their own "post-Marxist" political theory back in the Cold-War 1950s. According to this notion, democracy is best achieved and liberty best preserved in a society in which competition takes place not between classes but between a multiplicity of interest groups—precisely the kind of society, it turned out, that had been (allegedly) achieved in the liberal capitalist countries, and especially in the United States. It was this situation that allowed Dahl to say that "the political system of New Haven is an example of a democratic system, warts and all," Lipset to say that democracy [as above defined] "is the good society itself in operation," and Bell to argue that with the appearance of liberal-capitalism world-political development had reached its conclusion, and ideologies were no longer needed. The emergence of the new civil-society discourse has enabled Bell, who saw his *End of Ideology* become the laughingstock of the ideological 1960s and 1970s, to come back in the 1980s and say I Told You So. In a 1989 article titled "American Exceptionalism Revisited—The Role of Civil Society," Bell welcomes the "renewed appreciation for the virtues of civil society" as a step toward "achieving the goals of liberalism" and then goes on to boast that "the United States has been the complete *civil society* . . . perhaps the only one in political history."[19]

Similarly Edward Shils, who used the expression "the end of ideology" before Bell did,[20] joined the civil-society discussion in 1991 in "The Virtue of Civil Society," arguing that civil society is not the same as liberal democratic society but rather that it is what makes "the difference between a well-ordered and a disordered liberal democracy."[21] In Shils's image of civil society, the list of exemplary civic groups begins with "industries and . . . business firms"; in the political sphere only political parties are mentioned (p. 9). Unions, NonGovernmental Organizations, and movement organizations are not on the list (unless we are to assume they are included in the "etc."). According to Shils, such a society is harshly competitive, and this competition "supports the view that life is exclusively a matter of 'dog eat dog' " (p. 15). Civility, meaning "refined manners" (p. 8), can mitigate the harshness of such a society. "Without such civility, a pluralistic society can degenerate into a war of each against all" (p. 15): "Civility in the sense of courtesy mollifies or ameliorates the strain which accompanies the risks, the dangers of prospective loss and the injuries of the real losses of an economically, politically and intellectually competitive society in which some persons are bound to lose. Courtesy makes life a bit more pleasant" (p. 13). Moreover, civil society, far from being independent of the state, actually depends on it for its existence, as it "operates within the framework set by laws" (p. 15). In some cases it may even serve as an extension of state power, for "even the best police force cannot detect, trace and capture all criminals, to say nothing of juvenile delinquents" (p. 16).[22]

In this Hobbesian vision, the ability of people to form a civil society independent of the state is specifically denied. But if it "operates within the framework set by" Leviathan, still as liberals we do not give to Leviathan the total power that Hobbes did; rather we preserve an area of freedom in society, "freedom" meaning the partial return of the state of nature. To keep from falling entirely back into a war of each against all we need the state and its laws; to bear even the partial state of nature we need to be civil. Civilly we compete with our neighbors in a zero-sum game,[23] observe their actions carefully, and turn them over to the police when appropriate.

Far from being an agent of social change, civil society here is a technique for surviving in a hell from which there is no exit: the end of history.

One need not accept Shils's pessimism (or cynicism), but his account is helpful in reminding us not to be too romantic about civil society. If civil society simply means the nongovernmental sphere, it also includes EXXON, ITT, and Mitsubishi. Moreover, it is the stronghold both of racism and of patriarchal rule over women.[24] Civil society itself is no democratic force. David Held is quite correct to call for a "double democratization," described as "the interdependent transformation of both state and civil society."[25] But the idea is hardly new—the transformation of society, including the democratization of the economy, has been one of the chief aims of peoples' movements since the beginning of the rise of capitalism. It was precisely Marx's criticism of the French Revolution that it had been a political revolution only, rendering society, if anything, more oppressive than before. That's what people meant when they spoke of social reform and social revolution. Any democratic movement that accepts the basic conditions of competition and of work in the capitalist economy as unalterable, and seeks only to make things "a bit more pleasant," has conceded defeat from the beginning.

Václav Havel begins his essay "The Power of the Powerless" with the description of a greengrocer in communist Czechoslovakia placing between the onions and the carrots in his shop window a sign that reads, "Workers of the World, Unite!"[26] What message, asks Havel, is the sign meant to convey? "Verbally, it might be expressed this way: 'I, the greengrocer XY, live here and I know what I must do. I behave in the manner expected of me. I can be depended upon and am beyond reproach. I am obedient and therefore I have the right to be left in peace' " (p. 28). A government employee, the greengrocer lives in a world from which civil society has been abolished. He is skewered through with state power; the society around him is saturated to the bottom with state ideology. There is no occasion here for smugness on the part of ideologists of liberal capitalism. Havel makes clear that the communist bureaucracy that oppresses the greengrocer "is merely an extreme version of the global automatism of technological civilization. The human failure that it mirrors is only one variant of the general failure of modern humanity" (p. 90). Shils's citizen-as-informer offers a fair counterpart to the greengrocer.

Havel then goes on to describe a beginning of change:

> Let us now imagine that one day something in the greengrocer snaps and he stops putting up the slogans merely to ingratiate himself. He stops voting in elections he knows are a farce. He begins to say what he really thinks at political meetings. And he even finds the strength in himself to express solidarity with those whom his conscience commands him to support. In this revolt the greengrocer steps out of living within the lie. . . . His revolt is an attempt to *live within the truth* (p. 39).[27]

If the greengrocer gets away with this—that is, if he is joined by enough like-minded people that the state cannot repress them all—these actions amount to the birth of an autonomous sphere of society where people can think, speak, and act in freedom: democratic civil society. The important thing is that the change depicted in Havel's story is not organizational but mental. It is the kind of change that Marx meant to describe when he wrote of the workers "becoming conscious," and that liberation theologists mean to describe when they use the (in English) awkward expression "conscientization." This change is not a change from "incorrect" to "correct" knowledge: the greengrocer has not necessarily become aware of anything he did not know before. Something "snaps." It is an act of the mind: a decision.[28] Of course "a decision" means a decision to act; it comes not before but just at the moment the greengrocer stops putting up the sign. At that moment a free space has been created, without any organizational or institutional change whatever. After the greengrocer begins to act on his decision—and especially if he finds fellow actors—new organizations may emerge. Or he may act within organizations that already exist, working to change them. Though Havel does not mention this paradox, the greengrocer doesn't even need to change slogans: except that he and his fellow citizens are probably sick of hearing it, "Workers of the World, Unite" would serve quite well.

The change of mental state which Havel describes can also signify the difference between the dog-eat-dog liberal civil society described by Shils and the autonomous democratic civil society. For Shils's society of polite informers and backstabbers is also living within a lie: the politeness is a lie, and the notion that the human condition admits of no decent alternative to cutthroat competition is a deeper lie: the ideology of capitalism. Here too what gives birth to autonomous democratic civil society is not an institutional change but the decision to stop living this dual lie. Of course when a democratic civil society has a lively existence of its own, it tends to take on a typical form, developing a multiplicity of face-to-face organizations, some with the character of the political "councils" described by Arendt, some with the character of the mutual-aid organizations described by Pëtr Kropotkin, some with purely cultural or educational aims (producing music, theater, dance), and some combining these functions. But the shift to autonomy is not itself an organizational change; it occurs at a different level. This is why Havel sees (or in any case, saw at the time he wrote this essay) "systemic change as something superficial, something secondary, something that in itself can guarantee nothing," and criticizes violent overthrow of the government as "not . . . radical enough."[29] And it is why the difference between the dog-eat-dog civil society and the autonomous democratic civil society will be virtually impossible to explain for a social scientist who studies only organizations.

Thus although the definition of democracy given above—the state of affairs in which the people have the power—looks simple enough, it becomes more complex on closer analysis. It is more than a tautology to say that in order to hold the power the people must become a body by which power can in principle be held. Power cannot be held by people who live unresisting under the lie of state propaganda. It cannot be held by people who are convinced that dog-eat-dog competition is a doom from which human beings cannot escape, that the best we can hope for is a courteous state of nature. It is an illusion to think that an institutional change that drops power into the lap of a people stuck in such a state of mind will bring about democracy. The result may be as effective as pouring water into a sieve—unless, as can and does happen, the institutional change triggers a change in state of mind. But even to say that is misleading: democratic power does not fall from above, it is generated by a people in a democratic state of mind, and by the actions they take in accordance with that state of mind. It is the possibility of this change of state that is the power of the powerless.

At the same time, none of this means that democracy requires some leap of the consciousness into an uncharted future. Rather it only means returning to a natural attitude. What "snaps" in the mind are the ideological bonds that prevent one from assuming that natural attitude of democratic common sense. I shall have more to say on this in Chapter 5.

Borrowing the term coined by Jacek Kurón of Poland's Solidarity, Jean L. Cohen and Andrew Arato argue that the notion of civil society provides the basis for a "self-limiting" democratic movement. In this notion, the civil society does not seek to seize the state, abolish it, or replace it with itself. When the government is a dictatorship, the civil society may force it to undergo a "transition to democracy," meaning a transition to the institutions of representative democracy. But when the government already has those institutions, "we do not see social movements as prefiguring a form of citizen participation that will or even ought to substitute for the institutional arrangements of representative democracy. . . . Movements can and should supplement and should not aim to replace competitive party systems."[30] The idea is interesting. It is a great improvement over the strategy of first creating an authoritarian organization (the vanguard party) that needs to be run by authoritarian personalities (professional revolutionaries) and promises liberation to no one until after the massive institutional change of the revolution. As I wrote above, civil society does not seek to force the state to found liberty but rather struggles to found a space of liberty itself. It does not demand that we sacrifice the present in the name of an ideal future that will come "after the revolution"; as Havel wrote, we can begin today.[31] More accurately, the work was begun long ago. The movement to democratize civil society is self-limiting because it is not a force acting on society from the "outside" (e.g., a state seized by a revolutionary party), it is society itself—or rather, by the time it has become powerful enough to think of seizing the state, it will have become at least the great bulk of society. If a genuinely democratic civil society actually grew to such a proportion, would it leave the state structure intact? If it did, this would provide an interesting solution to the famous paradox posed by John Cotton. Q: "If the people be governors, who shall be governed?" A: The government.

Still, the statement that the democratic movement "should not aim to replace" the government system sounds less like a self-limitation than a limitation Cohen and Arato wish to place on it. A democratic movement embedded in civil society is self-limiting in the sense that it cannot in principle become a force to tear society—itself—apart.[32] But suppose, for example, that in the United States (Bell's "complete civil society") a genuine civil-society movement of the sort we are discussing here achieved the power and unity of purpose of, say, the movement led by Poland's Solidarity in 1980–81. Presumably if this were to happen the government would already be different. Managerial control over the people would have been weakened. State ideology would have lost much of its power to control. Different people would have been elected to office. The national political discourse would have been transformed, and even in Congress genuine political discussion would be taking place. If the spirit of civil society permeated the army, as it did during the Vietnam War, the government would face difficulty in embarking on neoimperialist adventures. I agree with Cohen and Arato that there may be no need to seize a state that can be permeated and transformed, or to abolish representative institutions in which the civil-society movement can itself be represented. Put differently, if the state with a central government at its head is to be retained, certainly the government institutions should be representative. At the same time we can imagine a civil-society movement acting to reduce state power radically, demilitarizing it and denuclearizing it, eliminating functions that have been made redundant by the autonomous organization of the civil society itself, reforming or establishing new government institutions appropriate to the new situation. Put differently, surely it would not be surprising if the people were to "provide for themselves, by erecting a new Legislature, differing from the other, by the change of Persons, or Form, or both as they shall find it most for their safety and good."

Let us try to be at least as radical as John Locke.

Radical Democracy and Political Education

In any case, democracy begins now. Just as it is not something that appears only "after the revolution," so also it is not something that appears after a period of political education. Of course, political education is vital, but the only truly effective education system for democracy is democracy—democratic action itself.

Aristotle taught that the essence of democracy is the system of choosing officials by lot, whereas choice by election is aristocratic by definition. Choice by lot presupposes, and operates to develop and maintain, a polity in which each citizen can stand for the whole. Similarly, Montesquieu taught us that the spirit of democracy is political virtue, which he defined as patriotism. In a democracy, it must be remembered, patriotism means the love that binds a people together, not the misplaced love of the institutions that dominate the people. Authoritarian patriotism is a resigning of one's will, right of choice, and need to understand to the authority; its emotional base is gratitude for having been liberated from the burden of democratic responsibility. Political virtue—democratic patriotism—is the commitment to, knowledge of, and ability to stand for the whole, and is the necessary condition for democracy. It is the condition that binds the people together into a body by which the power can in principle be held. Choice by lot, a symbol of radical democracy, is an expression of trust almost inconceivable to us who received our political education under governments managed by elected representatives: trust that no matter who is chosen he (or she, we say, though the Greeks did not) will not turn out to be a demagogue, or a political fool, or a knave who will run off with the public funds.

What would happen if, from tomorrow, the heads of state and lawmakers in every country were chosen by lot? A president or prime minister chosen by lot would receive no special honor by that choice. Though choice by lot presumes radical trust in the citizenry in general, there would be no reason to have exaggerated hope in the person chosen, no more, that is, than would be due your next-door neighbor. This would amount to the abolition of the modern Prince, the political Father, the great plaster statue/media star by which modern politics is dominated. Choice by lot would not have the power, which the election ritual does, of transforming an ordinary person into a superhuman.

The people, for their part, would be reluctant to hand over much of their power to a president or legislator chosen by lot. They (we) would be forced to the realization that the main responsibility for figuring out what to do about war, taxes, the economy, pollution, justice, national boundaries, and all the rest is theirs (ours). The selection by lot of the world's kings, prime ministers, presidents, and central-committee chairmen would amount to the abolition of those offices as they are presently understood. (As a side effect, we could expect that it would reduce the amount of graft and corruption in government: surely in virtually every country the crime rate among ordinary citizens is lower than that among professional politicians.)

Choice by lot is not radical democracy itself; I mention it here not as a proposal but as a symbol.[33] In it we can see the connection between democracy and human development: the development of political virtue. On the other hand, the key characteristic of modern representative government, as is explicitly stated in *The Federalist Papers*, is the severing of this connection and the construction of a government that is supposed to operate automatically to produce the result approximating what it would be if the people had political virtue, thereby making political virtue itself superfluous.[34] This is a brilliant move, and the government system for which the U.S. Constitution is the model has been an extraordinary success if the aim is, as the Founders believed, the establishment of lasting institutions that bring domestic order and national strength, to which *end* the people are the *means*.

Radical Democracy an End in Itself

But radical democracy sees it the other way round. Democratic institutions are means, but radical democracy itself—the people empowered—is not. It is no more a means than physical and mental health, or knowledge, or mature judgment are means; that is, it is a means precisely to the extent that human beings themselves are means. All these things, like human beings, have their uses. But this is not the locus of their value: the full development of the intellectual and moral powers in each human being is an end, not a means. What is radical democracy but the political expression of this end?

This end point sought by radical democracy, though as a practical matter no easy task to reach, should not be understood as a leap out of history as we have hitherto understood it, some awesome appearance of a collective Overman. Rather it is grounded in the common sense of our daily life; it is really no more than the end point of the process begun by every parent in raising children. Every parent knows that becoming an adult means taking responsibility for one's actions, that the only way a child learns responsibility is by having responsibility, and that a parent who never turns over responsibility to a child will raise a permanent child. In political terms, then, radical democracy is the end point in the process begun (for example) by Locke when he argued against Robert Filmer, in the first of his *Two Treatises of Government*, that political authority is not the authority of a permanent father.

If democracy is the end, all political institutions and arrangements, as well as economic systems and technologies, are means. Really to see things in this way would amount to a revolution in our understanding of those powerful words that so dominate our collective lives today: efficiency, practicality, and progress. For we often forget that these words have no fixed or absolute meanings: what is efficient depends on what effect we want to produce, what is practical depends on what practices we value, what is progressive depends in where we want to go. Taking democracy as the goal means stealing back these expressions from economics and technology, where they have been monopolized so long. It means rejecting such formulations as that there is a "trade-off" between efficiency and empowerment of the people. If empowerment were agreed on as the desired effect, any economic or technological arrangement that weakened the people would be inefficient by definition.

There may be some danger in describing radical democracy as the end point in the project of human development, because it implies that first there must be some long period of political education, lasting generations or centuries, only after which "democracy" comes as the prize. But this

delay is less of a danger if we remember, once again, that the only education system for democracy is democracy, that the only way to have it *then*
is to do it *now*.

The Madman and the Sword

Radical democracy can be thought of as having two aspects, one in the
realm of fact and the other in the realm of value. That all power is generated by the people is an assertion of fact.[35] It is an assertion that political
power is generated not by the rulers but by the ruled, that no one can be
king unless a large number of people are convinced that they are subjects,
and that on the day the subjects all decide that they are not there is no
more king.[36]

The value assertion is that the people who generate the power ought
also to have it.

There is a parallel here, as I suggested above, with the discovery of the
fact that labor is the source of economic value and the corresponding
conclusion that therefore the laborers ought to control that value. Political power held by the ruling minorities can thus be seen as something ex-
acted through a mechanism of exploitation, and the ruled as suffering
from power alienation and power impoverishment.

The move from fact to value here is based on one of the most ancient
formulations of justice, that it is just to return things to their rightful
owners. It will remembered that this is the definition of justice given by
old Cephalus at the beginning of Plato's *Republic*: justice means to deceive no one and to give back what one has borrowed.[37] The two fit together: "to deceive no one" includes not concealing the fact that one has
borrowed something and that the other party is the rightful owner; once
this point is clear, the justice of returning the borrowed item follows necessarily. (That is, the word "borrow," in addition to describing a fact, also
presupposes the obligation to return the thing borrowed.)

It is at this point that Socrates offers his counterexample that causes
Cephalus to retire from the conversation and launches the dialogue that
is the *Republic*, the dialogue that can be said to have founded Western
political philosophy: "But take this matter of doing right: can we say that
it really consists in nothing more nor less than telling the truth and paying back anything we have received? . . . suppose, for example, a friend
who had lent us a weapon were to go mad and then ask for it back, surely
anyone would say we ought not to return it. It would not be 'right' to do
so; nor yet to tell the truth without reserve to a madman" (1.331). It
seems strange that Socrates should bring in such an exceptional case to
make his very first point, until one recalls that madness is a theme run-

ning through the entire dialogue. Old Cephalus, after all, has just finished describing the peace that comes with age by saying, "For instance, I remember someone asking Sophocles, the poet, whether he was still capable of enjoying a woman. 'Don't talk that way,' he answered; 'I am only too glad to be free of all that; it is like escaping from bondage to a raging madman' " (1.329).

"Madness" (*mania*) is not an exceptional case. It is a metaphor describing the normal, or at least the most common, state of mind of people under bondage to "passions of that sort" (1.329). Later in the book, when Socrates describes the decline of the just polity and the just man into despotism and the despotic man, he is at the same time describing a descent into madness. The "democratic" man, having no principle to guide him and buffeted back and forth by the various principles, desires, and appetites to which he gives "equal right," is at the farthest edge of sanity. One step further and he becomes despotic man, "a soul maddened by the tyranny of passion and lust" (9.577). Put this being in the seat of power, and you have the despotic ruler: the madman with his sword.

The Republic can be read as a long argument showing why we should not give the sword to the madman.[38] At the same time it can be read as a cure for that kind of madness, or for the passions and temptations that lead one toward it.[39] The puzzle of whether the message of this many-layered book is in the end democratic or antidemocratic can probably never be resolved. That is, of course it is antidemocratic; there is no reason not to take the author at his word in this. But if so, why do democrats find such value in it? Partly because it presents *the* counterargument that democrats must answer: that returning power to the people cannot be just if you know that they will only use it to ruin themselves. At the same time it lays down the philosophical basis for an answer to this counterargument, for a cure to the madness. The forms, which are the same for everyone, have curative power. Even a slave boy who has never been educated can and must understand geometry, and therefore justice as well. The Socratic dialectic is founded on the belief that the capacity for political sanity is in each person. Can we call this democratic faith? The word "faith" may sound strange here, but how else does one describe the paradoxical contradiction between the Platonic epistemology and the Socratic teaching method? Epistemologically the forms exist, they are reality itself and the basis for all knowledge. To say that they are universal is to say that they are the same for everyone. But whether this is actually so can only be verified in practice through the method of the dialogue. And unlike so many later philosophers, Socrates engages not in a dialogue with the abstraction "humankind" but only with individual persons. The dialogue with "humankind" can be brought to an end, but the dialogue with individual persons cannot. All questions reopen with the appearance of each new person, and whether the truth will be found to be the same in the dialogue *with this person too* cannot be known in practice until the dialogue is actually carried out. According to Plato's epistemology, it ought to be true that if Socrates were able to talk to every human being long enough all would come to agree in the end. But this experiment can never be completed: there is no end to new persons. Driven by his demon, Socrates goes on and on with the activity of philosophizing, engaging the next person and then the next person in the dialogue. This activity makes sense only on the premise that the true forms of justice and virtue are knowable by every one and that knowing them can bring any soul out of its state of "madness" and into a state of health. The dialogue is premised on this axiom; at the same time the dialogue is the only possible demonstration that the axiom is true, a demonstration that must forever remain incomplete.[40] This is why we can say that while the Platonic epistemology is absolutist the activity of philosophizing carried out under it is democratic; that while the Republic is antidemocratic, the way Socrates talks to people is an expression of democratic faith. It is democratic because he sees each person as in principle capable of achieving the healthy state, which means becoming a person to whom the sword can safely be returned; it is faith because Socrates believes this and continues to act on his belief despite the impossibility of ever finally proving it—one must add, despite strong evidence to the contrary: there is still Thracymachus, refusing to believe that the world admits of any possibility other than dog eat dog. But if Socrates' position can never be finally proved, it can never be finally disproved either: it is always possible that in the next conversation something will "snap" in Thracymachus' mind, too. There being no final proof on either side, the choice between faith and cynicism is arbitrary. Socrates has no doubt about which to choose. And in the convolutions of his irony, he is occasionally candid enough to reveal to us just what sort of choice it is.

> *Meno*: Somehow or other I believe you are right.
> *Socrates*: I think I am. I shouldn't like to take my oath on the whole story, but one thing I am ready to fight for as long as I can, in word and act—that is, that we shall be better, braver, and more active men if we believe it is right to look for what we don't know than if we believe there is no point in looking because what we don't know we can never discover.[41]

Democracy presents us with a dilemma. On the one hand, the people are free and to be respected: they should be left as they are. On the other hand, if the people are to hold power they must form themselves into a body by which power can in principle be held. On the one hand, it is antidemocratic for authorities to wash everything out of the people's brains and pour in some unifying ideology. On the other hand, power cannot be held by *any* collection of persons, but held only by persons who have formed themselves into "a people" through their public commitment to political virtue. This dilemma for democracy is also a dilemma for the democratic educator: how to offer people a political education and still leave them free. Again, Socratic faith shows us a way out of the dilemma: faith that even if we use a teaching method that at all stages leaves the other free (this the significance of the fact that Socrates only asked questions: one is always free to say "no") we can come to an agreement on justice and political virtue.

Democracy and Cultural Relativity

If democracy faces a dilemma in a world of many persons, it faces a dilemma in a larger scale in a world of many cultures. In countries outside of Europe, the democrat is accused from two directions. The neocolonialist will say democracy is premature: "These people are not ready for democracy, they don't have a democratic political culture." The anticolonial traditional elitist will argue that it is cultural imperialism to try to introduce democracy in a culture based on different values. The democrat's answer, that democracy is common sense, runs into a powerful counterargument, that common sense is not the same in every culture.

In partial answer to this counterargument, the democrat can point out that democracy is in fact being demanded by at least some members of each culture in the world. Perhaps we could take, as a rough rule of thumb, that an outsider can legitimately advocate democracy in any culture where one can find genuine members of that culture who advocate the same thing. But this is only a practical strategy. Theoretically the democrat can only, like Socrates, operate on faith. Just as the Socratic dialogue is grounded on the faith that each personality contains in principle the possibility of a just version of itself, so democratic discourse is grounded in the faith that each culture must also contain the possibility of a democratic version of itself. If readers from the Western "democracies" think that this is too much to ask of democratic faith, they should remember that today, at the end of the twentieth century, the severest test may be in believing it about their own countries.

This faith is accompanied by a democratic critique of the "cultural relativity" argument itself. The radical democrat asks, Can oppression ever properly be called "culture"? When a class or group of people behaves in a certain way because they are forced to, is it fair to them to call their behavior their "culture"? Is it "culture" when serfs grasp their forelocks, when soldiers do close-order drill, or when slaves pick cotton? Would it not be failing to see the main point, to focus on the fine differences between the way people in different situations carry out these oppressed modes of behavior? Of course in reality in all civilizations oppression and culture are so intertwined that it is impossible for an observer to disentangle them. But this is a way of saying that all civilizations to some degree oppress, stunt, disfigure their own cultures. If they do, then the reverse should also be true, that the removal of oppression from any culture, the empowerment of any people, ought to result not in cultural destruction but in cultural elaboration and intensification.

But this suggestion is hypothetical. And because each culture is different, the hypothesis must be tested again in each case. Radical democracy can approach each culture only as Socrates approached each new person, bringing not sermons but questions and the faith that the transformation of each culture to a democratic version of itself would not lead to its destruction but its flowering.

2

antidemocratic development

Though written in large letters on the face of history, the fact that economic development is antidemocratic is hard to see. We have been taught just the opposite, that democracy and development go together. It is no coincidence, most historians argue, that the democratic movement and the industrial revolution appeared at the same moment in European history. The two support one another. On the one hand, they say, economic development is the necessary condition for democracy. Industrialization produces wealth, wealth produces leisure, leisure gives people the freedom to learn about and participate in politics, and this freedom makes democracy possible. On the other hand, the argument goes, economic development takes place most rapidly under conditions of democratic freedom. This interdependence seems to be borne out by the fact that most of the richest countries today are the ones we call democratic. At the same time the idea is an axiom in the ideology (though not in the practice) of Third World development. It is particularly hard to doubt today, when the peoples of Russia and eastern Europe seem to be opting simultaneously for democracy and economic development. The trouble with their "communism," we now hear, was that it brought political oppression and was an "obstacle to development." The establishment of "democracy" in those countries is expected to help their economies begin developing again. Surely the idea that development is democratic is one of the most powerful of our time.

The idea is powerful, but wrong. To see in what way it is wrong, it is necessary first to make clear what is meant by "economic development." The expression is not universal, but particular. It does not mean the development of any of the various ways that people have maintained their livelihood throughout history. Rather it means the elimination of most of those ways and their replacement by certain historically specific practices originating in Europe. "Economic development" means the development of *those* practices.[1]

That is, the word "economic" itself in "economic development" refers to a historically specific phenomenon. It means a particular way of organizing power in a society, and of simultaneously concealing this power arrangement—more accurately, of concealing that it *is* a power arrangement. If this formulation seems a surprise, that is a tribute to the effectiveness of the concealing function. If one were to say that the highest value of the economy is efficiency of production, no one would be particularly surprised. But this is only saying the same thing in a different way. The "economy" is a way of organizing people to work efficiently, that is, to do unnatural kinds of work under unnatural conditions for unnaturally long hours, and of extracting all or part of the extra wealth so produced and transferring it elsewhere. This process is equally true of capitalist and "socialist" countries. The economy is thus political, but pretends not to be. It is political in the most fundamental sense: it organizes power, distributes goods, and rules people. Aristotle called politics the Master Science (*Nicomachean Ethics* 1094 a,b.) because it is the process by which the basic ordering of society is decided. In the "economically developed" societies today, economics determines this basic ordering. We are taught to think of this determining relationship as inevitable. Even those who have never read Marx tend to see the economy as a substructure that develops according to its own Iron Laws and is beyond the power of human beings to change or choose against. Yet this inevitability exists only within the context of the ideology of development. Under the domination of this ideology, economics has replaced politics as the Master Science, but this political character of the economy is hidden. Through economic processes cultures are abolished or restructured, environments are destroyed or made over, work is ordered, wealth is transferred, goods are distributed, classes are formed, and people are managed. But the words for talking intelligibly about these things—words like "founding," "order," "lawgiving," "revolution," "power," "justice," "rule," "consent"—do not exist as technical terms in economic science.[2]

Economic development means, then, the extension and strengthening of this particular mode of economic power, order, and rule. To say that economic development is antidemocratic is not simply to say that it tends to produce undemocratic forms of rule in what we now consider the political sphere, but that it is an undemocratic form of rule in its own sphere. And keeping the vocabulary of politics out of economic discourse is part of what keeps it undemocratic.

Economic development is antidemocratic in several ways. It is antidemocratic in that it requires kinds, conditions, and amounts of labor that people would never choose—and, historically, never have chosen—in a state of freedom. Only by giving a society one or another kind of undemocratic structure can people be made to spend the greater part of their lives laboring "efficiently" in fields, factories, or offices and handing over the surplus value to capitalists, managers, Communist party leaders, or technocrats. One can make people do this by destroying their traditional means of livelihood or by forcibly separating them from it; the enclosure of land gave Europe its first generation of industrial workers. Or one can make people do it by drafting them as forced laborers; this is how the first generation of plantation and industrial workers was established in most of the European colonies.[3] One can arrange a society in which the only alternative to such work is the humiliation of poverty, or actual starvation; Karl Polanyi has shown how the free-market economists intentionally introduced the possibility of individual starvation into European society (e.g. by abolishing poor relief) as a means of labor discipline.[4] One can arrange a society such that virtually nothing of value can be had in any way other than by exchange for money, and industrialized work (yours or someone else's) is the only way to get money. Or one can put the economy directly under the power of the state—call this "socialism" or whatever—and use the iron fist of state power to enforce the iron laws of economic development and keep people at their jobs. All of these systems can be strengthened by the addition of an ideology that doing industrial labor is virtuous, or heroic, or patriotic, or a characteristic of "advanced civilization," or (for people who doubt their adulthood) mature, or (for office workers) prestigious, or (for men) macho, or (for women) liberating, or the like. The point is that to make people do unnatural kinds of work for unnaturally long hours under unnatural working conditions one must either force them or implant in their minds some ideology under which they will force themselves. The various "economic systems" we see in the world today are different combinations of these different sorts of force and ideology.

Economic development is also antidemocratic because it promotes social inequality (I assume here, as some theorists do not, that social equality is a democratic ideal).[5] Of course we have known for two centuries that this effect was true of capitalist economic development. Socialism was proposed as a solution, on the hypothesis that socialization of the ownership of the means of production would democratize the economy, that is, put it under the control of the workers and distribute power and wealth equally within it. This hypothesis is in the midst of a grave crisis today. If we grant that the pursuit of inequality ("getting ahead," "rising in the world," etc.) is the driving force behind the free-market economy, it seems that replacing this economy with a socialist economy *and still desiring economic development* requires finding a new driving force. The Leninist solution was to rely on the power of the state, supplemented by the power of ideology. The result is, as we know well today, only the replacing of one kind of inequality with another: a command economy needs commanders and foot soldiers. Where once workers in the capitalist countries hoped that socialism would bring the democratization of their economies, today workers in the socialist countries, at least some of them, hope that a return to the free market will bring them democracy. But this only takes the problem back to where it was in the nineteenth century.[6] The free market continues to generate inequality in wealth and power, as before. If "socialism" is not the solution, then what is?

Economic development is antidemocratic in that it is a process of establishing and strengthening an undemocratic form of rule over a central aspect of people's lives—their work—and also in that it generates inequality in wealth and power. In addition, it is antidemocratic in that it turns people's attention away from political goals and struggles and replaces them with "economic" goals. The economic-development ideology teaches that most of the things people really want are economic, hence most social problems are economic, so that the ultimate solution to them is economic development itself. It is no accident that the labor movement's shift from the struggle for power and for democratization of the workplace toward the struggle for higher wages is called "economism." The development ideology redefines the classical political demands: freedom becomes the free market; equality becomes equality of opportunity; security becomes job security; consent becomes "consumer sovereignty," and the pursuit of happiness becomes a lifetime of shopping. Economic development of the Third World countries is offered as a solution to the continued domination over them by the industrial powers, and to the vast inequality in wealth and power generated and maintained by that domination. Economic-development ideology transforms political domination, for which democracy is the solution, into economic domination, for which submission in the form of disciplined hard work, eventually leading to prosperity and "leisure," is the alleged solution. Economic development is antidemocratic in that it is the expansion of a sphere of life from which democracy is to be excluded in principle.

The Tenacity of the Belief in Development
The antidemocratic character of economic development may be hard to see, but not because it has been kept a secret. Development ideologists may speak highly of democracy in the prefaces and conclusions to their

works, but in the main body, where concrete forms of social organization are discussed, the concept does not appear. The undemocratic character of a society organized to maximize efficiency in production is well known among technocrats, economists and business managers all over the world. It is an axiom of management science, espoused especially fervently by advocates of the "Japanese system of management."[7] It has been considered as plain common sense by such development dictators as Benito Mussolini, Joseph Stalin, Auguste Pinochet, Pak Chung-hee, Lee Kwang-yu, Deng Xaioping, Nicolae Ceauşescu, and Ferdinand Marcos. Marcos, for example, organized a thinktank and had it put together an elaborate ideology to legitimize his martial-law regime, which Philippine scholar Alexander Magno analyzed and appropriately labeled "developmentalism."[8] And the scholars who wrote Marcos's books for him had no difficulty in finding firm grounds for martial-law development in mainstream Western (mainly American) social science.[9] What is remarkable is that the horrors perpetrated around the world under such developmentalist dictatorships do not seem to have discredited the idea of development itself. In many places development kept its good name because it could be argued that development was never really attempted: what was supposed to have been a team of technocrats turned out to be a band of robbers, and the painfully extracted surplus value went not into capital investment but into Manhattan real estate and Swiss banks. The "development debacle" under which so many crimes and horrors were committed could be denounced as an impostor. The genuine article (should it ever appear) would be a different thing altogether. Critics of development *as it has been* advocate development *as it might be*. Many seem to think that it can be a saved by finding just the right adjective for it: "true," "genuine," "alternative," "appropriate," "pro-people," "sustainable," or the like.

After Marcos's development dictatorship was overthrown, the Philippine government adopted a new constitution (1986) in which the word "development" appears thirty-four times,[10] as compared to four times for the 1935 constitution (five, if we include the provision added in 1945 allowing U.S. citizens equal rights in the development of Philippine natural resources) and seven times for the 1973 constitution. This increase in the use of the word reflects an increase in the number of entities seen as proper objects for development. In the 1935 constitution three things were to be developed: natural resources, the national language, and "the patrimony of the nation." In the 1986 constitution some of the things to be subjected to development are: the economy, the nation, humans, policy, rural areas, human resources, the national wealth, regions, self-government units, society, tourism, the cultural heritage, agriculture, science and technology, "a reservoir of national talents," health manpower, the family, Filipino capability, and children.

Whether or not this list is disturbing depends on what is meant by "development" in these several contexts. But it is disturbing to find passages in the People's Power Constitution in which development is recognized as a potential limiting factor to democracy. In particular the section on land reform—the key issue in the democratization of Philippine society and the one on which the Aquino government foundered—provides that "the state shall encourage and undertake the just distribution of all agricultural lands . . . taking into account . . . developmental . . . considerations" (Article XIII, sec. 4). Behind this bland language are the recognition that just distribution may turn out to be an "obstacle to development" and the implication that in that eventuality development should be given first priority.

Of course the People's Power Constitution was written largely by landlords, and one may suspect the sections on land reform of being insincere. But if so, we should expect to find different attitudes on the left. At least on the intellectual left, however, they are about the same. In the debate among Marxists over whether the mode of production in the Philippines is semifeudal or capitalist, and therefore whether Philippine revolutionaries should fight to establish capitalism or socialism, the key factor is development.[11] That is, the crucial failure of the present mode of production is not so much its injustice as the fact that it stands as an "obstacle to development." From this belief it is possible to conclude that in the determination of which new mode of production to fight for, the main criterion is development. In the postrevolutionary society, writes a Marxist economist, "the thrust of the overall program for agriculture is to make access to land be based on the ability to optimize resource use."[12] In other words, efficiency of production, not equality or the principle of "land to the tiller," will be the deciding factor. It would be a mistake to take this academician's statement as representative of the thinking of the farmers in this country, for whom land reform is the principal demand. Still, though the above statement may be extreme, the structure of its thought is common enough in contemporary Marxism around the world.

Development as Iron Law: Marx

Of course, those who already see Marxism as a theory of economic development may find nothing surprising here. After all, it was Marx who gave the word "development" much of its contemporary meaning. Before Marx, the word was applied in ordinary use only to a limited number of things: one could develop a chess position or a military attack, one could develop shafts in a mine, one could develop virtues, and one could develop the plot of a novel. In Hegelian philosophy, world history itself is the development (*Entwicklung*) of the human spirit, under the guidance of what Hegel was ready to call Providence.[13] Marx took this term, which Hegel had bloated to metaphysical proportions, and applied it to the field of economics. In this way he gave it a specific technical meaning without ridding it of its mystical overtones. Marx could write very concretely about the development of the forces of production and at the same time make godlike pronouncements about the development of entire countries, as in his famous passage in the Preface to *Capital*: "The country that is more developed industrially only shows, to the less developed, the image of its own future."[14] But this usage is still different from the way the term is used today. For Marx, development was never a project. It was not something intentionally to be brought about by means of a development strategy. Rather, it was, as he wrote in the sentence immediately preceding the one quoted above, a consequence of "laws . . . winning their way through and working themselves out with iron necessity." Development had no conscious author, but it had an unconscious agent. It was an unintended consequence of the quest for profits of the bourgeoisie.

And if development was not a project for the bourgeoisie, much less was it a project for the revolutionaries, because the particular actions that, taken together, constituted development were crimes. To transform the world into something from which it could systematically extract profit, the bourgeoisie were ripping it apart, tearing people from their homes, exploding their communities, trampling on their ancient customs and liberties, expropriating their craft skills, and placing them under an unprecedented form of oppression and in an unprecedented form of systematized poverty. It was precisely development that had created the situation Friedrich Engels described in *The Condition of the English Working Class*.

Of course Marx's attitude toward development was two-sided. On the one hand the bourgeoisie had done an awesome and useful piece of work. "It has been the first to show what man's activity can bring about. It has accomplished wonders far surpassing Egyptian pyramids, Roman aqueducts, and Gothic cathedrals."[15] But at the same time it had created a world based on "naked, shameless, direct, brutal, exploitation,[16] and for precisely that reason deserved to be overthrown, expropriated, and driven from the stage of history.

Development was no project for revolutionaries. Revolutionary action was in opposition to the developers and was justified by the crimes of development and by the fact that whatever good came of development had never been intended by the bourgeoisie. At the same time, revolution redeemed development by turning the newly created apparatus of production to just purposes for the first time. But the purpose of revolution was establishment of justice, not promotion of development.

Concentrating his attention mainly on France and England, Marx was able to believe that the new industrial order would be fully established before the anticipated revolution. This timing was, if one may put it so, a great convenience, for it meant that the bourgeoisie would do all the necessary dirty work, take its just punishment, and that the new industrial society—thus purged of the crimes that had brought it into being— could be inherited by the guiltless working class. The revolution, in addition to being an act of power, was also to be a ritual purification of industrial development. Obviously this script could not be followed where there was a Marxist revolution in a society that had not been industrialized, which is why Marx's writings on the nonindustrial societies of his day tend to be among his most obscure. And it explains why the Marxism of development-Marxists today is correctly called Marxism-Leninism.

not quite!

Development as Iron Discipline: Lenin

In V. I. Lenin's career we can see the historical moment at which "development" was transformed from a process spun out by the cunning of history to a project under the direction of human will and reason.[17]

In 1899, Lenin published what may have been the most widely read, or at least the most widely distributed, book ever written about development: over three million copies of *The Development of Capitalism in Russia* are said to have been sold.[18] In this work one can see the beginnings of the shift from Marxism to Marxism-Leninism. The basic structure is the same as Marx's: capitalism is subjectively criminal and objectively progressive. But the emphasis is on the progressive side. In the context of a Russia that had only just begun to industrialize, Lenin was arguing against the Narodnik position, which was that if capitalism was such a brutal arrangement it should be kept out of Russia altogether. The main text of Lenin's work is an account of the good and necessary things capitalism would bring, interspersed only occasionally with qualifying phrases such as "with the full recognition of the negative and dark sides of capitalism" (p. 602). Capitalism is progressive because it "separates industry from agriculture," that is, it takes farmers and makes them into industrial proletarians working in factories. It takes them from under the control of the traditions of agrarian society and places them under the control of industrial organization. It changes the nature of production by concentrating it and organizing it; it changes the nature of consumption by destroying subsistence and making people dependent on commodity consumption (this is the main theme of the book, as indicated in its subtitle, *The Process of the Formation of a Home Market for Large-Scale Industry*). "The progressive historical role of capitalism [i.e. its role as the agent of "development"] may be summed up in two brief propositions: increase in the productive forces of social labour, and the socialization of that labour" (pp. 602–3). This massive transformation from "natural economy" (p. 37) to industrial economy leads also to "a change in the mentality of the population" (p. 606), a change Lenin judges to be an improvement. He is so sure of this that he is ready to oppose efforts to ban labor by women and children in the factories as "reactionary and utopian." "By drawing them into direct participation in social production, large-scale machine industry stimulates their development and increases their independence" (p. 552). Development increases efficiency, raises production, and improves both the workers' society and the workers themselves. But, as with Marx, these cultural changes are not intentional. "Large-scale machine industry . . . imperatively calls for the planned regulation of production and public control over it" (pp. 549–50). That this is the natural order of societal evolution is taken for granted; public action is a result of development, not a cause of it.

The last section of *The Development of Capitalism in Russia*, titled "The 'Mission' of Capitalism," summarizes the progressive gains that capitalism was to bring to Russia. Less than twenty years after writing this Lenin found himself at the head of a revolutionary government in control of a country in which capitalism's "mission" had not been carried out. In March 1918, only months after the October Revolution, Lenin wrote in his essay "The Chief Task of Our Day": "Yes, learn from the Germans! History is moving in zigzags and by roundabout ways. It so happens that it is the Germans who now personify, besides a brutal imperialism, the principle of discipline, organization, harmonious co-operation on the basis of modern machine industry, and strict accounting and control. And that is just what we are lacking."[19]

Capitalism in Russia had been overthrown before its work was done; the Bolsheviks had no choice but to take over that work. Lenin saw this job as a major historical transition and as a fundamental change in the nature of development. Whereas "the chief organizing force of anarchically built capitalist society is the spontaneous growing and expanding national and international market," now after the revolution the reorganization of the society for factory production was "the principal task of the proletariat."[20] The Bolsheviks had "started from the opposite end to that prescribed by theory (the theory of pedants of all kinds), because in our country the political and social revolution preceded the cultural revolution, that very cultural revolution which nevertheless now confronts us."[21] The task was huge. It involved "the organizational reconstruction of the whole social economy, by a transition from individual disunited, petty commodity production to large-scale social production."[22] At the same time it was also necessary "to bring about a complete change in the mood of the people and to bring them on to the proper path of steady and disciplined labour."[23] This work is rather different from what Marx had described as the historical task of the revolutionary proletariat. But now "the proletariat has become the *ruling* class; it wields state power" and as a result faced "tasks which the proletariat formerly did not and could not set itself."[24]

Lenin was frank—"passionate" might be a better word—in emphasizing that in the field of economic development there is no room for democracy. One socialist notion has been that socialism was an attempt to extend democracy from the political to the economic sphere: the bourgeois revolutions had won democracy for the people as citizens; now socialism would win democracy for the people as workers. But this was not Lenin's idea. First of all, he saw a contradiction between economic development and what was supposed to have been one aspect of workers' democracy, economic equality. He had no hesitation about which to choose: "I insist that bonuses . . . mean a great deal more to economic development, industrial management, and wider union participation in production than the absolutely abstract (and therefore empty) talk about 'industrial democracy.' "[25] More important, he saw democracy itself as alien to the workplace: "We must learn to combine the 'public meeting' democracy of the working people—turbulent, surging, overflowing its banks like a Spring flood—with *iron* discipline while at work, with *unquestioning obedience* to the will of a single person, the Soviet leader, while at work.[26]

To make this point all the stronger, Lenin was willing to give a new definition to a key Marxist term—a definition which, I am sure, Marx never anticipated. The "dictatorship of the proletariat," Lenin said in April 1918 (three years before the announcement of the New Economic Policy), "by no means merely consists in overthrowing the bourgeoisie or the landowners—that happened in all revolutions—our dictatorship of the proletariat is the establishment of order, discipline, labor productivity, accounting and control by the proletarian Soviet power"[27] But mere dictatorship at the workplace was not enough. To make this dictatorship scientific and efficient, Lenin advocated the introduction of a management technology hated by the workers the world over:

> The Russian is a bad worker compared with people in advanced countries. It could not be otherwise under the tsarist regime and in view of the persistence of the hangover from serfdom. The task that the Soviet government must set all the people in all its scope is—learn to work. The Taylor System, the last word of capitalism in this respect, like all capitalist progress, is a combination of the refined brutality of bourgeois exploitation and a number of the greatest scientific achievements in the field of analyzing mechanical motions during work. . . . The Soviet Republic must at all costs adopt all that is valuable in the achievements of science and technology in this field.[28]

"The achievements of science and technology" are not to be used only for squeezing maximum productivity out of the individual worker; they are also to be employed in planning the development of the society as a whole. Lenin's famous remark that socialism meant "soviets plus electrification" is frequently quoted. There is a kind of charm in the seeming simplicity and straightforwardness of the formula. But it is often forgotten that for Lenin "electrification" was no simple matter at all. It was a shorthand expression for the planned reorganization of the entire society according to the logic of "large-scale machine production." The link can be found in the February 1920 Resolution of All Russian Central Executive Committee, which Lenin was fond of quoting and presumably wrote: "Soviet Russia now has, for the first time, an opportunity of starting on more balanced economic development, and working out a nation-wide state economic plan on scientific lines and consistently implementing it. In view of the prime importance of electrification . . . the Committee resolves: to authorize the Supreme Economic Council to work out . . . a project for the construction of a system of electric power stations."[29] Lenin believed that this was history's first comprehensive, scientific, written plan for national economic development. The weight he gave to it can be seen in the fact that he had the Eighth Congress resolve that "a study of this plan must be an item in the curricula of *all educational establishments of the Republic, without exception.*[30]

The massive uprooting of humanity from traditional community life and work, the rendering extinct of ancient skills, values, and ways of thinking and feeling to make society into an instrument of efficient factory production—a process of which Marx said, "World history offers no spectacle more frightful"[31]—were for Lenin the "new tasks" on which "we must . . . concentrate all our forces, with the utmost effort and with ruthless, military determination."[32] All of this must be seen, of course, in the context of the position of the fledgling Soviet government at the time. Ravaged by the war, surrounded by enemies, plagued by food shortages, trains that never ran on time and factories only sporadically producing, Russia was in a desperate situation, and Lenin's furious calls for sacrifice and discipline are perfectly understandable. At the same time the expression "ruthless, military determination" should be taken seriously: the imagery and ideology of development, as well as the actual organizational form it takes in factories and bureaucracies, owes much to the military model. Years later Karl Deutsch proposed the term "social mobilization" to capture the phenomenon of reorganizing a society for industrial production, saying that the expression came to him as a "poetic image" suggested by "the historical experiences of the French *levée en masse* in 1793 and of the German 'total mobilization' of 1914–1918."[33] And many post–World War II modernization theorists have pointed out the key role of the military in the "modernizing elites" and in giving the people their first experience in "modern forms of organization."[34]

Another peculiarity of Lenin's position is that the reorganization of the society which is to be carried out with ruthless determination using the deliberate power of the state is at the same time still the unfolding of a historically determined process. The iron laws of history become embodied in positive law, to be enforced under the iron discipline of the state. This peculiar combination, in which state power is seen as the medium for carrying out some metahistorical process, has often been noted as a characteristic of twentieth-century authoritarian rule and is identified by Arendt as a crucial factor in totalitarianism.[35] It is a kind of contemporary version of divine-right theory, depoliticizing political power by placing its alleged source outside of the realm of human choice. It puts the power holder in the position of being responsible for carrying out the iron laws of the process, while not being responsible for the consequences of doing so.

Consider this extraordinary method of reasoning: "In every socialist revolution . . . —and consequently in the socialist revolution in Russia which we began on October 25, 1917—the principal task of the proletariat . . . [etc.]."[36] Lenin wrote this in April 1918. According to this way of thinking, one learns one's tasks by reasoning deductively from the general principle to the particular instance, of which at the time of writing there had been only one in all history. This "task" then is not a choice made by fallibly human political leaders, grounded in past experience and a reading of the present situation. It is a fixed universal that existed before they came into power. The contribution of this strange form of duty-without-responsibility to what came to be known as Stalinism is well known. What is less often noticed is that the key to this mode of thinking—that is, the very content of this "task" that is commanded as a superhistorical duty—is the reorganization of the society for "large-scale machine production" and for mass distribution, that is, development.

Developing Other Peoples: Capitalist and Noncapitalist Paths

With the Russian Revolution development was transformed from a process to a project; grammatically the word "develop" was transformed from an intransitive to a transitive verb. At the initial stage described above, however, it remained a domestic project: the state and Party leaders were to develop their own country, not some other one. At what point did it come to be used transnationally?

Before World War II one can find two areas in which the notion was so employed. The first was in the expression "colonial development." The term, however, as used by European colonialists was purely pragmatic, containing none of the superhistorical or protoprovidential overtones that it has both in Marxist theory and in contemporary development theory. It meant, simply, development of resources, that is, organization of people and equipment in such a way that resources could be extracted at a profit. Though it was sometimes claimed that such organization would help native peoples "progress" or "become civilized," this social consequence was seen as a side effect, not the aim of the project. Thus in 1939 when the British government was forced to enact (at least on paper) a program for the welfare of colonized peoples, it replaced the 1929 Colonial Development Act with the Colonial Development and Welfare Act.[37] This way of seeing development and welfare as separate questions could be taken as evidence of the impoverished historic-philosophical vision of insensitive British pragmatists. It may also be seen as based on an honest, straightforward, nonideological understanding of the true character of development, by people who knew exactly what they were doing.

A second use of the word "development" to indicate a transnational process, not often mentioned in Western development writings, appears in the Stalinist period in the Soviet Union. It had been hard enough for the Bolsheviks to argue that the Russian economy had become sufficiently capitalist that Marxist revolutionary theory could be applied to it; that application was quite impossible for the peoples in the Russian Empire.

To describe the industrialization of these indigenous peoples under Soviet rule, the notion of the Noncapitalist Path of Development was formulated, as described in *The Great Soviet Encyclopedia*: "The idea of the noncapitalist path of development found definite expression in the transition to socialism under the new socialist state of the backward peoples of the Russian Empire (the peoples of Middle Asia, Kazakhstan, the Northern Caucasus, and the European Asiatic North)."[38] Here, "socialism" is no longer a rebellion against, or a solution to, capitalism: there is no capitalism for it to be a solution to. Moreover, it is no longer an ideal. To say that it is a "path" is to say that it is a means. Development is the end; socialism is a method of achieving it.

Cold War Development: Truman

In 1947, in the conclusion to his now-embarrassing *Lenin and the Russian Revolution*, Christopher Hill wrote, "Soviet experience in the bringing of modern civilization to backward peoples, and especially the development of the soviet system and collective farms as a means of self-government for agrarian peoples—this is bound to have enormous influence in eastern Europe, Asia, and perhaps ultimately in Africa and South America."[39] Hill did not, of course, think up this idea. It was in the air, and it had an extremely important influence in the formulation of the vocabulary of the Cold War discourse at the time. It formed the specific background against which the U.S. government became suddenly and unprecedentedly interested in "developing" countries other than the United States. Two years after Hill wrote his book, on January 20, 1949, President Harry S Truman announced that development was now U.S. government policy, and he introduced the newly coined term "underdevelopment" into public discourse: "We must embark on a bold new program for making the benefits of our scientific advances and industrial progress available for the improvement and growth of underdeveloped areas."[40]

Truman's speech was delivered at one of modern history's major turning points, the moment when the United States had emerged as a historically unprecedented superpower, inheriting proprietorship over the collapsed Japanese and collapsing European empires (a proprietorship that could no longer be exercised in the old colonial mode). And it was the moment of the beginning of the Cold War. And it was a time when the United States badly needed outlets for capital investment. Truman's "bold new program" to develop the "underdeveloped counties" brilliantly took into account all these elements. In his later *Memoirs* he described the program as a splendid venture "aimed at enabling millions of people in underdeveloped areas to raise themselves from the level of colonialism to self-support and ultimate prosperity." At the same time it "was consistent with our policies of preventing the expansion of Communism." And it was a good way to use "some of the capital which had accumulated in the United States. If the investment of capital from the United States could be protected and not confiscated, and if we could persuade the capitalists that they were not working in foreign countries to exploit them but to develop them, it would be to the mutual benefit of everybody concerned."[41]

Hidden in Truman's muddled prose one can see the basic outlines of the newly emerging ideology of development. Of course, Truman was not seriously proposing that the functioning of capitalism could be changed by persuading capitalists to develop instead of exploit. In fact, the sentences do not say that capitalists should do something different; they say that we should stop calling what they do "exploitation" and start calling it "development." And of course it was not the capitalists who needed to be convinced of this (they knew for what purpose they were working in foreign countries) but the people of those countries and the anticolonialists in the United Nations and among U.S. citizens.

In his biography, Truman described the program as "an adventurous idea such as has never been proposed by any country in the history of the world."[42] This boast should be taken seriously. It does not mean, as we have seen, that Truman and his advisers invented the idea of development as a national project, or were the first to use the term as a transitive verb. But it was with the Point Four Program that "development" took its full post–World War II form, to mean a conscious project of the industrial capitalist countries aimed at the total transformation of societies, primarily in the Third World, allegedly directed at curing a malaise called "underdevelopment." Before Truman's 1949 speech, the only object the dictionaries listed as possibly subject to underdevelopment was camera film. Only after his speech did "development," in the sense of the specific remedy for the disease called "underdevelopment," come to be established as a technical term in the social sciences in the capitalist countries. The announcement of this new government policy gave birth, in the United States, to an entire new paradigm for the social sciences, within which such fields as development economics appeared. Millions of dollars from such sources as the Ford Foundation and the U.S. Department of Defense were poured into "modernization" and "development" research, and they paid for hundreds and perhaps thousands of books and articles. Hundreds and perhaps thousands of promising young scholars were brought from Third World countries to the United

States on fellowships for the purpose of converting them to the new gospel and making them into "modernizing elites." In short, just when United States social scientists were trumpeting the superiority of their "value-free" methodology, the combination of a government policy decision and big money succeeded in conjuring up an entire new field of social science out of thin air.

The ideology of development has been immensely successful, not in actually raising the poor people of the world to the level of "ultimate prosperity" but in convincing millions that this is what capitalist activities in the Third World are intended to do. In fact, the expression "development of underdeveloped countries" refers to a set of activities which from another value perspective can be called "neocolonialism." Under this ideology was launched the most massive systematic project of human exploitation, and the most massive assault on culture and nature, which history has ever known. It was the extraordinary achievement of the development ideology to render the imperialism of the countries and corporations carrying out this project an arguable question. It has enabled development economists to write about all of this without using any of the old vocabulary of colonialism and imperialism, as if they not only no longer exist but never did, or if they did, didn't matter.[43]

Not that all these scholars were innocently unaware that they were turning their scholarship to the purposes of capitalist profiteering and government strategy. As one academic put it,

> Internationally known figures have said that competition between the two powerful opposing camps will increasingly shift from the military phase to the economic, and that success will hinge on their ability to develop underdeveloped areas. It might be remarked, with tongue in cheek, that so much attention has been focused on underdeveloped areas and their problems that the social scientists, if they could deliver, would gain increased prestige and status at the expense of the military.[44]

This professor who saw the common purpose shared by the military "phase" and the economic "phase" of the Cold War was not some Low Intensity Conflict theorist of the 1980s. This was written in 1957, which fact should help us to remember that Low Intensity Conflict is neither a new idea nor a bizarre set of schemes advocated by some group of adventurers at the margins of U.S. policy. This insight on which LIC is based—that military activity is more effective when it is supplemented by economic and social activity (technical assistance, development aid, Peace Corps volunteers, etc.)—has been the mainstream of U.S. foreign policy since Truman's speech. From the standpoint of U.S. policy, there is no distinction between LIC and development. From the beginning development has been seen as a form of LIC.

The concept of development, then, came to its present form in the context of the long dialogue between Marxism and liberalism. In the Cold War period the version put together by Truman and his advisers, backed by U.S. power, was successful in dominating the discourse in most of the world. At the same time, Truman development theory owes a debt to Marxism-Leninism which has never, so far as I know, been properly acknowledged. It is, in effect, a kind of liberal historical materialism, with the same mixture of voluntarism and inevitability (shifting from one to the other as the situation demands), the same notion of duty-without-responsibility. It is also a kind of economic-determinism-made-simple, so that positivist social scientists can understand it. As David Apter put it in 1965: "*In industrializing societies it is the economic variable that is independent. The political system is the dependent variable.*"[45] The point is that the "economic variable" is no longer seen here as developing according to its own laws, except in the prefaces to books, where the question is dealt with at the metahistorical level. As a practical matter, the "economic variable" is precisely the thing economic development is designed to bring under domination. To abbreviate the story somewhat: economic determinism was set in motion unconsciously by the capitalists, was discovered and analyzed by Marx, and then taken up consciously by capitalism again in the new form of economic-development theory. Now the message is: you control the economy, and you control all.

The next stage in the dialogue was the rebuttal from the Marxist side beginning with Paul Baran's book *The Political Economy of Growth* in 1957, said to be the first Marxist work to use "underdevelopment" as a technical term.[46] Again, the act of rebutting liberal development led to a further convergence of the two theories, as now some of the liberal terminology entered the Marxist discourse. Truman's picture of the world as divided between "developed" and "underdeveloped" countries is the presupposition that produces the shock effect of Andre Gunder Frank's famous paradox, "the development of underdevelopment." It was the very important work of Frank and other dependency theorists to show that U.S. development theory was a fraud, that the condition called "underdeveloped" was as it was not because it was traditional but because of the disfiguring effects of decades or centuries of colonialism and neocolonialism,[47] and that development (in this context, industrialization leading to prosperity in the poor countries) could not happen so long as this dependency relationship continued. The point is well taken, but from the standpoint of development theory itself it is a kind of insider critique. The critique "Capitalism can never put an end to underdevelopment" is true and important; the trouble comes with the implied conclusion, "And that's what's wrong with it." And this leads to the next troubling implication: "Whereas socialism can—and that's what's good about it." Liberalism and Marxism are set side by side as middle-level hypotheses within the general paradigm of development economics. The choice between them is no longer a matter of commitment or value but is pragmatic and empirical, depending on which turns out to serve best as the means to the shared end, economic development. Victory, in short, goes to Harry Truman. And the way is fully prepared for a Marxist economist to state that the criterion for a revolutionary government to use in its choice of land policy is the "optimization" of resource use.

The Development Metaphor

To understand the particular ideological power of the notion of development we should take careful note of the fact that it contains a half-hidden metaphor. In its original, nonmetaphorical meaning, its antonym was not "decline" or "stagnation" but "envelopment." "Velop" is not a word in English, but the same root appears in the Italian word *viluppare*, "to enwrap, to bundle, to fold, to roll up." To develop something means to unfold it or unroll it, to take it out of something in which it is wrapped. In this meaning, now obsolete, one could say, "He developed the contents of the package," meaning he unwrapped the package and took out the contents. The same image can be found hidden in the Italian *sviluppare*, the French *développer*, the Spanish *desarrollo*, the German *Entwicklung*.

From this beginning, the word was applied metaphorically to two kinds of situations. The growth of living organisms is called development, calling up an image of a form that had been "wrapped up" inside the immature organism (seed or infant) being "unwrapped" and revealed. Or the progression of a story is called development, calling up an image of a meaning hidden in the original situation gradually "unfolding" and becoming evident to the reader or listener. Combining and abstracting from these two processes, "development" took on a third meaning, that of a certain structure of change. Developmental change is change that takes a given entity through stages, such that a form that is latent in the earlier stage becomes manifest in the later stage. (This means, at least in the European languages, that the distinction sometimes made between exogenous and endogenous development is linguistically inappropriate. Strictly speaking it is incorrect to use "development" to describe exogenous change.)

In this still preideological sense, development does not necessarily mean change for the better. The desirability of change depends on what is developing. Fires and floods develop, enemy attacks develop and, as the *Oxford English Dictionary* carefully reminds us, diseases develop; the example *OED* offers is swine flu.

In the ideology of development, the power of the metaphor is that it gives the impression that the projects being carried out under that ideology are natural, inevitable, and bring about the proper and predestined future of the entity being developed. Development is portrayed as something that will happen by itself as soon as the "obstacles to development" are removed. In fact, virtually all of the changes that take place under the ideology of development are of an entirely different sort. Villagers are driven out and dams are built; forests are cut down and replaced by plantations; whole cultures are smashed and people are recruited into quite different cultures; local means of subsistence are taken away and people are placed under the power of the world market. It is not correct usage to apply the term "development" to the process of knocking down one thing and building something else in its place. Calling such activities "development" conceals the fact that they are human choices, that is, activities that human beings are *free not to do.*

This intentional misapplication of the metaphor of development is what gives rise to the semimystical notion, found both in liberal and Marxist development theory, that when political and economic leaders use their power to reorganize the natural and social world for maximum industrial productivity, they are only acting as agents of a vast historical force beyond human power to question or change, and so are not morally responsible for the consequences.

An additional message hidden inside the development metaphor (though hardly believed any longer by thoughtful people in the overdeveloped countries) is that the industrialization of the economy of a society corresponds in the long run to the development of the human spirit in some Hegelian or providential fashion—put simply, that economic development makes people better. This is a wonderfully self-satisfying thought for people who live in what are considered the developed countries. It is a slander against those who don't.

Underdevelopment, on the other hand, is a truly remarkable concept. It succeeds in placing the vast majority of the world's cultures into a single category the sole characteristic of which is the absence of certain characteristics of the industrialized countries. Is it proper social-science procedure to describe the absence of an efficient telephone system in, say, the town of Bereku in the Masai Steppe, in the ancient city of Cairo, and in the Republic of Belau as a "common characteristic"? But this was not the first time that Europe gave a single name to all who did not display some characteristic of European culture. Holders of civilizations other than European had from ancient times been called "barbarian"; believers in any religion other than Christianity had been called "pagan"; the original inhabitants of any country that Europeans colonized were called "natives"; and races any color other than white were called "colored." "Underdeveloped" was only the latest in this long series of labels for "the Others." However, it was in this form, Gustavo Esteva has argued, that the categorization acquired "its most virulent colonizing force,"[48] because this time millions of people were somehow convinced to accept it as their self-definition. Peoples whose cultures had for millennia taught them that the overt ("disembedded") and unlimited pursuit of material gain was offensive and dishonorable now began to reject this way of thinking as ignorant and backward: "Our culturally imposed limitation of economic ends has been constantly disqualified; it was seen as apathy, conformism and especially as a serious 'obstacle to development,' characteristic of a 'premodern mentality.' We ourselves came to see it like this."[49] The development metaphor, teaching people to see themselves as "obstacles to development," promotes a colonization of consciousness of the deepest sort and is profoundly antidemocratic: it "took away from the hands of people the possibility of defining their own ways of social life."[50]

Development Is Not a Universal Concept

Esteva is from Mexico, a Third World country where a European language is spoken. "Development" there is *desarollo* and contains about the same metaphorical and historical baggage as the English word. But most of the languages of the Third World presumably never had a word for "development" until the developers came. So they had either to coin a new word or find some word in their language to which this new meaning could be given. How successful are these new words in capturing the overtones and implications of "development," one wonders? I am not qualified to answer this question, but I can report what some native speakers told me while I was in the Philippines. "Development" is translated into Tagalog (or Filipino) as *pag-unlad* or as the Spanish-based word *progreso*. It is translated into Ilongo as *pag-uswag* or *asenso*. In Ilocano it becomes *progreso* for those who live in a town, or *rang-ay* for those in a barrio. I asked a native speaker of Ilocano what would be the most ordinary use of the word, *rang-ay*. His first answer was that if someone asked you how you are, you might answer, "*Awan ti pinag rang-ay,*" which means "No development" and may be close to the English "Oh, about the same." The implication is that *rang-ay* suggests getting ahead of your fellows in the world, and this is frowned on, so that to disclaim it for yourself is considered good manners and is a good way to get along with people in your town.

I asked a native speaker of Ilongo what would be an ordinary use of the word *pag-uswag*. His first answer was, "When a barrio becomes a town." He said that it could also be used to describe a pig or a plant growing to maturity, or a house being built. What these examples share is that in none of them is something hitherto unknown introduced into the world. From old times there have been towns, and from old times barrios have sometimes becomes towns, as when there is peace, health, and a series of good harvests.

To learn the meaning of the Tagalog (or Filipino) word, I chose the following passage on development written in English by a Filipino scholar:

> The intensification of poverty should be analytically dissociated from the advance of the forces of production. . . . it has often been taken as an assumption in the popularized version of political economy that intensifying poverty is the result of "backwardness." If "backwardness" connotes the undeveloped character of the forces of production, then this line of analysis is inaccurate. The rapid intensification of poverty during the last decade results directly from the *advance* of the monopoly capitalist forces of production. . . . The decisive factor in this development . . . [etc.][51]

I asked the author of this passage what Tagalog word could be used to translate "development" as described in it, and in particular whether *pag-unlad* would work. His first answer was that it would not, and that perhaps no other word in Tagalog would either. His second answer was that perhaps you could use *pag-sulong*, which means to advance as down a road. Here the figure is of motion in space, with no particular notion of improvement attached to it. His third answer was that you have to make a distinction between the Tagalog of Manila, where it takes the form of the national language Filipino, and the Tagalog of the surrounding countryside, where it takes the form of a local dialect. In the urban language, especially when it is spoken by people who know the English "development," *pag-unlad* could be used—which means only that here *pag-unlad* has taken on the meaning of the English word.

The absence of a word equivalent to "development" is by no means a case of the Philippine language's being inferior in sophistication to the English. On the contrary, in all cases the Philippine words are clear and precise. *Pag-unlad* means "to prosper." You use it when things prosper but not when people are starving or pigs have swine flu. What these Philippine dialects (except for the dialect of the Manila intelligentsia) lack is a word that tells you that things are getting better when you can see with your own eyes that they are getting worse. In short, they lack the ability to express what George Orwell called "doublethink."

Modern Architecture: The Slum

For what else can we call the development metaphor but doublethink? Consider its hypnotic power. We stand at the end of what may go down in history as the Century of Development. If we can tear our gaze away from the fantasies of futurology and look at the real world around us, what we see are unprecedented forms of mass poverty, unprecedented forms of mass killing, unprecedented methods of regimentation, unprecedented pollution, destruction, and uglification of the earth, and unprecedented concentration of wealth and power in the hands of the few. Knowing all this, and having understood Andre Gunder Frank's paradox, still we refuse to give up the idea, and tell ourselves that all of this must have been some kind of deception, an impostor, a false development, and that surely there must still be a "true development" yet to come.[52]

To demystify the gospel of development, a good starting place is to take the insights of world-systems theory seriously—one degree more seriously that they are usually taken. In discourse on development one sometimes encounters the assertion that development follows a certain "law of motion." This is, of course, a metaphor drawn from Newtonian physics, but it is never mentioned which of Newton's three laws is being referred to. If A. G. Frank and Immanuel Wallerstein are correct that development should be seen as a world-scale, and not just as a local or national, phenomenon, then the answer is clear. The law of motion that development has unvaryingly followed in this century is Newton's Third: "For every action there is an equal and opposite reaction." For everyone who has been enriched, someone has been impoverished. It would be pushing the analogy too far to insist that the numbers are just the same. In fact they are not: the impoverished far outnumber the enriched.

When we think of modernization and development, we tend to think of the International Style of the Bauhaus, high steel-and-glass buildings, quiet-running engines, airports, computers, and so on. We must recognize this image as a self-deception if we truly are to look at things scientifically, and in a world-systems perspective. If development is a world-scale phenomenon, then everything that it has produced, and not just those parts that are pleasing to the eye or to the moral sense, must equally be called modern and developed. "Modern architecture" must be seen as precisely what virtually every major city in the Third World actually has today: steel-and-glass high-rise buildings plus slums built by squatters. For the slums are just as new as the high-rises, or newer. Moreover, they are largely made of modern building materials: plywood, corrugated iron, fiberboard, plastic sheets, cement blocks. Or take Smoky Mountain, Manila's famous garbage dump: anyone who has ever walked over it knows that it is made up of very developed garbage: automobile tires, broken machine parts, rubber sandals, polyester cloth, and lots of plastic bags. (For that matter, "garbage" itself is modern; subsistence economies did not produce "garbage.") The work of the thousands of Smoky Mountain squatters, which is mainly collecting these bags, washing them in the river, and selling them to a company that reprocesses them into paint and plastic dolls, has become technologically possible only in the last few decades. We should think of it as a sunrise industry, like the computer-chip business. From a world systems perspective we should never fall into the sentimental error of talking about "poverty versus modernization" or "slums versus development," because this language takes our attention away from the very things that need to be studied, namely, the modernization of poverty and the development of slums.

Modernization and development never meant the elimination of poverty; rather it means the rationalization of the relationship between the rich and the poor. In this sense development includes not only the development of poverty but the development of the technology of management and oppression necessary to keep people in their position of relative poverty, quietly generating the surplus value that keeps the rich people rich. Thus world-scale development also includes the development of the police state, the martial-law regime, the company union, the strategic hamlet, scientific management, thought control, high-tech torture, the international network of the CIA—the list is as long as the history of the twentieth century.

Why Development Is a Losing Strategy

For democrats, then, to place their hopes on development, or to think of democracy as an eventual outcome of development, is to adopt a losing strategy, or rather it is to adopt a strategy that has already lost, one that has from the outset abandoned the vocabulary in which victory could be conceived or expressed. Democracy is a political state, which can be conceived only in political language, and can be achieved only through political struggle. You cannot talk your way to democracy in the language of development economics: "liberty" and "justice" do not exist as technical terms in economic science. And you cannot ride to democracy on the back of development. Development is not going there; and, anyway, to get to democracy you have to walk.

It is losing strategy because the "genuine development" dreamed of by good-hearted democratic developers will never happen. When Truman promised all the people of the world "ultimate prosperity" he meant, and everybody understood him to mean, life at the consumption levels of the U.S. middle class at least, that is, of the world's rich. This promise is a hopeless illusion. A second illusion is the notion that economic development can eventually bring the peoples of the world to a rough economic equality—that is, that the poor countries can "catch up." That these illusions still exist is a measure of how far we are from grasping the nature of the situation in which we find ourselves at the close of the twentieth century. It is worth mentioning some of the more obvious reasons why neither of these illusions can ever become reality.

Development Equality as a Statistical Absurdity. First, consider the gross statistics. According to the World Bank's 1988 *World Development Report*, the per-capita GNP for what they call Industrial Market Economies (i.e., the twenty richest capitalist countries) was U.S. $12,960 for 1986, with an average annual growth rate (1965–86) of 2.3 percent. A simple calculation gives for that year an increase in per-capita income of $298.08. The average per-capita income for the poorest thirty-three countries was $270, with a growth rate of 3.1 percent. The same calculation gives a one-year increase in per-capita income of $8.37. For these countries to equal the $298.08 increase in the per-capita income of the rich countries would require an annual growth rate of 110.4 percent.

Of course if the poor countries maintain a growth rate higher than that of the rich countries for a very long time, theoretically they could eventually catch up. How long would that take? Supposing the average growth figures in the *World Development Report* to remain unchanged, we can calculate that the poor countries will achieve the 1988 income level of the rich countries in 127 years. But of course like the hare fleeing Achilles, the rich countries will have become richer by then, so the poor countries will not actually catch up with them for half a millennium, 497 years to be exact. At that time the world average per-capita income will be $1,049,000,000.

If we assume the impossible, a sustained growth rate for all the poor countries of 5 percent, we can calculate that they will catch up in 149 years, at an average world per-capita income of just under $400,000 per year.

In fact the growth rate for these countries excluding India and China (it is mainly China's reported growth rate of 5 percent and vast population that skews the figures) is 0.5 percent. At that rate they will catch up never. And twelve of these countries have "negative growth rates."

Development Equality as a Structural Impossibility. These simple figures should help us avoid being unnecessarily surprised when we hear that after all the efforts that have gone into "development" the gap between the rich and poor countries continues to widen. But at the same time the figures are fanciful and misleading, in that they are not rooted in the reality of the economic system. That is, the *World Development Report* depicts the world as a collection of separate national economies rather than as a single economic system. The world economic system does not produce inequality accidentally, but generates it systematically. It operates to transfer wealth from poor countries to rich countries. A big part of the "economic development"—that is, the wealth—of the rich countries *is* wealth imported from the poor countries. From where could wealth be imported to create the same condition for all? The world economic system generates inequality and it runs on inequality. Just as the internal combustion engine is propelled by the difference in pressure above and below the piston, the world economy is propelled by the difference between the rich and the poor. So while we can fantasize statistics like a 5-percent growth rate for the poor and a 2.3-percent growth rate for the rich, we will not (under the rules of this game) see them in reality. It's rather like supposing a 5-percent growth rate in the winnings of the customers in a casino, with the house take remaining the same. The system is not built to do that.

If any doubt remains, we can refer to the authority of the former president of the World Bank, who in his celebrated speech to the bank's board of governors in 1973 said that for the rich to oppose development is "shortsighted, of course, for in the long term they, as well as the poor, can benefit."[53] We can be sure that any development that makes the poor a little better off will make the rich a lot better off.

"Ultimate Prosperity" as an Ecological Impossibility. Not only will the world economic system not allow "ultimate prosperity" for all; the earth itself will not sustain it. It is not clear whether the earth will be able to sustain even the present consumption levels of the minority rich. It has been estimated, for example, that for the world population to live at the present per-capita energy consumption of the people of Los Angeles would require five earths.* The statistic is dubious, but give or take a few earths, it amounts to the same thing. That consumption level cannot happen, it will not happen and we should stop talking as if it will.

The myth that it will is, of course, "functional": providing the fuel for the great engine that drives development forward; providing the spectacle that enthralls, transfixes, and draws the attention of the

---

* And it is important to remember that that consumption level has not produced economic equality, or eliminated poverty in that city. There are fabulously rich and desperately poor people in Los Angeles.

world's people from the real inequality generated by the world economy; providing the legitimation for the vast development industry that keeps many good-hearted people in it along with the development carpetbaggers. But the fact remains that in this or any other economic system the consumption levels of the rich, extended to all, would consume the world.

Why We Cannot All Be Rich. Development is a losing strategy for democrats because richness, which is the form of prosperity (and there are others) which it holds out as bait cannot be shared equally and in fact has a positive principle of inequality structurally within it. What, after all, is "rich"? The *OED* tells us that before it became an economic word, "rich" was political. It comes from the Latin *rex*, "king," and its oldest English definition, now obsolete, was "powerful, mighty, exalted, noble, great." Another obsolete form of the word is "riche," which meant "a kingdom, realm, royal domain" and is cousin to the German "Reich." Originally to be rich meant to have the power of the sort a king has, that is, power over other people. This is the kind of power one can have only when other people do not: where there are no subjects, there is no king. Only later was the word specialized to mean the particular kind of power one has over people by having more money than they do. Being rich does not mean controlling wealth; it means controlling people through wealth. Or, rather, the very "wealthiness" of this form of wealth is its capacity to control people. The value of money is not, after all, some magical property but what economists call its "purchasing power."* The point was made incisively a century ago by John Ruskin:

> I observe that men of business rarely know the meaning of the word "rich." At least, if they know, they do not in their reasonings allow for the fact, that it is a relative word, implying its opposite "poor" as positively as the word "north" implies the word "south." Men nearly always speak and write as if riches were absolute, and it were possible, by following certain scientific precepts, for everybody to be rich. Whereas riches are a power like that of electricity, acting only through the inequalities or negations of itself. The force of the guinea you have in your pocket depends wholly on

---

* Many "economic" terms originally had noneconomic meanings indicating naked power relations which are now hidden in the "free-contract" mythology of economics. "Purchase" (Latin *pro captiāre*, to catch, hunt, chase) originally meant "seizing or taking forcibly or with violence, pillage, plunder, robbery, capture." "Finance" meant "a payment for release from captivity or punishment; a ransom." "Pay" is from the Latin *pācāre*, to appease, pacify, reduce to peace. (*OED*.)

the default of a guinea in your neighbor's pocket. If he did not want it, it would be of no use to you; the degree of the power it possesses depends accurately upon the need or desire he has for it,—and the art of making yourself rich . . . is therefore equally and necessarily the art of keeping your neighbor poor.[54]

We think a person rich who has enough purchasing power to control the labor of a large number of other people. This control can take the form of directly hiring workers and servants or of arranging though the "service" industry to have other people do your work for you. We think a country rich when it has enough purchasing power to have a portion of its work done in other countries by "cheap labor." As Ruskin points out, this kind of purchasing power can be increased either by increasing the wealth of the rich or by increasing the poverty of the poor. Increasing the incomes of everyone increases the income of no one; this increase is not enrichment but inflation. So the old saying "The rich get richer and the poor get poorer" is not some kind of ironic paradox but an economic law as trim and tidy as Newton's Third Law of Motion: the rich get richer *when* the poor get poorer, and vice-versa.

Economic-development mythology is a fraud in that it pretends to offer to all a form of affluence which presupposes the relative poverty of some. Movies, television, and advertising originating in the overdeveloped countries idealize the lives of people who do less than their share of the world's work (because others do more), who consume more than their share of the world's goods (so that others must do with less), and whose lives are made pleasant and easy by an army of servants and workers (directly or indirectly employed). In an economy structured as a pyramid it is understandable that everyone might want to stand on top. But there is no way that positioning can be arranged. With everyone at the top, there is no pyramid, and no top.*

---

* In a famous passage in Aristotle's *Politics* (1253b–54a) the philosopher toys with the idea that perhaps slavery could be abolished if tools could be made to work by themselves, like the mythical statues of Daedalus (liberation through automation is a very old dream). He quickly dismisses the idea, however, pointing out that tools are instruments of production (*poiesis*), whereas slaves, like garments and beds, are instruments of action (*praxis*). Aristotle is reminding us of the tautology that the particular good attached to being served by others is being served by others. The master wears his slaves like garments, he walks around in them like shoes, he lies in them like a bed. They are not replaceable by moving statues, for without them the master is no master. So for the rich today there is no way the attentions of a top-class waiter (for example) can be replaced by the efficiency of a cafeteria or an automat.

This a priori inequality is also inherent in contemporary consumption. As we were taught a century ago by Thorstein Veblen, much of the consumption we associate with affluence is "conspicuous consumption," the specific pleasure of which is that there are others who cannot afford it. Nor is conspicuous consumption limited to the rich: establishing a mental association between a product and upper-class living is how unessential goods are sold to the poor—as every advertising agency knows. Nor is conspicuous consumption unknown in poor countries: the implantation of the desire for it is a big part of what modernization theorists have touted as the "revolution of rising expectations." In 1988 on Quezon Avenue in Metro Manila there was a huge, gross billboard advertising "Richgirl bras and girdles." The brand tells it all: how else do you convince people in tropical countries to buy girdles? By implanting in people the longing for elite status and by convincing them that bits and pieces of that status are infused in various consumer goods, the salesmen hope to guarantee infinite consumer demand and keep the development squirrel mill turning forever. Veblen's words take on an added significance today, when we know that endless growth can lead only to eco-catastrophe: "If . . . the incentive to accumulation were the want of subsistence or of physical comfort, then the aggregate economic wants of a community might conceivably be satisfied at some point . . . ; but since the struggle is substantially a race for reputability on the basis of an invidious comparison, no approach to a definitive attainment is possible."[55] It is by relentless logic, then, that "socialist" countries aspiring to achieve the standard of living of the overdeveloped capitalist countries break up into class structures in the process. That standard of living has class built into it. It is, as U.S. slang accurately tells us, "classy.

The Modernization of Poverty

Economists say that there are two types of poverty, absolute and relative. But the phenomenon can be further subdivided. Here I suggest that at least four distinct types of poverty can be differentiated.

First there is absolute, material poverty: the poor are those who do not have enough food, shelter, clothing, and medicine to maintain healthy life. This is the way poverty is usually depicted, and needs no elaboration.

Second, there are those who are called poor by outsiders but do not consider themselves to be so. A subsistence economy may appear impoverished to people from a different culture but may provide everything the people in it want or need, according to the standards of their own culture. Here it is important not to fall into the temptation of laying down a universal principle as to whether such outside judgments are always right or always wrong.

The extreme cultural relativist position, that such outside judgments are always improper, may be logically flawless in the abstract, but it is impossible to maintain in all concrete cases. People sometimes resign themselves to terrible situations and abolish from their cultures the language of criticism or protest. The fact that a culture may be arranged to accept chronic war or hunger or brutal oppression as fated does not mean that the pain is not felt and that the human spirit is not maimed by these conditions. On the other hand there are cases where the outside judgment is clearly absurd, as when indigenous peoples, for example, are declared impoverished by the absence of girdles, leather shoes, concrete buildings, street lights, or the like. The validity of such outside judgments can be determined only through a dialogue between the peoples of the different cultures on the basis of an equality and human respect which has been made almost impossible by the history of Western colonialism, chauvinism, and racism.

Third, there is social poverty. This is a relative poverty, but I do not mean here simply the poverty of one who possesses less wealth than others, as measured by some absolute standard (e.g., money income). I mean poverty as an economic and social relation, corresponding to the phenomenon of "rich" as described above. A person is poor who is controlled by the economic power of the rich. A person is poor who is one of those whose poverty generates the rich people's richness, whose labor generates their leisure, whose humiliation generates their pride, whose dependency generates their autonomy, whose namelessness generates their "good names." A person is socially poor who is organized as poor in the economic system.

A fourth kind of poverty is that produced by what Ivan Illich has called "radial monopolies."[56] This poverty occurs when people cannot have things they had never needed or wanted until these things were invented. Somebody invents the refrigerator, or the automobile, and succeeds in having it established as a minimum condition for ordinary living. This is a case not of meeting an existing need but of restructuring a society so as to establish a need where there had been none before, so that now the people who cannot buy this thing, including those who had never before dreamed of owing it, are to that degree impoverished. Through this process, people whose absolute standard of living does not change at all are driven deeper and deeper into "poverty" by changes that occur in distant places and over which they have no control. It is easy to see the deeply antidemocratic nature of this process. And it is also easy to see that this kind of poverty is not reduced by industrial development but is generated by it, and generated by it endlessly. Development does not bring people "freedom from want"; rather, it operates to keep people in a state of perpetual domination by want.

Absolute poverty is hard, but where it exists by itself—that is, where all are equally poor—it is not unjust. It is only poverty as a social relation that raises the question of justice and therefore is a political matter, a proper subject for reform or revolution. We often hear from development ideologists that the poor don't care about social poverty but only about material deprivation ("The poor aren't interested in politics and ideologies, what they want is roofs over their heads and food and clothing for themselves and their children"). This is a cruel slander against the poor, made by their self-appointed middle-class spokesmen. It is true that the poor will sometimes accept terrible humiliation to feed themselves and their families, but not because they don't mind humiliation. Although they are often forced to conceal their pride from the people on whom they are economically dependent, poor people care very much about it, and also about justice and decency in human relations. Surely they care more about these than the rich do.

Speaking roughly, we can say that what "economic development" has done (not in some hypothetical future but in real times and places up to now) is to transform the second kind of poverty into the third and fourth—while greatly increasing the number of people in absolute poverty in the world. Of course one cannot make a generalization that applies everywhere: the situation was very different in different places before the developers came. Where there had been subsistence economies, one could say that development transformed austerity into social poverty. Where there had been class-based traditional societies, economic development transformed one kind of social poverty into another. In all cases what economic development did was to shatter whatever economic system had been there and to recruit the resulting development refugees into the world economic system mainly as organized poor—organized in the sense of being under the increasingly systematic, rationalized control of the rich. This is what is meant by "the modernization of poverty."

The Political Substructure for Prosperity: Commonwealth

Economic development is an antidemocratic force. In its capitalist form it generates, and must generate, economic inequality.* In its "socialist" form

---

* The appearance of the so-called Newly Industrialized Economies (NIES) does not refute this generalization, any more than the rise of Andrew Carnegie from rags to riches proved the wealth of the proletariat in the nineteenth Century. The question here is not whether individuals or groups of people can get rich in this system (of course they can) but whether social poverty can be abolished from it. And today, as we hear that the NIES are subcontracting work to and importing guest workers from poor countries, we can see that their economic rise is business-as-usual.

it is economically equalitarian in theory (though not in practice), but it produces the inequalities inherent in a command economy. Again, "economic development" does not mean *any* form of growing prosperity, but refers to the expansion of a particular political-economic organization. Economic development means mobilizing more and more people into hierarchical organizations in which their work is disciplined under the rule of maximization of efficiency. And it means mobilizing more and more people as consumers, that is, people whose livelihood is dependent in the things produced by those big organizations. Both trends are antidemocratic. So even in a society with a "democratic" constitution, elections, free speech, and guaranteed human rights, economic development places a kind of antidemocratic Black Hole at the center of each person's life.

To point out the contradiction between democracy and economic development is different from taking a stand "against" economic development. A reader may want to protest, But look at all the good things economic development has brought us! Why, think of the automobile, the airplane, the washing machine, the wireless telephone. . . . Everyone knows the list. The objection is irrelevant. It would be nice if the various good things in the world came all connected together, but they don't. The goods of economic development are what they are. The good of a washing machine is that it washes clothes. Whether its manufacture by mass production tends to generate democratic workplaces is a separate question. The argument that economic development is antidemocratic is presented here as a fact, not as a value position. Knowing this fact, one may make a choice. It is possible to choose economic development over democracy. This choice is precisely what scientific managers, technocrats, development economists, and development dictators are making, all over the world.

But if we opt for democracy do we have to abandon all the good things development has brought? If democracy means that we must "go back" to the preindustrial form of society, wouldn't we experience not only an economic catastrophe but the collapse of the whole world in which our lives are embedded and to which we have become accustomed?

This question is also beside the point. Democracy is not a level of economic or technical development, either past or future. It is a way in which people order their lives together, through discussion and common action, on the principles of justice and equality. There is democracy where people desire it, struggle for it, and win the struggle. People are free to open a democratic struggle in any economic system, at any technological "level." In fact, this process is exactly what is happening all over the world today. How to democratize any particular antidemocratic organization—a kingdom in south Asia, a communist country in eastern Europe, a banana plantation in the Third World, a multinational corporation in capitalist country—is a question that can be answered in concrete form only through the process of an actual democratic struggle within each such organization. In this sense, radical democracy is different from utopianism. It does not seek to impose a preconceived model; such impositions always turn out to be antidemocratic, however "democratic" the model itself may be. It means a struggle carried out on democratic principles, a process from which new forms of organization emerge. Such a struggle can be begun in any organization, at any economic or technological level.

Radical democracy does, however, require a concept of wealth other than the condition of being "rich." Richness, as described above, is undemocratic in its nature, and the desire for it is an undemocratic desire. Richness means, exactly, economic power over other people. But there are other forms of wealth, which can be shared in common. And these forms of wealth are not purely economic but have an important political aspect. The expression "commonwealth" is, after all, a translation into English of the Latin *res publica*, public thing, that is, republic. The existence of common wealth in a society is not something achieved by economic development but by the political ordering of that society. This idea has been known to most of the world's peoples, including—perhaps especially—those with subsistence economies. And the idea is not unknown even in the most fiercely competitive capitalist societies. Common wealth may take its physical expression in such things as public roads, bridges, libraries, parks, schools, churches, temples, or works of art which enrich the lives of all. It may take the form of "commons": shared agricultural land or fisheries. It may take the form of shared ceremonies, feast days, festivals, dances, public entertainments.

The development ideology, placing the whole world under a single yardstick so that all forms of community life but one are disvalued as underdeveloped, unequal, and wretched, has made us sociologically blind. By eliminating this stupefying category from our minds, we should be able to look at the world and see not just two possibilities—development-or-its-absence—but a multiplicity of actual and possible ways of ordering communities. This ability to see a plurality of values is also in accord with the democratic spirit. Rediscovering the values in these communities does not mean discovering a value in being "poor," but means seeing that many of the things that have been called "poor" were different forms of prosperity. "Prosper" (Latin *pro spere*) originally meant "according to hope." How and when a people prospers depends on what they hope, and prosperity becomes a strictly economic term only when we abandon or destroy all hopes but the economic one.

If wealth is economic surplus, different communities may make different choices as to what form that surplus is to take. Surplus can be turned toward private consumption or public works. It can take the form of reducing work time and setting aside surplus leisure time for art, learning, festivals, ceremonies, sport, or simple play. These are not inevitabilities determined by "iron laws" but political choices, if by political we mean the fundamental decision making in a community as to how its work is to be shared and its goods distributed. And if the rule of just distribution is to give to each his or her due, we need to understand that there have been in the world communities that organized themselves so as to give the land its due, the forest its due, the fish, birds, and animals their due. These communities, defined by development economics as at the absolute extremity of poverty, actually maintained in this way a vast "surplus," the great common wealth that was the natural environment in which they lived. A marriage of the ancient idea of *commonwealth* with our presently emerging (or reemerging) understanding of *environment* could give birth to a promising new notion of what the "wealth" of this planet really is.

We may ask, What would happen to economic development if genuine peace and democracy were established in the world? This is a notion perfectly accessible to common sense; one could even say it *is* common sense. But at the same time, paradoxically, it is almost unimaginable. What would it really be like in a world where each society was free from the danger of military or economic invasion? A world where the rich-poor relationship had been abolished? Where there had been a successful consciousness-decolonizing cultural revolution, so that the specter of "Western capitalist middle-class life" no longer held the world in its spell, and the pride and integrity of all the world's peoples were firmly grounded in their own cultures? Where both local and international societies were founded on trust, and we were no longer afraid of one another?

The point of asking these questions is not to suggest that these conditions are easy to attain, but only to perform a mental experiment. By asking, What would happen to economic development in such a world? we can get a clearer grasp of its nature. It would be wrong, however, to attempt a futurology-type answer. So many of our needs have been implanted in us by professional needs-manufacturers, or disfigured by the envy and spitefulness of class society, or by the desire for enough power to protect ourselves against our enemies, that it is difficult to know what would remain were these extraneous factors removed. If Hobbes was right that our desire for "power after power, ending only in death," the engine that propels the possessive individualist, is grounded in our fear of our neighbors, what would happen to that desire if the fear were removed? Without the unnatural factors disfiguring economic activity, we can suppose it would return to its natural form. There is no reason this should mean that we would be thrown back into some dark age of abject poverty. It means simply that we would be free to decide for ourselves what we need and what we want, balancing those desires against how much work we want to do and how much leisure time we want to have. What is extraordinary is how far this common-sense image of democracy is from the "common sense" of our time.

In such a "natural economy" (ironically, Lenin's term) we can suppose that people would still have needs—if "needs" continued to be the proper word—and also wants, including wants for such "useless" things as toys, pretty clothes, music, pleasant rooms, and decorations for their hair. But these wants are not the kinds of things that should be decided in advance or that ruling parties should decide for the people by imposition of sumptuary laws (e.g., banning certain types of clothing or music) as we have seen in some socialist or theocratic countries. The sorting out of our true needs from those that are the maimed consequences of the fear and envy of class society would happen slowly and naturally in a society that was genuinely just, equalitarian, and safe. Quite probably after this process of "counterdevelopment" had continued long enough, "prosperity" would turn out to mean something quite similar to what *pag-unlad* once meant to the Tagalog people of the Philippines.

It may be worth noting, for those interested in such things, that adopting this view amounts to claiming that Marx needs to be turned on his head, making politics again the "substructure" (Aristotle's "master science") and economic-technological activity the "superstructure." (To say this is not necessarily to assert that Marx was wrong in his time to turn Hegel on his head: perhaps a theory is like an hourglass, which must be periodically turned on its head to keep it running.) To say that economic development is antidemocratic is to say that it is a political problem and admits of only a political solution. The economic disfigurement of the world is generated by economic activity within a disfigured political-economic structure; it cannot be remedied by further economic activity within that structure. On the basis of a radically democratized political-economic substructure, economic activity (production, exchange, and consumption) would take on an entirely different character. Shall we call this "the withering away of development"?

3

antidemocratic machines

To use the criterion of democracy to evaluate machines may seem a confusion of levels, for in Marxian terms, machines are part of the substructure, politics of the superstructure. Machines should be judged by the criteria appropriate to them—their ability to do the work they were designed to do, well and efficiently without too many undesirable side effects like noise or pollution. We don't require of a lathe that it produce sounds like a concert violin; why should we require that it be democratic? What would such a demand mean?

Even if such a critique were made, wouldn't it be an exercise in futility? There seems to be a kind of inevitability about machines. They change and improve with the advance of our technical knowledge, according to a seemingly inescapable logic. The secret of electricity is discovered, and soon we have the electric heater, the electric motor, the electric light, the telephone, the television, the computer, and the electric chair. What has this to do with politics?

This notion is itself part of the trouble. As I argued in the previous chapter, if something deeply affects the order of our collective life and we are taught that we have no choice about accepting it when in fact we do, that is a problem for democracy. In other words, the doctrine that machines should never be judged and chosen by political criteria is itself antidemocratic. The critique made in the previous chapter of the ideology of economic development could be applied to the ideology of technological development—as is natural because "economic development" and "technological development" largely overlap. But this is a critique of ideology. How does it apply to the machines themselves?

Machines as Reified Human Relations
What, after all, is a machine?

A machine is not an abstraction or generality; it has material existence. Of course we sometimes use the word in a different sense, as when we speak of a political machine or a war machine. In *The Myth of the Machine* Lewis Mumford uses the word to describe a fundamental way of seeing the world and of ordering society: a people under the enthrallment of a "mechanical world picture" will see even organic life as machine-life and will organize human beings as component parts in a great social machine.[1]

Mumford's argument is powerful and convincing, but here I want to begin at the other end, with the concrete things we call machines. (I shall use the term in its broad sense, to include instruments, apparatuses, and the like.) Is the shape that such things assume determined by strictly scientific-technological necessity? Is "efficiency" a universal principle of mechanical operation which works the same way in all situations?

We often forget the simple truth that what is efficient varies depending on the effect one wishes to produce. The principle of least effort applies well in a situation in which the means and end are clearly separable, and in which we love the end and hate the means, as with alienated wage labor. It does not apply in the same way where the means and the end are indistinguishably intertwined, as with playing music, making love, dancing, storytelling, or taking a walk in the woods. If you are exercising or eating a good meal with friends, it is not "efficient" to finish in the shortest time possible. There are many activities like these, which are most effective only if they are continued for the appropriate time and with the appropriate effort, and they are spoiled by either more or less.

The situation is still more complex. Take the lock, the development of which Siegfried Giedeon considered important enough to devote an entire chapter to in his *Mechanization Takes Command*.[2] There are societies that use locks, and societies that don't. Even in a society that uses locks, there are things we lock up, and things we don't. Locks presuppose theft, and theft presupposes not only private property but a situation in which one can gain by taking the private property of others without their consent. In Thomas More's *Utopia* everyone's clothing and furniture are about the same, and the doors have no locks. We need not think of this situation as wildly unrealistic: we all know of small towns where people do not lock their doors. This trust is not always simply the result of a high level of honesty. It also depends on the situation. If you and I live in a small village together and I steal your hat, where would I wear it? If we are on a camping trip and cooking together, what good would it do me to steal the frying pan?

The lock is not a universal necessity. Its usefulness is grounded in certain political, social, and legal conditions. In some societies the lock was and is not needed, and we can at least imagine changes in our own society which would cause the lock to lose its function and fade away.

In short, the lock is a reified *superstructure*, grounded in a political-legal *substructure*.

Those who would convince us that the lock is a universal necessity are in fact trying to convince us that the political-legal conditions that presuppose the lock's usefulness are themselves universal and unchangeable. The obvious example is Hobbes, who, immediately following his terrifying description of the natural condition of man as a state of war of each against all, seeks to convince doubters with the taunt "Let . . . [the doubter] consider with himself . . . what opinion he has of his . . . fellow citizens, when he locks his doors; and of his children, and servants, when he locks his chests. Does he not there as much accuse mankind by his actions, as I do by my words?"[3] Hobbes well understood the political meaning reified into the lock. If we swallow the lock, we swallow possessive individualism, and we swallow Leviathan. Or rather, Leviathan swallows us.

Like the lock, much of the machinery of industrial production is the reification of human intentions. It is a commonplace that the industrial revolution was more than a revolution in the hardware of production; it was also a revolution in the organization of work. This revolution does not simply mean that new machinery required new forms of work. It also means that new machinery was designed with the *intention* of reorganizing work and also of reducing the workers' power to resist. I am not referring to the division of labor, for that was achieved long before the industrial revolution and was a source of empowerment of workers. The division under which one worker becomes a potter, one a farmer, one a fisher, one a tailor, one a carpenter, one a blacksmith, and so on allows each worker—or community or guild of workers—to develop craft skills up to the level of an art. This kind of specialization produces more things of value than simply the objects of manufacture. It produces a certain kind of community, with traditions, songs and stories, artistic sensibility, and pride of craft. A worker who works for a lifetime at such a speciality becomes a skilled farmer, an expert potter, a master carpenter: a person worthy of respect, who has a legitimate authority grounded in real knowledge about things that matter. In this situation, as with dancing, means and ends become indistinguishably mixed together.

The reorganization of work in the industrial revolution unquestionably increased productivity and efficiency—if we agree that of all the values generated by a working community only the quantity and exchange value of the products count as legitimate ends. When nineteenth-century critics of capitalism railed at the "profit motive" their point was not so much that the desire for money was intrinsically bad but that it had come to be the exclusive yardstick of value, by which all the other goods generated by working communities could be disvalued and sacrificed. The machine, organized in factories, was a means of expropriating the skills of the worker. Skilled workers can demand high wages, are hard to fire, and when they go on strike are hard to replace. The machine enabled the industrialist to replace the skilled workers with unskilled machine tenders. The machine tenders—often children, before child labor laws were enacted—were cheaper and easier to manage. It is important to remind ourselves that these analyses were not invented by critics of capitalism but were matters of which the industrialists were perfectly aware. Karl Marx writes, "It would be possible to write a whole history of the inventions made since 1830 for the sole purpose of providing capital with weapons against working-class revolt."[4] In *Capital* he quotes the testimony of several industrialists on the disempowering effectiveness of the machine:

> "What every mechanical workman has now to do, and what every boy can do, is not to work himself but to superintend the beautiful labour of the machine. The whole class of workmen that depend exclusively on their skill, is now done away with. Formerly, I employed four boys to every mechanic. Thanks to these new mechanical combinations, I have reduced the number of grown-up men from 1,500 to 750. The result was a considerable increase in my profits."[5]

> "[The self-acting mule is] a creation destined to restore order among the industrious classes . . . This invention confirms the great doctrine already propounded, that when capital enlists science into her service, the refractory hand of labour will always be taught docility."[6]

Marx was aware of, and wrote eloquently about, the politics embedded in the machinery of industrial production. In the factory, he says in *Capital*, "the central machine from which the motion comes [is] not only an automaton but an autocrat" (p. 545). "The technical subordination of the worker to the uniform motion of the instruments of labour . . . gives rise to a barrack-like discipline . . . dividing the workers into manual labourers and overseers, into the private soldiers and the N.C.O.s of an industrial army" (p. 549). On the basis of the alleged technical necessities of the factory machinery, the industrialist becomes a "factory Lycurgus" (p. 550) who displays his law-giving powers in the factory code: "In the factory code, the capitalist formulates his autocratic power over his workers like a private legislator, and purely as an emanation of his own will, unaccompanied by either that division of responsibility otherwise so much approved of by the bourgeoisie, or the still more approved representative system" (pp. 549–50).

What was Marx's attitude, ultimately, toward machinery? It is difficult to tell. In one place he will describe the development of machines as an evolutionary process comparable in its naturalness and inevitability to the evolution of the species as described by Darwin (p. 493n.4). He often reminds the reader that he is criticizing not machinery itself but its misuse under capitalism. But how may one interpret passages like this?

> Factory work exhausts the nervous system to the uttermost; at the same time, it does away with the many-sided play of the muscles, and confiscates every atom of freedom, both in bodily and in intellectual activity. Even the lightening of the labour becomes an instrument of torture, since the machine does not free the worker from the work, but rather deprives the work itself of all content. (p. 548)

It is not clear how this description of the direct physical domination of the machine over the human body would decisively change if the machine were the property of the workers' state, or even of the workers themselves. What is the specifically capitalist element here? What is the exploitative *misuse* of the machine, over and above its technically "correct" use? I am not able to find where Marx makes this clear. His suggestions that factory work is less exhausting when it is alternated with schoolwork (p. 613) or when the workers have more than one skill and can alternate from one job to another (p. 618 and n. 31) are good, practical suggestions but hardly require a philosophy of *Aufhebung* to come by, as they imply no transformation in the essential nature of factory work itself. And it is notable that in Marx's famous comment that in a communist society one may "hunt in the morning, fish in the afternoon, rear cattle in the evening, criticize after dinner, just as I have a mind,"[7] he has given us a list of, with the possible exception of "criticism," not merely preindustrial but actually neolithic technologies. If he had written, "I may mine coal in the morning, tend a spinning jenny in the afternoon and assemble oil pumps in the evening," the affair would sound rather less idyllic. The "just as I have a mind" would turn to black humor; on the other hand we could probably expect a livelier result from the after-dinner criticism.

Is it the machine itself that is oppressive, or its misuse? It is difficult to think of radically different uses for, say, a power loom, an oil refinery, or an assembly line. The old saw "Technology can be used for either good or evil purposes" is not too convincing where technologies clearly have their purposes built into them. Perhaps we can escape this puzzle with a distinction and say that it is scientific and technical *knowledge* that is capable of being used for different purposes, whereas in the design of the actual machinery developed under capitalism, scientific knowledge has got mixed together with the intention to exploit. Science, one might say, is universal and neutral, but the hardware of production is a reified amalgam of science and the will to squeeze the maximum of surplus value out of the worker.[8] Charles Fourier's comparison of the factory to a prison is useful here. A prison—with all its locks and steel doors with peepholes in them, its guard towers and rooms for solitary confinement and execution chamber—has the intention architecturally built into it to confine people against their will. Of course, the building could be remodeled and turned into a theater or a museum, but it would require some very fundamental reconstruction. Probably the only way to destroy the prison character of the buildings on Alcatraz Island in the middle of San Francisco Bay would be to raze them to the ground. A prison is the reification of the social will to imprison. This will can also be found in the specific body of knowledge under which it was built, penology. But it is not to be found in the bodies of knowledge that went into building the walls or the roof, or installing the plumbing or the lighting. These can be used just as well in residences, libraries, or theaters. Similarly one could argue that the body of knowledge that, in the context of a society bent on extracting surplus value, took the form of the exploitive hardware of factory production, could in a different society with a different fundamental intention take the form of an entirely different hardware of production.

It is possible to make this argument; as I have shown in the previous chapter Lenin most emphatically did not make it. It was not his way of thinking, nor did the desperate situation of Russia after the Revolution leave much opportunity for leisurely experimentation. Far from rejecting the hardware of capitalist production, Lenin was eager to get his hands on as much as possible. And, as we have seen, he was always perfectly open about the consequences large-scale machine production would have on the freedom of workers at the workplace.

The above speculation was also one that never tempted Engels. In his notorious rebuttal to the anarchistic notion that after the revolution workers could take collective control of their factories, Engels raised the autocratic power of the factory machinery to the level of a universal principle:

> The ordinary machinery of a big factory is much more despotic than the small capitalists who employ workers have ever been. At least with regard to the hours of work one may write upon the portals of these factories: *Lasciate ogni autonomia, voi che entrate*! [Abandon all autonomy, ye who enter here!] If man, by dint of his knowledge and inventive genius, has subdued the forces of nature, the latter avenge themselves upon him by

subjecting him, in so far as he employs them, to a veritable despotism independent of all social organization. Wanting to abolish authority in large-
scale industry is tantamount to wanting to abolish industry itself, to
destroy the power loom in order to return to the spinning wheel.[9]

"Independent of all social organization": one's sense of the implausibility
of Engels's dual career as revolutionary theorist and industrialist somewhat lessens on reading these lines. Anyway, his point could not be more
clearly made: under socialism the wealth and the titles may be divvied up
differently, but the despotism of factory machinery over the workers is
here to stay.

To my knowledge the socialist who went furthest in the other direction
of exploring the possibility that in a society from which the exploitive intention had been removed the machinery itself might evolve into a different form was the man Engels dismissed as a "sentimental socialist,"[10]
William Morris. Morris was a rare figure among theorists of work in that
he not only wrote about work but also did it.[11] He was a true master at
many crafts—painting, printing, weaving, woodcarving, bookbinding—
and claimed to be a good cook as well. On the basis of this experience
Morris was able to produce a powerful and profound theory of what
work is and of what had gone wrong with it under capitalism. Central to
this theory was his insistence that work can and ought to be a pleasure.
This was not some strained utopian speculation, but something he knew
from his daily life. Making things with the right tools and materials, at
the appropriate speed, in an atmosphere of freedom is one of the great
human joys. For Morris the pleasure of work was part of the purpose of
work; from this position the means-ends "efficiency" of factory production is not efficient at all—if efficiency has to do with achieving the ends
that matter. Making things, and making them beautifully, are among the
chief sources of happiness for human beings on earth; to say that it is better to make more things in factories tended by miserable and barely
skilled workers is simply to miss the point. In "A Factory as It Might Be"
Morris concedes that even in a socialist society some jobs will be irre-
trievably tedious and that advanced machinery should be used to reduce
the time spent at this work. But in Morris's socialist society the disappearance of the profit motive will mean the disappearance of the motivation to produce useless and ugly luxuries—"illth" in the expression of
Morris's mentor John Ruskin. And all the idle rich will be put to work. In
this situation Morris estimates that factory work can be reduced to four
hours per day per person.[12] More important, interesting work will be
done not by machines but by hand. By stating this idea Morris does not
mean that everyone will have a "hobby"; he means that a major part of

basic productive labor will be handwork. Each worker, alternating shifts between machines and handwork, would come to know the pleasure of creative work and have the opportunity to become an artist.

Morris wrote his utopian novel *News from Nowhere* after reading Edward Bellamy's *Looking Backward* and being horrified by that picture of socialist society as an industrial army camp. In *News from Nowhere* machine production disappears almost entirely, as if Morris had taken seriously Marx's flat statement in *Capital* that "the machine is a means for producing surplus-value"[13] and had carried the insight to its extreme conclusion. If the purpose of the machine is extraction of surplus value, then in a society in which exploitation has been abolished and only use-value matters why would the machine not wither away altogether? The novel's protagonist, Guest, who has fallen asleep in the nineteenth century and awakened in the twenty-first, is surprised to discover not a technotopia but an age of handicraft. The Machine Period is an age long finished, preserved in museum and memory only. After the revolution establishing socialism, Guest is told, "the feeling against a mechanical life . . . [spread] insensibly; till at last under the guise of pleasure that was not supposed to be work, work that was pleasure began to push out the mechanical toil, which they had once hoped at the best to reduce to narrow limits indeed, but never to get rid of." "Machine after machine was quietly dropped under the excuse that the machine could not produce works of art, and that works of art were more and more called for."[14] It remains true as a principle that intrinsically irksome toil is done by "immensely improved machinery," but as we follow Guest on his travels through the English countryside about the only object we encounter that might fit this description is a motor barge on the river. And in Morris's "Nowhere" it is not only artistic creation that is a pleasure. The people take pleasure in activities such as rowing on the river (despite the existence of the motor barge) and harvesting. In fact, Morris managed to infuse the whole story with a magical charm by having Guest fall in with a group of young people traveling north to the hay harvest, which is a kind of annual festival they all anticipate with pleasure, as we might a sporting event. One of the characters describes hay harvesting as "easy-hard work": "I mean work that tries the muscles and hardens them and sends you pleasantly weary to bed, but which isn't trying in other ways: doesn't harass you, in short. Such work is always pleasant if you don't overdo it. Only mind you, good mowing requires some little skill. I'm a pretty good mower" (p. 162). The mowing, of course, is done by hand-wielded scythes. Part of the sadness at the end of the tale is that Guest wakes up before they arrive at the long-promised hay harvest.

Morris has been dismissed by many Marxists and Marxist-Leninists as a romantic dreamer and as unscientific. There is nothing wrong with his science, however; it is just that he is not a technological determinist. For Morris, machines and technologies are not causally prior to the society in which they are embedded; rather they are the embodiment of functions and values of that society and take on their character from the ethos of that society. A society with a different character will produce different technologies. For Morris, a free society with free labor would choose the technology of free labor, the technology that gives the most power and pleasure to the worker. If Marxist-Leninists dismiss Morris as a romantic, Morris would surely accuse the Marxist-Leninist economic developmentalists of simply having missed the point.

Noplace Technology

That most political of writers, Niccolo Machiavelli, once wrote that the wisdom of the founder of a new city can be "recognized by the selection of the place where he has located the city, and by the nature of the laws which he establishes in it."[15] Politics and place are deeply intertwined, though our contemporary political science has few words with which to talk about this idea. The common bond to a particular place is part of what holds a community together, and some of our most emotion-laden political expressions still reflect this fact: "homeland," "motherland," "country." People will struggle fiercely against forcible removal from their place. "Displaced persons" refers to people who have not only been torn from their native place but who as a consequence have no political existence as a community and no basis for their political rights as individuals.

A community partly takes its character from its place. By this statement I am not proposing some kind of climatic determinism: attempts to produce universal theories about the modal personalities of, for example, tropical cultures and temperate cultures will surely continue to fail. It is through work and the technology of work that a dialogue occurs between people and place, generating culture. When we describe a place as a fishing village, a farming region, or a trading port, we are asserting that the community is characterized by its chief work, and its work is rooted in its location.

The word "culture" in the European languages means both to till the soil and to refine customs and manners through education and training. This dual definition is not analogy. Human cultures *are* the product of ages of labor. Farmers dig the land and build the soil. They develop tools and techniques. From wild plants and animals they breed domestic plants and animals: rice, corn, wheat, pigs, chickens, cows. Their work gives rhythm and order to their year: the plowing season, the harvest season, with the ceremonies and festivals accompanying each. Their work generates certain human virtues: patience, attentiveness, orderliness, thoroughness. According to the *OED*, "cultivate" means "to bestow labor and attention upon (land) in order to the raising of crops." Labor and attention: *attentiveness* is the particular virtue of cultivation, not simply attentiveness in general but attentiveness to the land, to the place where one labors.

Through labor, human beings transformed the earth into the world, their own nature into culture, and space into place. Through labor, human beings developed the rich polytechnic craft tradition so eloquently described by Lewis Mumford in *The Myth of the Machine*. According to Mumford, the subversion of polytechnics began in the first industry to force people to work outside the biosphere, mining. Medieval mining, he argues, was the source of many of the technologies that became central to the industrial revolution: metal-tracked railroads, mechanical lifts, forced ventilation, artificial lighting, the twenty-four-hour triple shift, and (possibly) wage labor itself: technologies, in short, for working outside the world, in a place that is noplace. At the same time, mining was one of the first fabulously profitable capitalist industries. The conditions and technologies for working in the subterranean mine— "the destructive animus of mining and its punishing routine of work, along with its environmental poverty and disorder" (p. 147)—were a kind of prefiguration of work in the modern workplace that is noplace, the factory (including, of course, the white-collar factory: the office). The very unearthliness of the mine permits a kind of abstraction of the labor process; the uniform endlessness of mining and the absence of day, night, weather, or season in the shaft permits twenty-four-hour, year-round operation. In most human work *in* the world there is a beginning and an end, a time when the job is done and one can rest or turn to something else. The reproduction of the mine's unnaturally endless homogeneous labor in the factory is one of the secrets of the profitability of modern industry.

Marx claims that the first prime mover that was "of universal technical application, and little affected in its choice of residence by local circumstances," was Watt's steam engine.[16] The steam engine was of course fueled by coal from the mines, and Mumford points out that it "had first been used in Newcomen's cruder form to pump water out of the mines" (p. 147). The dis-located steam engine became the prime mover in the new dis-located workplace, the factory.

In one of her wonderful and puzzling insights, Hannah Arendt once argued that in addition to the world alienation generated by modern economics, our age also suffers from an "earth alienation" that began when science became astrophysics, left the biosphere, and took its standpoint in outer space: "Without actually standing where Archimedes wished to stand . . . , still bound to the earth through the human condition, we have found a way to act on the earth and within terrestrial nature as though we dispose of it from outside, from the Archimedan point. and even at the risk of endangering the natural life process we expose the earth to universal, cosmic forces alien to nature's household."[17]

Strictly speaking it is not science that is at issue here, but technology: we have found not a new way to think but a new way to act. It is not the discoveries of Galileo or Newton or Einstein that are the cause of earth alienation, but earthly technologies that require unearthly work and produce unearthly human environments. Gertrude Stein's famous remark about Oakland, California—"There's no there there"—was somewhat unfair to that working-class city. There's no reason to pick on Oakland—the comment applies to a large and growing number of cities. Some years ago Nakao Hajime and I took a group of Japanese students to the Hanford Nuclear Reservation in eastern Washington State, where the plutonium for the Nagasaki bomb had been produced and which had since turned into a nuclear-power center and research facility. As our bus entered the company town of Richland, Nakao said, "Take a good look, everybody, this is atomic culture." In the middle of the beautiful and awesome expanse of the eastern Washington desert was a town that had absolutely no relation to the place on which it had been built. Its architecture showed no hint that anyone there had ever been a rancher or a farmer. In fact, the few farmhouses that had been there were all razed in 1943, and the town was built simultaneously. Richland was the famous "atomic town"; the prime mover that not only sent electricity into its air-conditioned homes but also supported its entire economy was nuclear power. In honor of its great energy source it had streets named "Proton Lane" and "Electron Lane"; its high-school football team was called the "Richland Bombers." Richland could almost as well have been underground or in outer space as in eastern Washington. It is not accurate to say that it could be anywhere; rather, it is essential that it be *nowhere*: the desert was about as close to nowhere as could be found in the North American environment. Noplaceness is not just a characteristic of peculiar cases like Richland or like Houston, Texas (whose two big industries—oil and space—operate above and below the biosphere and whose contribution to the environment was a product with a perfect noplace name: Astroturf), or like Kuwait (also on a desert, where oil is burned to make seawater into drinking water). Noplaceness threatens to become characteristic of everyplace. I live in the city of Tokyo. Tokyo was once fed by fish from its bay and vegetables from its surrounding farms. Today the bay is nearly dead and the farms are paved and housed under, and Tokyo eats food imported from abroad. I don't know, but I suppose houses are torn down ("consumed") and rebuilt here at a faster rate than in any other city in the world. Since World War II, Tokyo has been an ugly city, but the most recent generation of houses is not so much ugly as chilling. There is no longer any craft or cultural tradition in Tokyo strong enough to sustain an architectural style. Houses can be any architectural style, and are, which means of course that they are no architectural style at all. They are not buildings, but manufactures. The workers do not build them but assemble them, rather as one would assemble a steel bookcase or a plastic model. I saw some workers unload a truckload of brightly colored metal parts, like parts of a giant toy, and bolt together a house frame, following a set of instructions, in a day.

In 1989 Ailton Krenack, from Brazil's Amazon, passed through Tokyo on his way back from an indigenous people's conference sponsored by the Ainu people in Hokkaido. At Hokkaido he had said:

> I remember in 1950, the Brazilian government took the last families of my tribe and put them in a truck bound for other regions. It relocated them. . . . This new village had much better facilities, and the main argument of the government was that we were being relocated to a better place. . . . Our struggle was to show the government that there is no other village in the world where we can live, die, or travel through the world, because any other place would be an exile.
>
> This isn't a feeling of borders, but of a sacred place, where the mountains are not only mountains, where the rivers are relatives. . . . It's a place where each spot bears the memory of the creation and reminds us and gives us a feeling of continuity.[18]

I was sitting next to him on the monorail coming into Tokyo from the airport. We passed some giant new apartment buildings constructed on reclaimed land and I asked him if he was aware that people were living in those buildings. "Yes, I know," he said, and his face went sad. "And if they go on living there for three generations, their grandchildren will know *nothing*."

What has any of this to do with politics? The question itself can be asked only by one who has forgotten the essential nature of politics. Politics is the activity by which humans choose and build their collective life together. The ideology of technological determinism, which pretends that this choice is not a choice, is antipolitical and antidemocratic in that it takes from us one of our avenues of self-rule. The "politics" with which these questions have nothing to do is what Jacques Ellul called "the political illusion": a politics that places outside its sphere of concern the really important choices—the choices that most powerfully affect the quality of people's lives, the order of their communities, and the way they are ruled—and concentrates on deciding all sorts of secondary and trivial matters by "democratic processes" is illusory politics, no politics at all.[19] The choice of noplace technology comes with a staggering political price, which in this century we have paid and paid again. If we could only grasp that it really is a choice, perhaps we could start to choose differently.

Technology and the Order of Work

At the beginning of all political discourse is the question of order, not only of what kind of order is best but of how communities can achieve order at all. There are many different answers. The policeman's answer is that order can be achieved by establishing law and bringing state violence to bear on those who disobey it. The schoolteacher's answer is that order can be achieved through universal compulsory education, through which a unified value system can be instilled into the pupils before they achieve adulthood (though today in the United States and elsewhere real teachers might laugh at this idea). The manager's answer is that people's behavior can be ordered by manipulation of their interests, putting them into situations where cost-benefit calculation will channel then into orderly behavior patterns. The conservative's answer is that people will be orderly if they follow the customs and traditions handed down from the past. The demagogue's answer is that the people's lives will be orderly if they follow him. The contract theorist's answer is that we can achieve order by making promises to one another and keeping them. The anarchist's answer is that for one reason or other order is natural to human communities and can be achieved without state power ("anarchism" means no government, not no order). And so on.

Most forms of government, actual and proposed, use a combination of these strategies. Even Thomas More's Utopia has a penal code; even Rousseau in *The Social Contract* talks about customs and mores; even Machiavelli advises the Prince to watch after the fundamental interests of the people; even Plato's Philosopher King is ready to use the Noble Lie, that is, propaganda. My intention here is not to present a complete taxonomy of theories of order and of their various combinations. I wish only to point out that there is another solution to the problem of order that is rarely taken up by political theorists but is part of the experience of peo-

ple who live in working communities. To my knowledge the only political theorist (if he may be so called) to propose it formally was Gerrard
Winstanley.

Winstanley, it will be recalled, was the leader and main pamphlet
writer for the Diggers in the English Revolution. At the beginning of the
plowing season of 1648 Winstanley and a small group of his comrades
began digging the commons at a place called St. George's Hill and passing out pamphlets calling for the common ownership of land. They were
attacked from all sides and finally driven away in early 1650. Later Winstanley published his *Law of Freedom in a Platform*, a detailed program
for a polity founded on common ownership, prefaced by an appeal to
Oliver Cromwell saying that the only way the revolution could achieve
true liberty would be to carry it to its conclusion by abolishing private
property.

In *The Law of Freedom* Winstanley lays out an elaborate social order,
working from the bottom up. It is the statement of general principles at
the beginning of his discussion that is of interest here.

> First, there must be suitable Laws for every occasion, and almost for every
> action that men do: . . . As for example,
>   There is a time to plow, and the Laws of right understanding attends
> upon that work; and there is a time to reap the fruits of the Earth, and the
> Laws of right observation attending thereupon.
>   So that true Government is a right ordering of all actions, giving to
> every action and thing its due weight and measure, and this prevents con-
> fusion, as *Solomon* speaks, *There is a time for all things. . . .*[20]

This is not everything Winstanley has to say about order. He is a chilias-
tic Christian, who in his earlier pamphlets had argued that the English
revolution was the occasion whereby people could purge themselves finally of the prideful desire to profit from buying and selling and live together in peace; on the other hand in *The Law of Freedom* he provides
punishments for criminals.[21] Nevertheless it remains true that in the latter he places the foundation of healthful government on the order of
work.

Writers on Winstanley tend to be embarrassed by his lower-class background, seeing it as a handicap he was only partly able to overcome.[22]
This embarrassment is a reflection of the class prejudice that has distorted
political theory in all ages. Political theorists have tended to be members
of privileged classes, and whatever their theories of order might have
been, they have typically seen order as something correctly understood
by, and therefore properly enforced by, people like themselves. Unless
ruled from above—whether by kings or charismatic leaders or benign

teachers or elected legislators or managers or technocrats—the ordinary people will be incapable of maintaining order and will fall into "anarchy." In fact, throughout history the world's working communities—farm villages, fishing villages, market towns, craft cities—have tended to stay orderly on their own, without the help of state violence. Their order has been largely founded on the order of work.[23] Political theorists ignore this historical fact probably because they typically have no experience in doing this kind of collective work. Winstanley's lower-class background was not a handicap but an advantage. In *The Law of Freedom* he was able to express something of which upper-class theorists are ignorant but which is common sense to working people.

Work in the world has a natural order. Every job of work has a beginning, a proper sequence of tasks, and a time when the job is done. I say this order is "natural," but it is also artificial: man-made. That is, work is artifice itself, but what the worker works on comes from nature, and has natural characteristics. A farmer works the field with tools invented and improved upon through millennia of farming, tools that have been shaped in accordance with the natural characteristics of soil, water, weather, and growing plants. A carpenter uses a plane or a chisel on the basis of a rich understanding of the complex characteristics of wood. All the crafts—cooking, pottery, glassblowing, fishing, animal husbandry— are orders of knowledge and action in which the natural characteristics of the substances and creatures of the world are mixed together with human reason, experience, and need. A skilled worker is not a loose, flying object, an uprooted individual who will thrash around randomly unless restrained by superiors. A craft worker lives a life ordered by the work, and lives in a community whose structure is ordered in large part by its common work. The day is ordered by the work and also the year. There is, as Winstanley says following Ecclesiastes, a time to plow and a time to reap.

From time to time in this book I have used expressions such as "natural" economy and "natural" (or "unnatural") work. Logically these expression may seem self-contradictory. Work means artifice; if work can be natural, then what could "artificial" possibly mean? The expression might not be the best, but what I mean by it is work as described above, which still maintains its character as a dialogue with nature and whose order is in part a reflection of the order of nature. This work and its products cannot be described as "natural" if that word is used in its strictest sense, but can be if it is used in a softer sense, to denote modes of work and of life which have been proved over time to be fitting for human beings to do and a fitting way to create a home for human beings out of the natural environment of this planet. It is distinguished from those modes of life and work which are based on the fantasy that human beings can "conquer" nature, to produce a world from which its influence has been expelled.

This order of work can be compared to the order of common law. Like common law, it is derived from the nature of things, mediated through human reason and long experience. But the "nature" in which the order of work is rooted is not a philosophical abstraction nor is it the nature only of the psyche or society of human beings considered separately from their environment. It is Nature itself, the nature of wind and weather, rivers and rain, stones and cedar trees. Its laws are not arrived at deductively; they are built into the properties, motions, and transformations of the substances themselves. The imperative that they be obeyed is not simply a matter of ethics. No king's decree, no philosopher's discourse, no saint's prayer will cause lead to turn to gold, or petroleum to wheat.

This is an order of life which people can obey without humiliation or servility. As Rousseau points out, it is obedience to the wills of other humans, not obedience to the laws of nature, that threatens our freedom. In this sense the craft worker, *qua* craft worker (that is, in his or her relation to the work), is as free as Rousseau's "natural man"—and in fact freer because the craft gives the worker the power to do more things. The craft worker neither conquers nature nor is conquered by it. It is a question of learning what can and what can't be done: conquest has nothing to do with it.

The order of work is a form of obedience to nature mediated and moderated by human skill. It may also take the form of obedience to specific persons: the masters of the craft. *The Law of Freedom* provides for magistrates; according to Winstanley the legitimate origin of magistracy is the appeal of children to their father, "do thou teach us how to plant the earth, that we may live, and we will obey" (p. 85). Winstanley provides for overseers, whose work, in addition to keeping the peace, is "to assist any Master of a family by his advice and counsel in the secrets of his Trades, that by experience of the Elders, the young people may learn the inward knowledg [sic] of the things which are, and find out the secrets of Nature" (p. 95). The overseer is also to see to it that no man become head of a household who has not served a seven-year apprenticeship. The head of a household, in Winstanley's half-medieval communist society, is a patriarch who governs the family. The point in this context is that the family is a working unit and what is governed is the work, so that the only legitimate authority to govern is that which comes from mastery of a craft. Consider how different a notion of work this is from our own. Far from being degrading or debilitating, work is enriching: seven years of apprenticeship in a craft makes one into a person whose authority should be respected. We tend to hand over political authority to people who have never worked with their hands, who were born rich or have spent their adult lives managing the work of others, or who are lawyers. In Winstanley's community, none of these categories of human beings exists.

Perhaps we cannot fully grasp what Winstanley means by "master" until we rid our minds of the prejudice that is ingrained in the language of political theory as a result of centuries of contempt for work. In the context of a discourse on politics if we encounter the word "master" we immediately associate it to the words "and slave." For Winstanley, the words that naturally follow are "of a craft." The difference is very great between being master over people and master over a skill. The craft master's secondary mastery, that over the apprentice, is aimed at teaching the apprentice also to master the skill, not at keeping him or her in permanent subjection. And incidentally, the word "mistress" once also had the same meaning, "mistress of a craft," vestigially preserved today in the word "schoolmistress." It seems likely that the words "mister" and "missus," which are derivations of "master" and "mistress" and are used today as respectful titles for adult men and women of any class, have evolved from this meaning of the terms: craft mastery, not slave mastery.

I have used the word "work" here to include both sides of Arendt's famous distinction between work and labor. In saying that in following the order of work the worker is free, I seem to be contradicting Arendt's assertion in *The Human Condition* that labor is necessity itself, the very negation of freedom (chap. 3). For Arendt, work is the making of things ("works") that have a lasting existence and become stable parts of the human-made "world" that serves as the stage set before which human beings act out their individual and collective stories. Labor, on the other hand, is dictated by the needs of our bodies and must be endlessly repeated as it "leaves nothing behind" (p. 76). "Of all human activities, only labor . . . is unending, progressing automatically in accordance with life itself and outside the range of willful decisions or humanly meaningful purposes" (p. 91). Arendt avoids—rather carefully, it seems—telling us just which jobs she has in mind. Her description of labor as taking place in "nature's prescribed cycle, toiling and resting, laboring and consuming" (p. 92), sounds a lot like farming. In another place she seems to offer bread baking as an example (p. 81). But to say that either of these is "outside the range of willful decisions" is to ignore the craft of the farmer and the baker. In the case of the farmer it would be utterly false to say that nothing permanent is left behind. Farming not only produces crops that are eaten, it produces the entire rural countryside. It was farm labor that gave birth to the whole agrarian world, from provincial France to the rice terraces of Benguet, so loved by landscape painters, poets, and musicians. Leave nothing behind indeed! Farming is one of the most architectonic of human activities.

It is equally false to say that bread baking (or any other form of cooking) makes no contribution to "a world . . . whose durability and—relative permanence makes appearance and disappearance possible, which existed before any one individual appeared into it and will survive his eventual departure" (pp. 84–85). Not the loaves themselves that are eaten every day but the *craft* of bread baking has precisely this worldly quality. The world as Arendt means it, the humanly made framework for human life into which we are born and which outlasts our life thus alleviating the meaninglessness of our short lifespan, is made up of more than houses with furniture in them and streets in front of them. It is also a world with "bread" in it, and bakers with the skills to bake it, skills that have been handed down through the generations from ancient times. Of course this craft is a collective product, and probably most bakers go through life without contributing much to it that is original. But in mastering the craft and handing it on to apprentices, the baker is doing more than simply responding mechanically to the body's needs by producing food; he or she is actively reproducing the human world.

By "labor" can Arendt mean laundering, dishwashing, and other forms of cleaning? (cf. p. 87). From the standpoint of its tedious repetition and inability to leave a clear product behind, cleaning seems to be good candidate. But it does not fit Arendt's chief criterion. It is not something that is required to sustain "life itself." We wash dishes and clothes *after* we have used them, and these activities are demands not of life but of culture. Cleanliness is needed not to sustain life but to live the way we would like to; it is not a demand from nature but a demand we make of ourselves. It is, in short, well within "the range of willful decisions or humanly meaningful purposes."

In the end, as brilliant as Arendt's description of labor is, I doubt that one could find any traditional job of labor which would quite fit it. This failure may not matter much for the argument she wanted to make, which was to criticize the modern economic world as having been transformed into a meaningless cycle of factory production and consumption, as having, in her terms, come to be dominated by the principle of "labor": "The industrial revolution has replaced all workmanship with labor, and the result has been that the things of the modern world have become labor products whose natural fate is to be consumed, instead of work products which are to be used" (p. 108). It is here that Arendt's concepts really begin to take effect: her description of how the needs of the modern economy have transformed all the things of our world into consumer goods, so that the very world on which we had depended for stability has been dissolved into a state of meaningless flux is wonderful, accurate, and chilling. But whereas Arendt argues that the modern economy has taken on in its entirety the characteristics that labor (but not work) has always had, I think that what she has really done is retroactively to apply to traditional labor the characteristics of the modern economy, characteristics that traditional labor never actually had. The description of labor "outside the range of willful decisions" is unconvincing when applied to the crafts of farming, fishing, dairying (the labor most directly related to the necessities of "life itself" presumably being food production and preparation). It becomes more plausible when applied to, say, labor on an assembly line, labor from which most of the craft has been removed and about which most of the decisions have already been made, so that workers move their bodies not in accordance with the operation of their wills but in accordance with the necessities of the machine.

Moreover, Arendt's way of formulating the problem conceals the changes that have taken place in labor itself. Her criticism that the principle of labor has taken over all of human activity makes it impossible for her to look at a change such as the industrialization of farming, the transformation of the farm into a factory run by agribusiness. Here we see the very change Arendt wanted to describe: the once-stable agrarian world has been swept into the torrent of frantic and endless technological change under the leadership of the corporation, and farmers have increasingly become assembly-line workers, moving down the rows of crops carrying out instructions given them by experts from the agricultural chemical companies. Although traditional labor was never free in the sense of the "freedom" that Arendt says comes from collective political action, it was not unfree in the way she has described it. Do not misunderstand here, I am not saying serfs or slaves were not oppressed by landowners and masters. Arendt has asserted that labor was unfree *in itself*, independent of whether the laborer was under a master or a landowner. Blind spots like this are part of the stiff price we have so long been paying for being heirs to tradition of political philosophy founded by slaveowners.

Machines and the Managerial Order

The order of work in the factory and the office is very different from the order that grows up from craft work. This new order is a managed order, as it must be. Though one can still find some craftspeople in factories, the ideal factory worker (much less office worker) is not a craftsperson with the order of the work engraved into the rhythms of body and soul. The factory worker does not know how to make whatever it is the factory produces. Separated from the factory, the worker becomes one of the "unemployed," separated long enough and that worker risks becoming one of the "underclass." To put order into the activity of such workers is the job of management. By definition management is from the top down. The order is not produced out of a dialogue with nature; management science is a result of a dialogue between the principle of least action and the capacities of the machinery ("machinery" including the worker's body and—for "humanistic" management science—the worker's spirit). The order need not be internalized or understood by the worker—it is enough that it be followed.

Managerial order is built into the machine itself. Think again of an assembly line. An assembly line is a managerial ordering of work congealed into hardware. It is the reification of a set of orders: you install this part, you weld these parts, you tighten these bolts. The product as well has the order of managed work built into it. It is *designed* as a thing to be made on an assembly line by managed workers and by no one else. We all learn in school that standardized, interchangeable parts made the assembly line possible, but we have not learned to think of this means of production politically. Products made of standardized, interchangeable parts are products that demand a managed order of work. True, an unexpected side effect of this form of production was a kind of democracy of amateur repair, for owners could easily repair their own automobiles and washing machines by buying and installing new parts. But recently this option too is being done away with, as more and more products are manufactured in such a way that we cannot repair or even disassemble them. Products are sealed in plastic, or put together with those maddening screws with the slot that is flat against the screwdriver only in the clockwise direction and an inclined plane in the counterclockwise direction. These products have built into them a command to the owner: You shall not repair this; you must buy a new one or go without. Increasingly, homes are built so that about the only repair work possible is the changing of lightbulbs or faucet washers.

Choose a technology and you choose the politics—the order of work—that comes with it. Choose mass consumption and you choose mass production and a managed order of work. Choose the big factory and you choose managerial oligarchy and social inequality. And again, there is a sharp difference between the inequality separating manager and worker and that separating master and apprentice. The manager/worker relation is (as Marx points out) more like the officer/enlisted relation in the army. With very rare exceptions workers never become managers, and with very rare exceptions managers have never done the work. The mass-production of the automobile by advanced industrial countries was a choice. People were perhaps not fully aware that they made that choice, partly because they believed strongly then in the beneficence and inevitability of techno-logical "progress," and partly because they had not the dimmest idea of the vast changes the automobile would force on civilization. Nevertheless it was a political choice, even then—as for example when governments began shifting funds from railroads and other public transportation to highway construction. Would people have agreed to massive public high-way construction if they had known how many would die on those high-ways, how much pollution would go into the air from them, and that someday we would have to fight oil wars to get fuel for the cars on them? Would they have chosen the automobile if they had known exactly what life would be like in Detroit, Michigan, or Toyota, Japan, by the end of the century? Well, they didn't know these things. Now we do.

A Note on Technological Conservatism

The spirit of conservatism teaches that the techniques, institutions, tradi-tions, and manners that have developed over the centuries have hidden within them more wisdom and more uses than we know and can possibly know, so that if we start knocking them down we are likely to lose things we do not want to lose and begin a chain of destruction beyond what we intended. The spirit developed in response to Jacobinism, seen by the con-servatives as the notion that the world can be reshaped, by violence if nec-essary, to conform to an ideal pattern dictated by abstract reason. Here, too, language in this century has become muddled, and we need a radical rectification of names. The ruling-class "conservatism" of today is the di-rect historical heir of Jacobinism, and the institutions it seeks to preserve are institutionalized Jacobinism. What ruling-class conservatives are in-terested in conserving are the institutions that maintain and extend their power, and to that end they are perfectly ready to bulldoze hills into val-leys, transfer populations, or raze to the ground any building, neighbor-hood, or town that stands in their way. Tennyson wrote,

> That man's the best conservative
> Who lops the mouldering branch away,

but the ruling-class conservatives seek to save the branch by going after the root, and the economic and technological system they seek to con-serve has eradicated more traditional techniques, customs, and institu-tions than has any other force in the history of the world. To give the name "conservative" to this kind of economic and technological Jacobin-ism is like calling a strip miner a conservationist because he conserves the institution of strip mining.

The ecology movement in recent years has found the proper domain for the spirit of conservatism. Here the classic conservative argument is right: when the industrialist tells us that his science guarantees that little will be harmed by logging off the Amazon jungle for pulp or by leaking a bit more radiation or by adding another chemical to the food, it is not ignorant know-nothingism but conservative wisdom to answer, *Your science cannot know that much.*

Politically, the ecology that is important here is less the ecology of the wilderness (which has a different importance of its own) but rather the ecology that has been developed in the centuries of dialogue between nature and the people who do productive labor: between farmer, soil, and season; between carpenter, tools, and wood; between potter, clay, and fire; between fisherman, sea; and weather. As I mentioned above, these are dialogues that the ruling class has rarely participated in and knows little about. Their product has been the culture of the people, the culture of productive labor, that in its tools and techniques carries on the most ancient traditions known to humankind, and compared to which every tradition and inheritance Edmund Burke sought to protect is a newfangled invention. It is this ecology, the infinitely complex set of relationships between the human culture of production and that part of nature on which production has been based—rather than the "ecology of games" which connects the institutions of big government, big business, and high finance—which is the proper sphere of conservatism. It is here that change must be slow and watchful, or in some cases stopped altogether, and it is precisely here that the ruling-class "conservatives" send in their bulldozer brigades. Ordinary people, however, whose lives are embedded in this ecology, have been naturally protective of it, and this motivation has been a large part of the history of people's struggles since the early days of capitalism, from Luddism, through factory-workers' movements, through anticolonialism, to the antiredevelopment, antipollution, antinuclear movements of today.

It is said that the people are natural conservatives, which is true if understood in this way. The spirit of technological conservatism is, from the standpoint of the ruling-class "conservatives," one of the most subversive forces operating in the world today.

Nuclear Power

When I visited the Hanford Nuclear Reservation with the group of students from Japan, we were given a brief lecture tour of the site. We had timed our trip so as to be there on Hiroshima Day. The guide was a little nervous and defensive and skipped the big panel of photographs showing

Hanford's crash program to build the Nagasaki bomb and the celebrations in Hanford and Richland when they learned it had exploded successfully. Instead of talking about the war, he talked at length about the safety of nuclear power. The waste, he said, would not only be buried safely but would be carefully monitored throughout its danger period. I raised my hand and asked him, "You said the waste produced here will be dangerous for 25,000 years. Who is going to monitor it that long?"

"The U.S. government, of course."

"Have you ever heard of any government lasting for 25,000 years?"

The man stared at me in cold anger and refused to answer. Apparently he thought my question unpatriotic. I, on the other hand, realized I was talking to a fool. Critics of nuclear power who are not themselves nuclear physicists are often accused of intruding into matters of which they have no expert knowledge. I realized then that this man was intruding into the field of politics—my field—about which he had not a grain of common sense.

The argument that nuclear power plants are safe is not only a technological argument, it is also based on ideas about politics and history. It presupposes a degree of political stability which history has never known. It presupposes not only that the United States and every other government that builds nuclear power plants will last for 25,000 years but also that there will be no major war for 25,000 years. These bomb manufacturers seldom mention the vulnerability of their power plants to bombs. The Japanese government, which during the Cold War built its entire military self-defense system around the hypothesis of an invasion from the Soviet Union, also built a row of nuclear power plants along the edge of the Japan Sea, to which Soviet submarines would have had easy access. To support the claim that these plants are safe the government would have to "know" that there would be no war with the Soviet Union. Unfortunately, however, this cannot be "known," least of all by the science of nuclear physics.

Moreover, the argument for the safety of nuclear power presupposes a theory of history. It is notorious that no adequate technology has yet been discovered for the safe disposal of nuclear waste. The "experts" assure us, Don't worry, it will be invented before long. On what sort of knowledge is this assertion based? Not, again, on science: science as it exists has produced no such technology. The assertion that it will produce one is not a scientific statement but a historical prediction. It is based on the notion not only that science will progress but that it will progress indefinitely. To say that it will surely solve this problem can be justified only on the assumption that it can solve any problem. This is a strange sort of statement coming from experts whose methodology is supposed to be grounded on empirical evidence: to get empirical evidence about what science may do in the future, all we can do is wait and see. In fact, the statement that science will surely solve this problem is no more than a guess based on a very trite and muddled analogy: well, it solved a lot of problems in the past, didn't it? This retort ignores the fact that there have been lot of problems it failed to solve as well, though scientists tried quite hard, for example, to turn lead into gold or to discover the elixir of eternal youth.

So scientists who say nuclear power is safe, or safe "enough," are stepping outside their field of expertise: in saying these matters should be left up to scientists they are trying to usurp a legitimate political question and put it within the exclusive jurisdiction of the class of scientists: they are, in short, trying to usurp political power. Whether a technology is safe "enough" is not a scientific question but a choice, and it is a choice that can be legitimately made only by the people who will be hurt if the choice is wrong.

After the nuclear accident at Three Mile Island, Nakao Hajime traveled from Japan to interview people who lived in the area. He discovered he was the first to do so: the U.S. scientists believed that the way to find out what happened was to look at their instruments, not to ask people. Because Nakao is not a scientist, he had the liberty to observe things and think things that the scientists were prevented by their science from observing and thinking. He decided to adopt a method of research which is in a way more empirical than that of the scientists: to take the experiences of the people as the primary data, and the readings on instruments as only secondary data.

Many of the victims told him that on the day of the leak they had had some strange experiences: a deafening roar, a metallic taste on the tongue, a choking feeling in the throat, nausea, a burning around the eyes (as after welding without goggles, one said), a dryness on the skin like a light sunburn, which flaked off a few days later.[24] Many also observed dead pets and other animals; many driving cars hit birds with their windshields.

The scientists, on the other hand, asserted that, judging from the readings on their instruments, the radiation levels were too low for the residents to have felt any effects. Consider what a remarkable form of "empirical science" this is. On what experience or experiment could such a conclusion be based? There had never been a big nuclear-power-plant accident before. Who knows what happens when a radioactive cloud passes through a city? The scientists' conclusions were based on models and speculation, not on experience.

Nevertheless when it was announced on the authority of "science" that the radiation had been too low to be noticed, many people began to doubt their experiences or even began to feel ashamed of them as if having had them was a sign of scientific backwardness, ignorance, or even weakness. These reactions were made worse when the scientists began defining these experiences as the "psychological effects" of the accident. Reddened eyes, nausea, and so on were diagnosed as manifestations of panic. Put bluntly, people who said that they felt radiation attacking their bodies—radiation that did not register on the instruments—were being told that they were cowardly and neurotic.

Determining what people have experienced by the method of deduction from readings on scientific instruments—instead of asking them—is, when you think about it, a strange scientific method. When the people themselves become so mystified by the "science" that they will believe the instruments rather than the messages from their own bodies, they are radically disempowered. In fact, the people of the area surrounding Three Mile Island overcame this disempowerment by organizing their community. By gathering often and telling their experiences to one another, they came to understand that the experiences were real. It remains true, however, that so far the only lawsuits waged against the power company have been for psychological distress.

Leapfrogging

Some may object that it is futile at this late date to lament the passing of the preindustrial craft worker. Industrialism is here, and "You can't turn back the clock." What a poor analogy this old saw is: in fact, you can turn back clocks: they have handles for doing just that. What you cannot do is make the past itself happen again: the events cannot be repeated, and the people are gone. But the things known by the people in the past can be known by us as well. As if I couldn't break a walnut with a hammer, wear cloth of woven wool, or drink water from a clay cup because these are neolithic technologies! Yes, industrialism is upon us—and it has us organized into a lockstep march toward ecocatastrophe. We would do well to seek wisdom wherever we can.

Moreover, to say that it is too late is to be Europocentric. If there are no places untouched by industrialism, there are at least some less saturated by it than Europe, the United States, and Japan. Instead of being doomed to follow mechanically the whole miserable history of European industrialization, perhaps Third World countries could learn from the European experience and move directly into a better future.

The idea is suggested, for example, by Roger Posadas of the University of the Philippines in his article "Leapfrogging the Scientific-Technological Gap."[25] He argues that a country like the Philippines is in a position to select from the industrialized countries whatever technologies it chooses, without having to go through all the stages those countries went through to develop those technologies. The argument is persuasive and presents interesting possibilities. For such a path to be a genuine alternative for the Third World countries, however, the idea needs to free itself entirely, not just partly, from dogmatic belief in technological progress.

Posadas says that the goal of his program for the Philippines is "national scientific mastery." To this end he proposes the complete reorienting of the educational system, the economic system, the culture system, and the political system: "In short, the successful implementation of the strategy of technological leapfrogging entails the overhaul of our present system and the establishment of an entirely new social system" (p. 37). Notice the ordering of means and ends here. Technology is originally, generically, means par excellence: a way to get something done. We value good technology when it helps to do good work, cuts down time spent at drudgery, or liberates time for education, culture, play, or the pursuit of free politics. But here it is the other way around. Technology itself is the goal, for the achievement of which the entire social, political, economic, and educational system should be made over—that is, treated as means.

I agree with Posadas that the introduction of new technologies entails changes in the political system: that is precisely what I have been trying to argue in this chapter. But to begin with the assumption that the technologies "of the future" are the goal, and then to propose that the society be reorganized so as to produce them, is to stand the natural order of priorities on its head.

This tendency to see science and technology as having a transcendent rather than an instrumental value sometimes takes on an almost religious quality and makes it difficult to have a scientific discussion about science. Statements such as that we should leap into the scientific future, presented as self-evident, are themselves without scientific (i.e., empirical) foundation. The *scientific* future means whatever "comes next" in the logic of scientific advance. To say that this must necessarily be good for human beings and their world is not to make a scientific statement but is rather to make a profession of faith in science. As for what "comes next" technologically, nuclear holocaust or the invention of some robotic/biotechnological cyborg that renders human life "obsolete" are as easy to predict as any other scenario.

Posadas's list of the "Third Wave" technologies which the Philippines ought to consider includes "micro-electronics, robotics, computers, laser technology, opto-electronics and fiber optics, genetic engineering, photovoltaics, polymers and other synthetic materials" (p. 33). Although I don't know much about these things and I suspect that most ordinary people in Manila, Tokyo, or Berlin don't either, I do know that a big part of what is produced by these technologies goes for military use, for toys (including big expensive toys for adult scientists), for so-what products (a radio the size of a calling card), for technological exhibitionism—in short, for what Ruskin calls illth, as opposed to wealth.

Posadas writes, "The *intermediate*, *appropriate*, or *alternative* technologies based on the Schumacherian philosophy of 'small is beautiful'" fall under the category of preindustrial First-Wave technologies and are "based on empirical rather than on scientific knowledge" (p. 33; italics in original). The assertion is not true, but what is remarkable is that the form of knowledge on which a technique is based should be proposed as a measure of the value of the technique. The assertion that technology increases in value as it advances in scientific sophistication cannot itself be supported by the scientific method of any Wave. It is liberating, I think, to remind ourselves that most of the technologies that a human being really needs to live an orderly, comfortable, and healthy life are ancient. Would anyone really want to seriously argue that robots are more important to human beings than cloth woven from spun thread, or computers more important than the house with roof, walls, and windows? It is these technologies—cultivation of the soil; domestication of animals; fishing with nets, hooks, and traps; making pots from clay and glass from sand, extracting metals from ore; cooking food with fire; singing and dancing to the accompaniment of musical instruments; making imaginative figures by painting or dyeing or by sculpting in wood, stone, or clay—that have made human society, and not one of them has been made obsolete by any Third-Wave technique.

This is not to make the opposite and equally mechanical argument that all new technologies are valueless or harmful. As in any mixed bag some are valuable, some are harmful, and much comes under the heading of "so what?" The point is that the value of a technology must be judged by its effect on people, society, and the natural environment, not by when it was developed.

Moreover, there is an illusion that the technologies that are the most "advanced" are the ones that have the most money and power attached to them. The technologies presented to us as "Third Wave" or whatever are almost always those that have big money behind them, that are developed by vast armies of scientists and technologists supported by grants from governments or multinational industry, and that produce the technological "spectacles" that dazzle the world. It is easy to forget that other more democratic technologies may be equally new and advancing, though they produce fewer spectacles.

Recently I saw, in a book about China, a photograph of a bicycle and a truck going down a road, with a caption something like "The old and the new go side by side." This well illustrates the illusion: because the truck is motorized and bigger than the bicycle we think of it as "newer." The fact is, of course, that the bicycle and the automobile became operational at about the same time, the bicycle being only a few years older. Moreover, measured by the technological criterion of energy efficiency—calories expended per distance traveled—the bicycle is said to be unmatched by any other means of land transportation. And it is still improving.

"The bicycle" would look silly on Posadas's list. Bicycle technology is not high-tech or powertech; producing it does not require scientists with doctorates from big-name universities; it does not require huge factories for its manufacture. Yet there is no question but that Posadas's Philippines needs a bicycle industry more than it needs, say, fiber optics. As it happens, the Philippines is virtually unique among Asian countries in its devotion to the internal combustion engine, to the exclusion of the bicycle. Probably this obsession is a by-product of colonization by the United States, the world center of automobile fetishism. Most other Asian countries are flooded by bicycles. Even in metropolitan Tokyo bicycles probably outnumber automobiles. In these countries bicycles are not toys but a means of transportation for commuters and shoppers, and they are used as a light truck for mail carriers and delivery people. In South Korea heavy-duty delivery bicycles are manufactured which are capable of carrying remarkable loads. In the Philippines a useful bicycle sidecar is manufactured in tiny welding shops, but the bicycles themselves are mostly imported, either ten-speed racing bikes or small-wheeled bikes like the BMX, both of which are designed for sport, not for work. With a little encouragement the expert welders and machinists of the Philippines (of whom there are many) could easily manufacture an inexpensive working and commuting bicycle as sturdy and stylish as the wonderful jeepney. Consider the effects that increased bicycle use would have on (1) carbon-monoxide pollution (Manila is under a permanent brown cloud), (2) noise pollution, (3) the efficiency and safety* of the traffic flow, and (4) the amount of wealth that leaves the country each year to import automobiles, automobile parts, and oil. It is the illusion that the bicycle is "an earlier stage of technology" and that one must go "forward," not "back," that prevents us from seeing facts as obvious as these. An addi-

---

* That is, if some streets were set aside for bicycles only.

tional factor is that the bicycle is the sort of technology which takes power and initiative away from the university-trained scientific and technological elites and places it in the hands of the workers: welders and machinists. Scientific and technological elites, however well intentioned, are unlikely to waste time advocating technologies that do not require their services. In these senses the bicycle can serve as an approximate model for democratic technology. Many other such modest technologies are improving. Hand tools, for example, are being made with greater precision and of harder steel. Since the oil crisis of the 1970s there have been remarkable improvements in the design of wood-burning stoves in North America, leading to much greater energy efficiency. A few years ago I talked to a house carpenter of the Kalinga-Apayao region in northern Luzon. He told me that he used a chain saw to cut his boards, the local sawmill being too expensive and the old handsaw method too time-consuming. But it is very hard to cut straight with a chainsaw, so that he had to plane each board level laboriously. I asked him if he knew that a guide apparatus had been invented which can be attached to a chainsaw, making it easier to saw boards, and he said he did not. The chainsaw guide is not Third Wave, but it is new, and it is what this worker can use on this job.

Leapfrogging is obvious, and it happens. Surely we needn't think a country in the technological situation of the Philippines is doomed to go lumbering blindly through all the stages and horrors of industrialization followed by England, France, Japan, or the United States. To say so would be as absurd as saying that the farmers in the Cordillera and other regions who transport their loads on wooden sleds pulled by carabaos are obligated to use the wooden wheel and the greased axle before they can put rubber tires and ball bearings on their carts (which in fact they actually do in addition to using sleds). Leapfrogging is inevitable, but the question is which frog to leap? It would be simple enough if all the frogs were lined up in single file, as some people think technological development is ordered. But it is not in the nature either of frogs or of human inventiveness to line up like that. So there are frogs hopping in all directions. One can leap into a high-tech future of ecocatastrophe, or into a future in which the human being has become totally degraded by the machine, or in which human body parts have been largely replaced by machine parts (like Robocop), or one in which we see the most dazzling display of Third-Wave technological prowess possible: nuclear war. Just choosing high-tech because it's high, or Third-Wave tech because three is the next number after two, provides us no defense against these kakotopian futures.

There is also the question of how far to leap. The expression "Leap into the twenty-first century" is no longer impressive: we'll get there soon enough even if we crawl. What Ivan Illich has called the "hyperindustrial nations" are now in a state of deep technological confusion, and it is not clear whether they will succeed in shifting to a mode and a level of production that will stop their present rush toward ecocide and therefore suicide. Rather than leap forward smack into the middle of the problem, why not try to leap over it into a solution? Illich has written: "Two-thirds of mankind still can avoid passing through the industrial age, by choosing right now a postindustrial balance in their mode of production which the hyperindustrial nations will be forced to adopt as an alternative to chaos."[26] To call the building of a society with democratic tools and a nonecocidal level and mode of production "a leap into the far future" is not to return to some kind of technological-determinist theory of development; it is nothing more than an expression of hope. It is determination, not determinism, that will get us there.

Does This Matter to Workers?

Just as the well-off sometimes argue that the poor care only about food and shelter, so elites sometimes argue that workers care only about getting the job done and getting a paycheck. Empowerment or disempowerment of the worker is a subject intellectuals like to split hairs about but matters little to the men and women at the workplace.

This is hard to prove decisively one way or the other. Certainly after many generations of the factory system it is possible to find workers who will say they care nothing for the work and only for their pay. But statements like these are in reality bitter charges against the system, rather than affirmations of it. On the whole one can say, contrary to the above, that probably the only people that really believe that work satisfaction doesn't matter to workers are people who have never themselves done productive labor.

In 1987 I traveled to the Philippine province of Negros Occidental and visited a tiny cooperative workshop there. At this time the collapse of the sugar industry had brought Negros real starvation, and this workshop had been seeded with aid funds from Canada. The shop was operated by women who lived in the company town of a sugar refinery that had been shut down. It was giving them the first work they had had in two and a half years, a time during which they and their families had survived on UNICEF feeding programs. They were making stuffed dolls for a company in Taiwan. It was pitifully low-paid work, and it was tragic to see, in a region in need of so much, people set to work making junk. (Moreover, learning that they were working on a subcontract from a Taiwanese company helped me to demystify the Newly Industrialized Economies success story.)

In any case, the project was set up so that the women were self-managing. There were two remarkable things about the way they had ordered the work. They had adopted microdivision of labor—one making arms, another heads, another hats, and so on. But they were also rotating the jobs so that by the time each contract was finished each woman would have made the complete doll, part by part. That is, they had arranged the work so as to squeeze out of it whatever training value it had. Moreover, they had arranged that each worker could get the satisfaction of having made something. This choice no doubt slowed down their productivity, a serious matter for people working at the edge of starvation. Yet as they talked to us visitors they made it very clear that this ordering of the work mattered very much to them.

They had also arranged their sewing machines (their own, mostly battered antiques, which they had brought from their homes) in a way never seen in a factory: in a circle, facing the center. I did not really need to ask why, but I did, and got the answer (and the laughter) I expected: "So we can talk to each other while we work, of course!" Again, at a cost to productivity which would make any factory foreman grind his teeth, these workers had transformed their work from dreary drudgery to a pleasant social occasion. What grounds other than elitist arrogance is there for saying that arrangements like these would matter less to the poor than they would to anyone else?

Another striking example also comes from Negros. Farmers in the National Federation of Sugar Workers (NFSW) and also in the Small Farmers' Association of Negros (SFAN) are trying to develop a farming technology that will bring them not only a steady supply of food and income but also "self-reliance."[27] When they use this expression they are not talking about the North American ideal of "individual self-reliance" but of the self-reliance of farm communities and the farming class as a whole. To this end they are relearning organic farming.* To them, of course, "organic farming" is not the fashionable new idea it is to some urban health-food advocates; it is the way farming was always done in the Philippines until a couple of decades ago. They want to go back to organic fertilizer and organic pesticides not only to grow more nourishing

---

* For the sugar workers, "relearn" may not be the right expression. Labor in the sugar fields is not really farming at all, and many sugar workers need and want to learn farming from the beginning.

and less poisoned food (a matter of life and death in a region where children are dying of malnutrition) but also to liberate themselves from the grips of the multinationals who sell them the seeds and chemicals for high-tech agriculture at prices that keep them impoverished and at the mercy of the usurers. The rice farmers, in particular, want to get away from high-yield variety seed and are presently experimenting with what they call "traditional seed" for the same reasons (the Green Revolution was one high-tech leapfrogging experiment that was far from liberating for the Philippine farmer).

Notice how these farmers have corrected the means-end relationship between technology and social purposes. Their slogan is not "productivity" but "self-reliance." Their idea is not first to introduce whatever are the most advanced high-tech farming methods and then accept as "inevitable" whatever production relations and social forms emerge from these methods. Rather they begin with the kind of communities they want to live in (self-reliant communities) and then search for the farming technologies that will make this possible. This stance is what it means to control one's tools and not to be controlled by them. Of course neither the sugar workers nor the small rice farmers can fully succeed in these aims without genuine land reform, which the government has so far refused to give them. And at the time of writing they are being fiercely repressed in Negros for trying these experiments. For a government of landowners the image of a country of economically and technologically self-reliant farmers is the worst nightmare of all.

4

democracy's flawed tradition

Let us coin the expression "state of democracy." As a metaphor calling up the image of a change of state in physics, the term may help us to distinguish the phenomenon of democracy itself from the institutions that people build hoping to establish and maintain it. This distinction in turn may help us to clarify what category of thing democracy is. As I argued in Chapter 1, it is an error to refer to institutions as if they were synonymous with the conditions they are intended to promote. We tend to think about institutions of learning or the Department of Justice or the religious establishment as the locuses of learning, justice, and religion. We would be less likely to make the analogous mistake of thinking of institutions such as, say, beauty parlors, fitness centers, and penitentiaries as the locuses of beauty, fitness, and penitence.

According to Montesquieu, democracy requires, in addition to law and the power to enforce it, "one spring more . . . , namely virtue."[1] That is, there can be democracy where there is political virtue, not otherwise. Modern political scientists have labored hard to produce definitions of democracy which have no need of this intangible quality, definitions that assert democracy exists where certain laws and procedures are in effect, certain rules of the game are followed, a certain decision-making progress prevails. But the political form characterized by the people's following certain rules and procedures is something Montesquieu places in an entirely different category. It is not in a democracy but in an aristocracy, where they do *not* rule, that "the people . . . are restrained by their laws." In this situation, Montesquieu adds, "They have, therefore, less occasion for virtue than the people in a democracy."[2] For Montesquieu, democracy is the name of a form of rule, not of a form of obedience. It is the name of a situation in which the people are in the sovereign seat of power, which means that they have power *over* the law. In this situation, nothing but political virtue can lead them to use that power in an orderly and restrained way. Thinking about this makes political writers nervous, and they like to move quickly—as Montesquieu himself did—to the business of describing various checks and balances or other institutional arrangements that would render people's political behavior orderly and predictable. But a situation in which people's behavior is orderly and restrained because of their virtue, and one in which it is orderly because it is restrained by institutions and laws, though in real life these two factors generally appear mixed together, are in principle two quite different states of affairs. If Montesquieu is right, the state of democracy is preinstitutional. It is the position of the Lawgiver occupied by the people themselves. Its virtue is the positive, creative virtue capable of establishing just law, not simply the passive virtue of obedience to the law. To define it thus is different from saying it is anti-institutional or antilaw. There are certain laws, institutions, and procedures that have an affinity with democracy, that democrats have fought for from ancient times and still do. Equal rights as citizens, fair procedures known to all, public discussion of public choices, rough equality in wealth and in control over the means of production, regionally dispersed power—all of these are essential democratic demands. But even if they are all won, if they are simply then accepted passively in ignorance of the political virtue that lay behind them, the result will not be democracy. It will be more like the situation in More's Utopia, where the laws laid down by the Lawgiver keep the people forever in a state of happy childhood.

My argument here corresponds to the classic typology of forms of government, in which the three basic forms—government by one, few, or many—are further subdivided into their corrupt and uncorrupt modes. What I mean by the state of democracy corresponds to the uncorrupted rule by the many. But it would be a mistake to think of virtue and corruption as merely intangible "normative" elements, whose presence or absence leave the political form itself unchanged. "Change of state" is an apt figure precisely because there is such a sharp change in *form*, though the element itself remains the same, as when ice turns to water and water to steam. In a state of democracy the political molecules come into different relation with one another, behave differently toward one another. As in the case of the transformation of water into steam, this change can generate extraordinary power.

The power generated by the state of democracy is hard to explain or even to form a conception of in an age in which we are taught to believe with Max Weber that the basis of state power is its monopoly of legitimate violence. When democratic power appears it is typically unpredicted and unexpected, even by the actors themselves. And as it is not easy to account for in the language of contemporary political science, it is erased from the record of political phenomena by an "explanation" of it in some other terminology. One may kick it either upstairs by describing it as a miracle, or downstairs by describing it as a riot.

The February 1986 presidential elections scheduled in the Philippines were boycotted by the most realistic forces on the left. The boycott did not stem from ignorance. It was backed by most of the collected wisdom of modern political science, Marxist or liberal: dictators are not overthrown with civil elections. This idea comes close to having the status of a law of power politics. It doesn't happen. Then it happened—not only that there was an election but the great mass of the Philippine people rose up to enforce the results of that election. The dictator's power disintegrated.

Remarkably, after this event the "political realists" of all persuasions began thinking up arguments to prove that it had never happened. Actually, we were told, it was a military coup. Ronald Reagan was behind it. The CIA engineered it. Juan Ponce Enrile had it all planned. Anything but that a military dictator was defeated by democratic power. It is true that the moment of People's Power soon ended, that the Philippine people were induced to put their trust in the wrong place and are paying a bitter price for that choice today. The point here is that, at that moment, People's Power was real power.

Power politicians and cynics like to believe that their power and cynicism are protected by iron laws. They are uncomfortable when these iron laws begin to dissolve before their eyes, and reassured when the laws reassert themselves. I am prepared to believe that there are such iron laws of power in politics and social science. Only, people sometimes disobey them. That is the peculiar characteristic of laws in social science. We can make them or discover them, and they may be accurate, but that accuracy in itself does not stop people from choosing to do something else. When enough people do something else, there occurs what amounts to a change of state, and the old laws no longer work. You cannot learn what steam will do by watching ice.

In *On Revolution*, Hannah Arendt notes that since the rise of the modern nation-state, revolution after revolution has produced, at least in the first stages, a peculiar political form she calls the council system. Again and again, in the phase when the revolution was still revolutionary, the polity has broken down naturally into units small enough that the people can confront one another in genuine communities, talk to one another, and choose and act collectively. What is remarkable is that people in sharply different cultures and historical circumstances have consistently fallen into this political form even in the absence of any political theory or ideology advocating it or capable of explaining it. It has even appeared where revolutionary theory dictated an altogether different sort of political organization for revolution, the revolutionary party.[3] This form can be understood as the state of democracy struggling to reassert itself in an age in which it has been theoretically ruled out. When "democracy" was redefined as government by elected representatives in the huge nation-state, the actual state of democracy became a political phenomenon without a name. But stealing its name and abolishing its theoretical status do not eliminate it as a possible phenomenon. Some things cannot be "progressed" out of existence. It is just as true as it was before that the state of democracy is a possible configuration and that it seeks a human group small enough to make the formation of a visible public possible.

It's not surprising, then, that people who have experienced a state of democracy typically have trouble finding words to express it. In the Philippines people still talk about the "miracle" of EDSA (the acronym for Epifanio de los Santos Avenue, where unarmed people stopped the advance of Ferdinand Marcos's armored infantry). A Polish member of Solidarity I interviewed in 1987 changed the tone of his voice when he began talking to me about "those days," and he told me that he did not believe the essence of the thing could be comprehended or believed by one who had not been there. It was not an ordinary union struggle, and it was not aimed at throwing out the men in power, and it was not about the price of meat or the long waiting lines. It was a situation in which the political and military institutions of dictatorship had remained fully intact and yet were powerless to rule over a society that had undergone the democratic change of state.

Many people who had participated in the movements of the 1960s experienced something similar, albeit on a smaller scale. I was at the University of California during the Free Speech Movement of 1964 and have never been able to look at politics in the same way since. What started as a small picket line seeking to influence the policy of the university grew until it *became* the university, or at least a big section of it. The university could not attack the movement without hacking away at itself. During that fall semester an entirely new communications system grew up on the campus. I remember thinking that one would be able to tell by looking down from an airplane that the university was in an extraordinary state. Instead of streams of mutually alienated students marching dutifully to and from class, everywhere there were little knots of from five to twenty people, talking, exchanging information, arguing furiously. Every time one of us met someone we knew we would ask, "What have you heard?" and pass on anything we might know ourselves. I remember many times leaving to go to work in the library, getting caught up in a discussion at the edge of the campus, then another, and another, and then realizing that it was 6:00 P.M. and I had spent the day standing and talking in the Plaza. So much information was communicated through these word-of-mouth channels that the ordinary channels of information became useless. We always had more information about the situation than what the radio, television or the newspapers could tell us, and we also knew more than the campus administrators. Moreover, participating in this culture of marathon discussion gave us an excellent political education. Suddenly what the students had been studying in the class room . . . *mattered*. At the same time human relations became warmer and less competitive. People became more able to make friends and more willing to help out strangers. Could this, we wondered, be a small, frail sample of that legendary entity that haunts the imagination of liberal politics, the political community?

In the early 1960s, when the civil-rights movement and the first campus movements were still using the tactic of nonviolent civil disobedience, liberal critics opposed them with a slogan they repeated endlessly, as if it had the magical power to make the whole thing go away: "We agree with your goals but not your methods." This objection was often accused of being hypocritical, but it was not. The goals of the civil-rights movement and the Free Speech Movement were unobjectionable to liberalism, being demands for rights guaranteed in the U.S. Constitution. But the methods were the methods of radical democracy and subversive to the liberal notion of politics. And it was an open secret in the movement that for many activists the method had become a big part of the motivation for participation. The sense of hope, trust, community, and joy of action which people experienced at least at the best moments in the movement brought with them a feeling of happiness totally different from the simple means-end satisfactions offered by competitive liberal society ("success," "getting ahead," "the satisfaction of a job well done"). It is significant that after the brutality of the U.S. attacks against the Vietnamese people led the movement to turn to violence, the criticism "We agree with your goals but not your methods" was no longer heard. Of course the liberal establishment did not like the violence of the antiwar movement, but they understood it and knew how to handle it. It didn't put them in that state of fear of the unknown which the method of radical democracy had.

Radical democracy does not simply mean people acting in concert. There are many ways to get people to do so: the threat of punishment or the promise of reward, manipulation, indoctrination, the raising of false hopes, psychological conditioning, scientific management. The study of the ways to organize action is a central concern of political science. But one way is different in kind from all the others—when people act together spontaneously, joined by the trust they place in one another. When this happens, vast, unexpected power is generated, the power of people acting together not ignorantly, or under orders, or in accordance with someone else's plan, but in freedom.

Sometimes this power is greater than the power of guns and tanks, sometimes it isn't. What matters is that it is different in kind, and can do what no other kind of power can do. The other powers—military power, state power, technological power, bureaucratic power, or money power— may be stronger in the sense that together or alone they can defeat democratic power. But the one thing they cannot do is to bring into being a new world of public freedom. Democratic power, the state of democracy, brings that world into being not by "making" it but by becoming it. The other kinds of powers may prevail, but after they do, the political world is the same as before—a world we can endure only thanks to our long training in cynicism.

Democratic power is the one sort of power which can bring the world of public freedom into being. It can dissolve the most powerful-seeming institutions—as when the people who are the building blocks and cogs and motors and fuel of those institutions decide to stop being those objects and simply walk off and do something else. It is the ever-present danger that people may vote with their feet which reveals the fragility of institutionalized power.

Yet the state of democracy is also fragile. When the occasion passes— the strike is won, the demands are met, the dictator falls—people return to what we call (with more significance than we realize) "business as usual." Radical democracy takes place outside the sphere of the institutions by which we sustain our lives, the economy. Those institutions patiently await our return: The strikers will return when they get really hungry, the student activist will return to mainstream society after graduation, the drop-out will eventually decide that it's better after all to have a job. The state of democracy is exhilarating but exhausting, and soon people return to the quiet stability of managed life. Power reverts to the managers, and people's free action reverts back once again to institutionalized behavior. Revolution leads to thermidor, the people rally to Napoleon or elect the likes of Corazon Aquino, Lech Walesa metamorphoses from union leader to business promoter, and public freedom is replaced by "free trade."

The state of democracy presents a problem similar to the old alchemists' puzzle: how can one make both a universal solvent and a vessel in which to contain it? Or, to take a metaphor from modern physics, how can one both sustain and control a fusion reaction? The classic answer, again, is that the only force that can contain the democratic fusion reaction without destroying it is the powerful magnetic field called political virtue. If this is so, radical democracy is operating at a great disadvantage today: as mentioned above, the expression "political virtue" is hardly a part of our political vocabulary. We can barely use the expression without embarrassment, although we can speak with sure confidence about such matters as rights, law, power, voting, taxes, interest. People who inadvertently find themselves in a state of democracy are groping in theoretical darkness. Without the language for grasping the situation they are in or for understanding what is needed to sustain it, they soon find that they have been outwitted, as it were, by the institutions of management.

This limitation is important, but there is another way of looking at the short-livedness of the state of democracy in our time. Modern democratic theory is sustained by two great models from the European classical past, the political fusion reaction of demonic power that was democratic Athens, and the mighty seat of law and of the ideal of the citizen, the Roman Republic. Both of these models, great as they are, are from the standpoint of radical democracy fundamentally flawed. And their flaws correspond in a remarkable way to the flaws in our own conceptions of democracy. Their flaws and our own have a way of concealing each other from our view. Conversely, taking up the flaws in the Athenian and Roman models can serve as a method of addressing the flaws in our own. This is what I propose to do next.

Democratic Empire: Athens

In the West, Athens in the Age of Pericles has been the traditional archetype of democracy, an archetype that causes some embarrassment to those who hold modern democratic values: Athens was a patriarchy and a slave society. It is a tribute to the dazzling attraction of the Athenians that they make us want to forget these failings, and we should evaluate the Athenians for what they achieved in their age and not for their failure to achieve what a modern person would consider an ideal society. The Athenians did not invent slavery and patriarchy, neither did they abolish them; what they did do was to discover public freedom. Among the minority who were citizens, something close to a state of democracy prevailed, and we can learn much from them.

That democratic Athens was also an empire is a criticism that modern observers make less often. (This omission is rather strange, because this is the criticism, and not that against slavery and patriarchy, that contemporary Greeks were ready to make.) But modern "democrats" (British, French, U.S., and others) have had their own historical reasons for not wanting to raise the question of a possible contradiction between democracy and empire. Significantly, in the period of reflection following the Vietnam War, Athenian imperialism has begun to become more visible to scholars.[4]

Few contemporary writings in praise of Athenian democracy have survived. Historians rely heavily on the Funeral Oration of Pericles, as recorded by Thucydides. Textbooks often refer to this speech, typically emphasizing the paragraph on the constitution and on the spirit of equal justice and mutual tolerance that prevailed among the citizens (*Peloponnesian Wars* 2.3).[5] It is important, however, to read this paragraph in the context of the whole speech, and moreover to consider the speech in the context of the entire work of Thucydides. In that context, the historian intends the speech to explain not so much Athens's domestic happiness or justice as its extraordinary and unprecedented form of power.

Thucydides, the first political historian (arguably the first historian) in the West, begins his work by seeking to demonstrate that the war he is chronicling is "a great war, and more worthy of relation than any other that had preceded it." Not only is it the greatest war, but "the greatest movement yet known in history, not only of the Hellenes but of a large part of the barbarian world—I had almost said of mankind" (1.1). He does not simply make this point in passing, but argues it at length. In ancient times, he says, there was nothing to compare to this war: "Before the Trojan War there is no indication of any common action in Hellas" (1.1). Agamemnon's expedition against Troy "may be pronounced on the evidence of what it effected to have been inferior to its renown and to the current opinion about it formed under the tuition of the poets" (1.11). As for the tyrants, "their habit of providing simply for themselves, of looking solely to their personal comfort and family aggrandizement, made safety the great aim of their policy, and prevented anything great proceeding from them" (1.17).

Finally, the historian says, the tyrants were overthrown and two great powers emerged. The first of these he introduces by reference to its political institutions; Lacedaemon had "enjoyed a freedom from tyrants which was unbroken; it has possessed the same form of government for more than four hundred years . . . and has thus been in a position to arrange the affairs of the other states" (1.18).

The other power was Athens, but here the historian says nothing about the form of government of the polis. Instead, he introduces the Athenians by telling of something they did: at the time of the second Persian invasion "the Athenians, having made up their minds to abandon their city, broke up their homes, threw themselves into their ships, and became a naval people" (1.18).

In modern times we have examples of peoples' abandoning their cities in the face of enemy invasion but always in the form of fleeing streams of refugees, taking with them as many of their possessions as they can carry. The transformation of citizens into refugees also amounts to a kind of political change of state: the dissolution of the city as a political entity. The Athenians, Thucydides tells us, left architectural Athens behind them, even destroying the buildings so as to emphasize the point, but brought the *polis* with them. Let us admit that Thucydides is exaggerating (in fact some Athenians stayed behind), as he sometimes does to make his idea clear. What he has done in this short sentence is to give us a brilliant image with which to grasp the unprecedented nature of the power generated by this fusion reaction called Athens.

Thucydides details the many circumstances that led to the war, but the "real cause," he says, was "the one which was formally most kept out of sight." This was "the growth in the power of Athens" (1.24). Thucydides does not romanticize what the Athenians did: the war was "without parallel for the misfortunes that it brought upon Hellas" (1.24), and the book's descriptions of the horrors of war are without parallel in historical writing. At the same time it is the power of the Athenians that gives the historian a tale to tell.

Thucydides tells us that one of his historiographical innovations was "computing by summers and winters" (5.19) rather than by using genealogies or the names of magistrates as the way of ordering the events in time. This method was not simply a clever new discovery that earlier historians had not hit upon. The point of Thucydides' opening paragraphs is to tell us that until now the method of ordering the events of Hellas according to summers and winters would not have yielded a story. Chroniclers up to then had told the different stories of separate cities, for which the genealogies of leading families were adequate to order the events. Thucydides' narrative is "more worthy of relation" than any other because this is the first time that all Greece was entangled in public events on such a scale. It is the first time that public events on that scale have been ordered so as to be tellable. Thucydides is able to be the first political historian because the world itself was forcibly reordered into "historical" form. And, Thucydides says, what forced the world into that form was Athenian power. All Greeks had to be either participants or audience: the leading cities joined one side or the other, "while the rest of Hellas stood straining with excitement" (2.8).

This history forms the context for Pericles' speech. Seen in that context, some of the sections we might tend to dismiss as mere bombast take on new meaning. Thucydides, who has already said that his book will be "a possession for all time" (1.22), has Pericles say,

> "The admiration of the present and succeeding ages will be ours, since we have not left our power without witness, but have shown it with mighty proofs; and far from needing a Homer for our panegyrist, or other of his craft whose verses might charm for the moment only for the impression which they gave to melt at the touch of fact, we have forced every sea and land to be the highway of our daring, and everywhere, whether for evil or for good, have left imperishable monuments behind us." (2.41)

If Arendt is right that for the ancient Greeks "being remembered" was the high goal of action, this paragraph becomes the keystone to Pericles' speech. This is a chilling realization. Pericles is saying, in effect, that in order to be remembered, the Athenians have used their power to compel the world to take on the structure by which such memory could be held. The Athenians, who "forced every sea and land to be the highway of our daring," ensured thereby that the monuments they leave behind will be imperishable. What they have done is written not simply in a poem or book, it is written directly on the world.

Not all societies are historical, in the sense that they structure their collective past in the form of a story so as to be remembered publicly. Thucydides has Pericles tell us that the Athenians forced events to take on that structure for the very purpose of ensuring that they should "have the whole earth for their tomb," in which they would be "eternally remembered upon every occasion on which deed or story shall fall for its commemoration" (2.43). And they did so, Pericles adds (almost as if he were anticipating that one day he would have Nietzsche among his readers), "whether for evil or for good" (2.41).

State of Democracy/State of Plague

We should not forget that this speech was given at a funeral. The bodies of the first young men to die in the war had been laid out for three days in public, there had been a procession with wailing, the bodies had been buried. Before Pericles stand the parents, sisters, brothers, wives, children of these dead young men; his task is to induce them to shift their attention from the brute fact of the dead bodies they have just seen go into the ground to the political body for which the men had died. In this sense it is a classical wartime speech, a kind of battle between the eye and the ear, in which Pericles works to convince his audience to grant less credibility to what they have seen than to what they can hear: his words. "You must yourselves realize the power of Athens, and feed your eyes upon her from day to day, till love of her fills your hearts [and until] all her greatness shall break upon you" (2.43). Then you will be able to see that the men who died here are not the most miserable of persons, but are "fortunate indeed" (2.44; he says this directly to their parents). They are fortunate because they died heroically and gloriously, and because there is a metaphorical sense in which such people are not quite dead: they "live on" in memory. In Pericles' telling, the spirit is victorious over the body, honor overcomes the misery of physical pain and death, the memory of life compensates for the loss of life, the living body of the polis signifies more than the dead bodies of these sons. The speech is a brilliant success; it is all that its reputation says it is. One can sense that Pericles knows that he has done his job well when he concludes, "And now that you have brought to a close your lamentations for your relatives, you may depart" (2.46).

In the very next paragraph Thucydides tells us that soon after this speech the plague appeared in Athens. Let us assume that it is no accident that this subtle historian placed his descriptions of the Funeral Oration and of the plague back to back.[6] For the description of the plague is precisely the logic of the Funeral Oration turned on its head. It is as if the repressed body has returned to take vengeance on Athens for having been slighted and to remind the Athenians that according to *its* logic death is merely death. If Pericles' speech is a triumph of the mind over the body, the plague "first settled in the head, [and] ran its course from thence through the whole of the body" (2.49). Against the blank absurdity of death Pericles has set the beautiful order of the city, an order in which a just relation of cause and effect is guaranteed: sound policies bring good results, virtue is recognized and rewarded, and the future is guaranteed as a space in which actions in the present will continue to ramify and in which they will be remembered. The plague, Thucydides tells us, overturns precisely this logic of cause and effect. The disease itself, he says, had "no ostensible cause" (2.49). Moreover, no sort of medical treatment had any effect on it: "Some died in neglect, others in the midst of every attention. No remedy was found that could be used as a specific; for what did good in one case, did harm in another. Strong and weak constitutions proved equally incapable of resistance, all alike being swept away"

(2.51). And if wisdom brought no result, neither did virtue gain a reward: "There was the awful spectacle of men dying like sheep, through having caught the infection in nursing each other. This caused the greatest mortality. On the one hand, if they were afraid to visit each other, they perished from neglect; indeed many houses were emptied of their inmates for want of a nurse: on the other, if they ventured to do so, death was the consequence. This was especially the case with such as made any pretensions to goodness" (2.51).

With no reasonable relation between cause and effect, the future disappears as an intelligible category, and neither wisdom nor virtue remain as sensible guides to action. What is left is the present and the body; and the body alone (as Hobbes, the first translator of these lines into English, knew so well) does not provide us with a basis for social order. Lawlessness begins to break out: "Fear of gods or law of man there was none to restrain them. As for the first, they judged it to be just the same whether they worshiped them or not, as they saw all alike perishing; and as for the last, no one expected to live to be brought to trial for his offenses, but each felt that a far severer sentence had been already passed upon them and hung over their heads, and before this fell it was only reasonable to enjoy life a little" (2.53).

Finally, as if the plague were determined to drag the logic of the Funeral Oration down to its final degradation, it made even proper funerals impossible. Only a few pages after Thucydides has described the very careful and formal sacred ritual with which the young heroes had been buried and through which they would always be remembered, he tells us how the plague victims were thrown into nameless graves:

> All the burial rites before in use were entirely upset, and they buried the bodies as best they could. Many from want of the proper appliances, through so many of their friends having died already, had recourse to the most shameless sepultures: sometimes getting the start of those who had raised a pile, they threw their own dead body upon the stranger's pyre and ignited it; sometimes they tossed the corpse which they were carrying on the top of another that was burning, and so went off. (2.52)

Earlier in his scientific description of the disease, Thucydides notes, "All the birds and beasts that prey upon human bodies, either abstained from touching them (though there were many lying unburied) or died after tasting them" (2.50). In Sophocles' *Antigone* the most extreme expression of the pollution brought down on Thebes by Creon's refusal to bury Polyneices is that domestic dogs ate of the body and "brought the stench of [his] great crime back to each hearth" (1082). With what extraordinary, dry restraint does Thucydides conclude the previous passage: "But of course the effects which I have mentioned could best be studied in a domestic animal like the dog" (2.50).

What shall we make of this description? Of course we know that the plague really happened; at the same time we know that Thucydides must be exaggerating again: otherwise Athens could not have continued to exist, let alone continue to fight the war for decades after. There is no question but that these paragraphs are written not only by Thucydides the chronicler and natural scientist but also by Thucydides the artist and theorist.

Should we read him the way Hobbes undoubtedly did, as showing us how even the simplest structures, those on which we depend for giving order to our daily lives and which we take for granted, are in fact conditional, and that to maintain them we must never waver in our trust in the polity and our obedience to the law, as Pericles has instructed; otherwise we are lost? This interpretation would be too simple. The plague, was, after all, a sickness, which the polis was no more able than anyone else to cure. And it is simply not possible to forget, once we have seen it, the cool irony with which Thucydides—when the reader's head is still reverberating with Pericles' thundering words, THE FUNERAL IS OVER! ATHENS HAS DEFEATED DEATH ! GO HOME!—writes, "In the first days of summer the Lacedaemonians . . . invaded Attica . . . and sat down and laid waste to the country. Not many days after . . . the plague first began to show itself among the Athenians" (2.47).

Athens's state of democracy, as Pericles describes it, and its state of plague are mirror images of one another. The latter is the deconstruction of the former, which helps us to see what it is made of. Here too, the description of the state of plague resembles the methodology of Thomas Hobbes. But Thucydides is no objective social scientist; he has a moral tale to tell as well. And the state of democracy in Athens is not only democracy, it is democracy-at-war, democratic empire, "to speak somewhat plainly, a tyranny," as Pericles says later (2.63). The absolute sacrifice of the body to the city which Pericles calls for in the name of democracy is actually needed to protect and expand the empire. Athens is a fusion reaction without a vessel to contain it. While political virtue and their laws keep the Athenians mostly just to one another, outside the polis is a moral void, with little to slow them down. The Athenians are pure action, "they were born into the world to take no rest themselves and to give none to others" (1.70), said a Corinthian speaker at the beginning of the war; "We cannot fix the exact point at which our empire shall stop" (6.18), says Alcibiades toward the end.

Yet Thucydides suggests that there is something, a kind of rudimentary principle of international justice, which the Athenians could have used to contain their endless expansion. He mentions it several times, most forcibly through the lips of the people of the tiny island of Melos.

From the Island to the River

You will remember the story. It is a time of truce between Athens and Sparta. The Athenians have landed on Melos and invited the citizens to try to show them why they should have any choices other than to surrender or to die. In an eerie parody of the Socratic method, the Athenians propose that instead of exchanging speeches, the two sides could better get to the truth of the matter by engaging in a dialogue: "Take us up at whatever you do not like and settle that before going any farther" (5.85). The Athenians further propose that both sides dispense with "specious pretenses": the Athenians will not argue that they have a right to their empire, and in return the Melians should not argue that they have done the Athenians no wrong, "since you know as well as we do that right, as the world goes, is only a question between equals in power, while the strong do what they can and the weak suffer what they must" (5.89).

In response, the Melians, under the Athenian demand that they speak only from interest and never from justice, argue that the Athenians would find it expedient that they "should not destroy what is our common protection, the privilege of being allowed in danger to invoke what is fair and right, and even to profit by arguments not strictly valid if they can be got to pass current" (5.90).[7] The argument is remarkable. In the international (or strictly speaking, "interpolitical") arena, there is no law; fairness and right do not exist, but it is expedient to act as if they do. For whom is it expedient? Fairness and right, apparently, are useful only for the weak. But the Melians argue that the strong, even when they have the power to ignore and destroy these principles, should not, but should leave them intact as a "common protection." They should do so because of the factor of fortune, which is "sometimes more impartial than the disproportion of numbers might lead one to suppose" (5.102). You are the stronger now, but you cannot know that you will be the stronger forever. So even the Athenians ought to leave these principles intact, against the day when their power may fail them. Or, rather, *especially* the Athenians, "as your fall would be a signal for the heaviest vengeance and an example for the world to meditate upon" (5.90). But the Athenians' power is too great for them to take such a possibility seriously. They cannot form an image of themselves reduced to the position of pleading for just treatment. One can almost hear the amused contempt in their voices when they reply to the Melians, "This . . . is a risk that we are content to take" (5.91).

After more fruitless exchange, the dialogue ends, the Melians resolve to fight, and the siege of Melos begins. The Melians soon surrender to the Athenians, "who put to death all the grown men they took, and sold the women and children for slaves, and subsequently sent out five hundred colonists and inhabited the place themselves" (5.118).

What is this grisly little tale about? We are not told that the capture of Melos was of any particular strategic importance in the war. Clearly the historian is using the incident to set down the dilemma of interpolitical justice in as lucid a form as possible, to engrave it in his reader's memory. The Athenian argument appears cool and logical; we learn in the final paragraph that it also transforms them into monsters. The Melian argument appears sentimental and muddle-headed, but it gives the Melians a basis for acting honorably and bravely. But still, weren't the Athenians right, at the height of their power, to reject the argument that they should respect justice merely because someday they might find themselves in a weak position? The historian gives his answer in the way he has located this dialogue in his narrative. As with the Funeral Oration, the meaning of the Melian Dialogue is revealed in the sentence that immediately follows it. The sentence is, "The same winter the Athenians resolved to sail again to Sicily" (6.1).[8]

The Melians were not sentimentalists, but seers. In the dialogue they exactly prophesy the Athenians' fate, and in the Athenians' inability to conceive of such a fate we are given an exact measure of their hubris. Thucydides hammers this point home. He has already told us that this war was the "greatest movement yet known in history"; of the Athenian defeat at Syracuse he says: "This was the greatest Hellenic achievement of any in this war, or, in my opinion, in Hellenic history; at once the most glorious to the victors, and most calamitous to the conquered. They were beaten at all points and altogether; all that they suffered was great; they were destroyed, as the saying is, with a total destruction, their fleet, their army—everything was destroyed, and few out of many returned home" (7.87).

The historian's description of the last battle is a vision of ultimate human horror. If the final degradation of the State of Plague is the pollution of the dogs, at Syracuse the Athenians themselves are reduced to dogs. In an agony of thirst they are driven into a river, where the Syracusan and Pelopponesian soldiers "came down and butchered them, especially those in the water, which was thus immediately spoiled, but which they went on drinking just the same, mud and all, bloody as it was, most even fighting to have it" (7.84).

The Two Bodies of Rome

In the year 494 B.C. the Roman Republic was engaged in fierce class struggle. The chief issue was the same as the chief issue today between the rich countries of the north and the poor countries of the south: debt. The property-owning patricians were driving the commoners deeper and deeper into debt, and when they could not pay were seizing their property if they had any, or throwing them into prison or taking them into slavery if they hadn't. Whenever the commons showed signs of rebelling the Senate would declare a military crisis, put them under military oath, and send them off to war. Seeing through this tactic, the commons began to respond in kind, by organizing mass refusal of military service. The consul Servilius, and later the dictator Valerius, responded by issuing edicts making it illegal to fetter a Roman soldier (so that men in chains for debt could free themselves by volunteering) and also edicts making it illegal to seize or sell the property of a soldier while he was out on campaign. On these conditions the men took the oath, went off to war, and returned to find that when they were released from their military oaths they were put back in chains. The second time the army returned, the Senate, fearing an uprising if the army were disbanded, refused to release the men from the military oath and ordered the army to march against the Aequians. The soldiers considered freeing themselves from the oaths by assassinating the consuls but were advised that the oaths, made to the gods, would still hold. So they went to a place outside the city called the Sacred Mount, set up a fortified camp, and waited. In his *History of Rome* Livy tells us that ten legions had been raised for the campaign; if all of them deserted that amounts to a general strike of a very large section of the Roman population. In Roman history it came to be called the Secession of the Plebs (2:23–33).[9]

The Secession was a great moment in the history of people's struggles, and through it the commons managed to wrest from the Senate a major concession: the creation of the institution of Tribunes of the People, the final element completing the complex political and legal structure of the Roman Republic. This remarkable set of compromises arising out of bitter and brutal struggle, which established a balance of power and a set of procedures able (just barely) to keep the Romans from assassinating and enslaving one another, corresponded rather closely, as it turned out, to the constitution considered ideal by most Greek political philosophers, the one that mixes elements of kingship, aristocracy, and popular power.

Thus, Polybius wrote in his *Histories*, while Lycurgus discovered this constitution through reason, the Romans discovered it "rather through the lessons learned from many struggles and difficulties; and finally, by always choosing the better course in the light of experience acquired from disasters, they have reached the same goal as Lycurgus, that is, the best of all existing constitutions" (6.10)[10]

This opinion has had a vast influence on the political thinking of the modern period. As Marx commented (in "The Eighteenth Brumaire of Louis Bonaparte") the French Revolution "draped itself alternately as the Roman Republic and the Roman Empire.[11] Similarly James Madison, Alexander Hamilton, and John Jay signed their theoretical defense of the proposed U.S. Constitution with the collective pseudonym "Publius." Revolutionaries on both sides of the Atlantic believed that they were presiding over the rebirth of the form of the Roman Republic, adapted to modern conditions. If what J. G. A. Pocock has named "the Atlantic Republican Tradition"[12] has its modern origins in Machiavelli, for Machiavelli the great wellspring of republican wisdom and virtue was Rome.

I do not question the value of the Roman notions of law, *res publica*, virtue, and citizenship to our political life. I want only to make the lesser point of noting that the citizens of Rome were organized not into one body, but two: not only the Republic, but also the army. Or one could say that the Roman citizens lived alternately in two cities, the city of Rome and the army camp.

Polybius, the Greek historian, wrote *The Rise of the Roman Empire* while living in Rome, where he had been taken as a hostage after the defeat of the Achaean League. In his cool assessment of the causes behind Rome's incredibly swift conquest of Europe, his section on the republican constitution is followed by a section approximately three times as long on the organization of the Roman army, and in particular on the way the army camp was laid out. Here are the very same people that live in the city—patricians, plebeians, consuls, tribunes—but now bound under an utterly different order and law: "The whole camp is laid out as a square, and the arrangement both of the streets and the general plan gives it the appearance of a town" (6.31). But unlike a normal city it is no chaotic jumble of streets and alleys. It is laid out with perfect precision: "Everyone knows exactly in which street and in which part of that street his tent will be situated, since every soldier invariably occupies the same position in the camp, and so the process of pitching camp is remarkably like the return of an army to its native city" (6.41). The night watches are organized so that soldiers pass on tablets from one watch to the next in such a way that if anyone does not keep the watch a superior can always discover his identity by examining the tablets and questioning the other men. In this event the man is tried by court-martial and if found guilty is sentenced to punishment by beating, "whereupon *all the soldiers* fall upon him with clubs and stones" (6.37; italics added) and either kill him or drive him into lifetime exile. "The consequence of the extreme severity of this penalty and of the absolute impossibility of avoiding it is that the night watches of the Roman army are faultlessly kept" (6.37).

All other military laws are enforced with the same precision and severity, and "unmanliness" in battle is equally punishable. If too many soldiers flee for the officers to execute all, the notorious method of decimation—execution of one in ten chosen by lot—is used. "For this reason the men who have been posted to a covering force are often doomed to certain death. This is because they will remain at their posts even when they are overwhelmingly outnumbered on account of their dread of the punishment that awaits them" (6.37).

Here is a body of men whose virtue is its unsurpassed ability to wreak death upon outsiders, held together by a system of total control and total violence, enforced by each upon all and by all upon each. In full recognition of the ahistoricity of such a comparison if carried too far, I think it is fair to say that the Roman army is the classic prototype for totalitarian rule. There is no reason to accuse Benito Mussolini of slandering one of our revered symbols when he chose the Roman *fasci* as the emblem for his movement. The difference, of course, is that the modern totalitarians sought to organize all of society under this model and keep it there for good. The Roman army contained only a portion of the male citizens, and in times of peace they were able to return to their other city, the Republic.

The utter difference between Rome's two bodies is illustrated in the story of Appius Claudius. In 471 B.C. an electoral measure was proposed that would make it difficult for patricians to use their influence over personal dependents to get themselves or their nominees elected as tribunes. The Senate chose Appius Claudius, a fierce enemy of the plebeians, as consul, in the hope that he could use the position to defeat the measure. After a long and furious struggle the measure was passed, and the proud Claudius was humiliated. Then the Senate decided to make war on the Volscians and the Aequians. As consul, Claudius was put in command of the army to march on the former. Claudius, Livy tells us, "was a proud man at the best of times, and in his rage and indignation at what had occurred he was driven to exercise his authority over his men in the most savage and brutal way" (2.58). The men were insubordinate, dragged their feet at every task, and refused to fight. Faced with imminent mutiny,

Claudius ordered the army to march out of the camp and directly into the arms of the enemy, which routed them. Claudius collected the survivors, put them in parade formation, and then "gave orders that every soldier who had lost his equipment, every standard-bearer who had lost his standard, every centurion, too, and distinguished-service man who had abandoned his post, should be first flogged and then beheaded. The remainder were decimated" (2.60). But when the remains of the army returned to the city and disbanded, Claudius no longer had the power to behead his enemies; on the contrary in the Republic it was the people who had the authority to pronounce the death sentence. Claudius, now busy working to defeat land-reform legislation, was arrested and put on trial before the people. We do not know if they would have put him to death: he died of sickness before the trial ended.

Again and again this pattern was repeated. The cycle of war and peace in Roman history was, for the people, a cycle between the state of Republic and the state of army. Once, Livy says, when the city was struggling over a proposal to limit the authority of the consuls with codified law, the consul Quinctius, saying that the people were still under their military oaths from the previous military crisis, ordered them to report for duty at a location outside the city. The news was circulated that the augurs were also being sent to the site: "This meant that . . . political questions would be able to be brought up there for public discussion. . . . Everyone, [the tribunes] were convinced, would vote as the consuls wished, for there was no right of appeal outside a radius of one mile from the City, and the tribunes themselves . . . would be subject like everybody else to the consular authority" (3.21). A compromise was reached, and this attempt to enact legislation under military law was not successful. But from this example we can see what a limited and fragile thing was Roman republican justice at this time: a short walk outside the city gates could take a person beyond its protective screen. And whenever the power of the plebeians got too strong that is where the Senate would try to send them. The tribunes knew the trick well, as we can see from Livy's paraphrase of their speeches in another dispute: "The Senate, they declared, deliberately tormented the commons with military service and got their throats cut whenever they could, keeping them employed in foreign parts for fear lest, if they enjoyed a quiet life at home, they might begin to think of forbidden things—liberty, farms of their own to cultivate, the division of the public domains, the right of voting as their consciences dictated" (4.59). The tribunes were probably wrong, though, if they meant to suggest that Rome could rid itself of its army-camp alter ego and remain in its republican state permanently. The army state was part of the

Roman system of rule, an institution as central as the Senate or the consuls. Just as Jekyll and Hyde were in fact one man, so the Republic and the army were a single ruling system. If the army was a central political institution, it was also an essential economic one. War and plunder were, after all, indispensable to the Roman economy. Such populist demands as land reform must be looked at in that context. When, for example, two tribunes proposed a measure for distributing among the people all land acquired in war, Livy points out that this request amounted to a demand for the whole country, "for Rome having been originally founded upon alien soil had hardly any territory but what had been acquired in war" (4.48). When Augustine asked his famous question, Is there really any important difference—other than size—between a kingdom and a band of robbers,[13] it was of course Rome that he mainly had in mind. If we believe the legend of the Rape of the Sabine Women, the Romans founded their city by stealing not only land but also women. The Republic maintained this character throughout its history. In the early days the soldiers received no pay: pillage was their salary, and pillage remained an important industry. Examples appear repeatedly in Livy's work:

> [Servilus] turned his troops over to pillaging; this was carried out over so wide an area and on such a devastating scale that he returned to Rome with a quantity of plunder many times as great as what had previously been lost. (2.64)

> The town and the camp were both sacked; next day every cavalry trooper and every centurion drew lots for a prisoner apiece—two prisoners being granted for specially distinguished service (4.34)

> The three contingents were allowed to sack the town; a long period of prosperity had made it rich, and this act of generosity on the part of the three commanders was a first step towards a better feeling between the commons and the patricians. (4.34)

Rome was indeed a great band of robbers, so successful that it eventually stole the whole Mediterranean world. Its land—the very seven hills of the city—was booty; its slaves who did the work were booty; booty from pillaging defeated towns made the city rich, and later taxes and tribute from the conquered empire were institutionalized booty. Rome was a band of robbers from the ground up, and it is idle to imagine a situation in which the citizens could enjoy the virtues of the Republic alone without the necessity of shifting over from time to time to the military (i.e., robber) state. And when we praise the great struggle of the plebeian class for republican justice, we should remember that among the main issues of the struggle (e.g., land reform) was fair distribution of the booty.

This is the Roman Republic that Machiavelli dreamed of restoring in Italy, that the American Federalists sought to capture the essence of in the federal constitution, and in whose togas the French revolutionaries draped themselves in 1789. And it is the Roman Republic that generations of British schoolboys were taught—under the rod—to revere in their Latin lessons. It is this republic that stands at the head of the "Atlantic Republican Tradition" and after which those modern nation-states that called themselves republics named themselves. Given these origins, there is no reason to consider Machiavelli's military/totalitarian side as a contradiction to his "republicanism"[14] or that it was a betrayal of principles when the French revolutionary army swept into northern Italy, or when the Americans began their bloody march of conquest across the North American continent to the Pacific. Napoleon was only living out a foreshortened version of Roman history when he began fighting for the Republic, became "consul" and then "emperor." British men were only following the same honored tradition when they alternated between the two bodies of their own policy, protecting republican principles at home, fighting for the empire abroad.

The modern European nation-state, in short, also has its two bodies, or two phases. It is not one system of rule, but two. Its military phase has its own hierarchical system of rule, its own law, and its own traditions that can be traced back to those of the Roman army. Why else should the U.S. Marine Corps emblem be the Latin *semper fidelis*? The army hovers always alongside the republic as an alternative form of rule, actually ruling a sector of the population and with the potential for ruling all of it should the republic fail. Martial law is a Roman invention, and means applying the military form of rule to the whole polity. And incidentally, the fact that the full system of the modern state is the republic/army duality is one factor that has made it difficult to grant full equality to women within it. Conquest, with its historical and psychological associations with pillage and rape, is not an activity that women in large number have participated in directly in any culture we know of. For millennia of Western history women were prizes of conquest, not conquerors. Their exclusion from the military phase of the body politic has been crucial to their exclusion from the rest of it. Put differently, given the Roman notion of what a citizen is, full citizenship for women is inconceivable.

It is interesting that Japan's notorious system of "moral education" (*shushin kyoiku*), which until the end of World War II taught militaristic patriotism to children by having them memorize tales of heroic soldiers and patriots, is often thought of as uniquely Japanese. As an educational device for building nationalism, however, it is certainly borrowed from the West, along with the notion of compulsory education itself. The story patterns are perfectly recognizable: if Japanese children read again and again of the heroic deaths of Private Yamashita and Sub-Lieutenant Hachida, their European counterparts had for generations been brought up on the stories of Horatio at the bridge, Mucius Scaevola holding his hand in the fire to show his captors the futility of their torture, and so on.

I hope not to be misunderstood here. I respect these heroes as people who acted as I cannot. I could not have died clutching my rifle to the end as Sub-Lieutenant Hachida did, and in Horatio's place I would have jumped into the water a lot sooner. I admire people who can do these things. If anyone wants to honor the Roman Republic as the founder of the Atlantic republican tradition I have no objection.

Just let's don't confuse the matter by calling it the founder of the *democratic* tradition.

The Two Bodies of the Modern Industrial Republic

In his discussion of the constitution of Rome, Polybius noted that the Senate also exercised economic power. Through the personal wealth of its members and through its control over public property and public works, it had the power to give or withhold employment. "The result is that all citizens, being bound to the Senate by ties which ensure their protection . . . are very cautious about obstructing or resisting its will." These ties are part, he argues, of what maintained the balance of power among the classes and functioned in a way similar to that of the city's military phase, which caused the people to "think twice about opposing the projects of the consuls, since they will come both individually and collectively under their authority while on a campaign" (6.17).

In the overindustrialized states in this century the role of military organization and military virtue in counteracting the fluidity of republican politics has declined. In World War II fascism, Nazism, and Japanese military-statism gave militarism a bad name—something, we must remember, it had not had earlier. The European countries' loss of their colonies brought an end to direct rule and made the military phase of these countries somewhat less of a structural necessity, while the Vietnam War brought the military to unprecedented disgrace in the United States. The governments of some of these countries—particularly those of the United States and Great Britain—are struggling to restore the central role of military virtue. Their struggle is not over and they may yet succeed, but at this point it seems that the importance of the military phase of the Atlantic republics is less than it was in the nineteenth century. As Sheldon

Wolin points out, the other body of the republic today is "the economy."[15]

I do not mean to repeat here my argument in Chapter 2 that what we call "the economy" is a system of rule. I wish only to point out that the economy has not only taken over some of the ruling functions of the military, but has also taken on many of its characteristics. Polybius' description of the Roman army, with its hierarchical chain of command and its strict system of accountability, is a description of the basic structure of a corporate bureaucracy. The picture he draws of the army camp, in which the order of command is laid out physically on the ground would, if put in three-dimensional form, become the very picture of a factory or corporate office building. The two tracks of company employment—white collar and blue collar—correspond to the ancient class division in the military, maintained to this day, between officers (patricians) and enlisted soldiers (plebeians).

Moreover, it is in the context of the economy and through the medium of the corporation that we hear today the most strident calls for virtue, loyalty, and patriotic service. As I was writing this chapter I heard on the radio the tale of an employee of Chrysler who won a Toyota automobile in a contest, refused it out of loyalty to her company, and was rewarded with Chrysler automobiles given her by three different executives of that company. Here is our modern Horatius at the bridge, with the difference that now patriotism is mediated through the institutional form not of the army but of private enterprise.

The most successful of the industrial republics today is, as we know, Japan. I believe that an important reason for this success is that after World War II Japan was more successful than any other country in transferring the spirit of the military into its economy. Of course this transference took place during the war as well, when company employees wore military insignia indicating their ranks. When Japan lost the war, the prestige of its military fell virtually to zero, and the people made a choice to opt, genuinely, for the peaceful way; most of them still do. Japan's unconstitutional Self-Defense Forces are given little public honor and tend to stay out of sight. For almost half a century now no one has died at the hand of a Japanese soldier acting under the right of belligerency of the state. The Self-Defense Forces are in fact a strong military force, but they are peripheral to Japanese society. The "other body" of this republic, the body that corresponds to the Roman army, is the corporatized economy. Seen in this light, the so-called Japanese management system becomes less enigmatic, and also less unique. Its difference from other management systems is only a matter of degree. Japanese corporate managers have been highly successful in transferring the military ethos into the corporate economy. Perhaps managers in other countries have been less so because the military itself enjoys higher prestige in those countries. Americans and Europeans who laugh at the idea of Japanese workers' singing loyalty songs and doing morning exercises together forget that they themselves do these things with little hesitation when they are in the army.

To place the ethos of the military into the corporate economy is not to make an erroneous confusion of spheres. Economic activity is, after all, the most important "warfare" of the postwar period. It is the principal activity through which the big powers struggle for relative advantage, and it is the principal activity (as I sought to argue in Chapter 2) through which they maintain and extend control over former colonial regions. It is also the activity that has the best chance of mobilizing the people into a patriotic community, for the purpose of instilling into them the virtues of loyalty and obedience. And this phenomenon is not peculiar to Japan; in fact, it may be strongest today in the United States: witness the mutterings about Pearl Harbor when Sony purchased Columbia Pictures.

The corporate economy is the other body of the industrial republic, not as an abstraction but as the concrete organizational structure that, like the Roman army, regulates in detail the activities of each worker each day. It maintains its discipline not through flogging or execution but rather through giving or withholding raises and promotions, suspensions, firings—with the extreme penalty being exile into the permanently unemployed underclass.

Perhaps it is more accurate to call the corporate economy not the "other" body but the main body of the industrial republic. In Rome, after all, the army was disbanded in times of peace, and citizens could return to life in the Republic. Today the corporate body is never disbanded: in the economic war there is never peace. Here in Japan, where much overtime is required, workers stay under its control until late at night. A strong union movement can be thought of as an invasion of the corporate body by the republic, the attempt to transform it in accordance with republican principles, or even democratic principles. A weakening of the union movement, or its transformation from a movement to democratize the economy into a movement only to get adequate wages from it, amounts to a defeat of this invasion, and a purification of the corporate body as an antidemocratic, managerial system. And because the working population spends most of its waking hours under this rule, political activity is pushed to the peripheries of life. Even the most dedicated political activists must schedule their rallies and demonstrations on weekends or holidays, during what we now call our "free time." Because college students are under a relatively less strict management system than either high-school students or workers, they have been one of the most important politically active groups since World War II. In Japan today, in a reversal no one expected, unemployed housewives have replaced students and blue-collar workers as the most politically active group, for largely the same reason: they are outside the sphere of direct bureaucratic management.

This scarcity of people with unmanaged time is one of the reasons that, as I mentioned in the first part of this chapter, those rare moments when the polity undergoes a change of state into the democratic mode do not last long. The people are rather like the Roman soldiers sitting on the Sacred Mount: they have achieved their freedom only by leaving the city. They cannot stay there forever: eventually they must return to "daily life." And "daily life" is the economy, the very control system we have been talking about, captured in the ominous expression "business as usual." I know that I contradict Arendt and Aristotle when I say that democracy cannot be satisfied with a politics defined as a leisure activity, driven out of the center of life into occasional bits and pieces of "surplus" time. The democratic project will not be complete until it has succeeded in democratizing work. When the leaders of the capitalist world announce that socialism is dead and that the issue now is democracy, I am ready to agree. If they want to talk about democracy, let's talk about it. On these terms.

Against Democratic Empire
The tales of ancient Greece and Rome, as they have been handed down in mythical form through European history and, as a result of European colonial power, today passed on to a large part of the non-European world, are tales structured to teach us the dangers of pride and corruption. Athens thrived under Pericles; its defeat began when it started to listen to that very embodiment of hubris, Alcibiades. Rome, when it was a vigorous young republic, was a model for us to emulate; it was only after a long period of internal corruption that it became a cruel empire.

These readings may satisfy a soldier, but a radical democrat will see things differently, noting trouble from the start. The one who reminded the Athenians that their rule over their colonies was, "to speak somewhat plainly, a tyranny" was, after all, Pericles. And as Augustine pointed out,[16] the rape of the Sabine Women comes at the beginning of the Roman chronicles, not the end.

Arendt has given us, derived largely from the model of Periclean Athens, her wonderful concept of political action: action that is neither labor nor work, that is different from making things or enacting plans; action that is pure freedom, power, and political happiness; action that gives birth to new beginnings in the flow of history. One may, with due respect to the brilliance and beauty of the concept, ask, Action means . . . doing what, exactly? We may accuse Arendt of never giving a clear enough answer to this question, but in the case of the Athenians, there is no puzzle: the main content of their collective "action" was conquest. After they defeated the Persians, they busily set about building themselves an empire. According to Pericles, it was the fact that they did so of their own collective free will, rather than under a severe regime of authoritarian masters, which gave them their extraordinary military power. Athens was awesome, it was a fusion reaction, but it does not provide us with an answer to the puzzle, How do you make a fusion reaction and a container in which it can be held? Athens did not have the power to contain itself, but could only expand. There was, as Alcibiades correctly said, no way to fix the exact point at which the Athenian empire should stop. It was stopped, finally, by bitter military defeat.

We puzzle over the enigma of democracy: what does it mean for the people to rule themselves? How can they be both ruler and ruled? What does "rule" mean in this case? Again, this question was no puzzle for the ancients. What they ruled over—collectively—was others. Athenian democracy was a democracy among the masters by which, according to Xenophon, they could "ward one another . . . from their slaves and from evildoers, to the end that none of the citizens may perish by a violent death."[17] The same could be said for Rome.

We must ask directly, What is wrong with this? The precedent is one of great authority; what ground have we for rejecting it? Of course we have rejected slavery but we have not rejected class society, and, more to the point here, we have not rejected (in deeds, that is, not just in words) "democratic empire."

In a world in which it is beyond our power to establish democracy universally, a possible strategy is to seek to establish it in one or several states by surrounding them with a wall of military force and social discrimination, particularly against those in other states whose labor is exploited to provide the economic base for the leisure and liberty of the democratic citizens. There is little purpose in preaching retroactive moral sermons today against those who attempted this strategy in the past. The past is done; it is we in the present who still have choices before us. The question is, Can democratic empire, or "democracy in one country," be a viable strategy today? Would it be possible to establish a "democracy" by surrounding it with a buffer of Third World puppet dictatorships to ensure the markets, raw materials, and cheap labor needed to provide the leisure for politics? Given the growing awareness of Third World people themselves, the chances of such a strategy succeeding for very long are diminishing. But the question here is different. Even supposing that it were militarily possible to hold such an empire, what are the prospects of establishing a democracy at the imperial center?

One might respond, "But isn't that what we have now?" And with this the question has been answered. Two centuries ago Edmund Burke feared that the breakers of law in India might return to become the makers of law in England; his fears have proved well founded. The citizen must live in both bodies—the "democratic" one and the imperial one. And inevitably the second invades the first. The spirit, the technology, the forms of organization used for exploitation and oppression in the colonies and economic dependencies are brought home. Union busting and cheap labor under military regimes abroad become union busting and wage cuts under the regime of the "democratic" free market at home. In short, yes, the attempt to establish democratic empire produces precisely what we have now, a situation in which radical democracy is subversive in the "democratic" countries.

This result is obvious and need not be dwelled upon. But there is a further reason that the democratic movement must take a clear stand against democratic empire. The divided consciousness that once could sustain the idea of democracy for some and slavery for others can no longer be maintained, though not because the moral character of civilization in the twentieth century has improved over that of earlier times—surely it has not. It is because the myths on which these mass exclusions of human beings were based have been exploded and revealed as self-deceptions. Notions of natural slaves, or of civilizations at lower levels on the evolutionary scale, or of the natural inferiority of certain races or of women, are no longer available in the way they once were. Once they were considered beyond doubt. Backed by the religious or "scientific" authority of the time, they could be espoused with a minimum of bad conscience. Today they can be revived only through the crudest hypocrisy.

It is still possible to cut ourselves off from the fates of our fellow human beings, but we know now that the cutting, as it were, must go on within our own nervous systems. What we cut off is not other people but one of our own sense organs, that special organ that gives us the capacity, when we see the faces and hear the voices of others, to recognize them as human beings like ourselves. Aside from the general inadvisability of this kind of self-mutilation, it directly contradicts the essence of radical democracy. That is, it is a lobotomy of the very sense that radical democ-

racy must seek to develop, the sense that makes political virtue possible—
what might be called the *democratic sense*. The movement for radical
democracy aims to sharpen and extend this sense; it cannot at the same
time participate in a project to mutilate it. For the radical democrat, imperial democracy is no longer a possibility. Lest it corrupt its own spirit,
the struggle for democracy must be not the struggle only for a democratic country but for a democratic world.

Transborder Democracy

One may ask, This sounds fine as an abstract ideal, but does it mean anything from the standpoint of concrete action? To answer, let me borrow
an expression proposed by Muto Ichiyo in an address in 1989. "Transborder participatory democracy," he argues, "is the name both of a goal
and of a process:" As a goal, admittedly very distant, "it is a picture of a
world order clearly distinct from the conventional idea of world government or world federation, which presupposes states as the constituent
units." As a process, it is a direct and practical response to the present situation. Today imperial power is incarnated in three bodies: pseudo-
democracy at home, vast military organizations, and the transnational
corporations that are seeking to put all of humankind and nature under
their managerial control. The result is that "major decisions which affect
the lives of millions of people are made outside their countries, without
their knowledge, much less their being consulted."[18] These decisions are
made by big governments, by transnational corporations, by the International Monetary Fund, by the World Bank, and so on. Participatory
democracy means the right to participate in the making of decisions that
affect one's life. If the power making the decision can cross national
boundaries, then doesn't the right to confront that power cross them as
well? As Muto argues, "The situation calls for the declaration of a new
right of the people: the right of the people to intervene in, to modify, to
regulate, and ultimately to control any decisions that affect their lives, no
matter where those decisions are made. This should be established as a
universal right which recognizes no borders" (p. 124).

Muto is intending here not to propose something new but to give a
name and a theoretical ground for something already going on. When
South Pacific islanders come to Japan to protest the dumping of nuclear
waste in their sea, or go to France to protest nuclear-weapons testing;
when Central Americans come to the United States and lobby for an end
to U.S. intervention in their countries; when forest dwellers from the
Amazon, or the Cordillera, or Sarawak travel to countries of the north to
protest the destruction of their world by the logging companies, they are

exercising this right. But, Muto argues, this action is not simply lobbying by some new kind of pressure group. These people speak the language not of interest but of justice: their message is universal. It must be, if they are to find supporters in the northern countries. By appealing in this way, they may convert people in those countries to a new way of thinking, or they may assist people there who are already trying to change their countries. Coalitions are formed, which may in turn lead to something altogether new: "a transborder 'people,' by which the division of the world into North and South can be overcome" (p. 123). The idea is perfectly in accord with fundamental democratic theory. It is the basic idea of democracy that the people are sovereign: their power is prior to the power of the state. The state and its laws exist by their consent alone. This statement means that it is up to the people, and not to the state, to determine who "the people" is. There is no reason in principle why the people cannot form itself into an "international civil society," a body transcending the state, capable of developing "law" and asserting new rights that states must honor. If the people so decide, then so be it.

If there are no obstacles in principle, there are plenty in practice. This transborder "people" is powerless and without authority if it exists only as an abstraction. To be formed concretely as a conscious public will require a long and painful process of practical action. There is no sense being romantic about this project: the difficulties are immense. Most are obvious: cultural, language, and religious differences; the need to maintain contact over great distances; direct oppression in many countries; possible creation of a new class of conference-going elites. Moreover, many of the world's peoples are engaged in fierce ethnic struggles and murderous tribal wars, which the state is only too happy to utilize to maintain its supremacy over them. The dream of a transborder civil society is just that, a dream; concretely, it is a dream that an alternative can be found to Samuel Huntington's nightmare vision of an era of hopeless war between "civilizations."[19] Huntington's nightmare is not simply the product of a cynical mind; it is grounded in political realities we can read about in the newspapers every day. But the hope for a transborder (and "transcivilizational") civil society is also grounded in political realities: the actual existence of a transborder political movement with its expanding worldwide network of information exchange, personal contact, common understanding and joint action.

Projected imaginatively into the future, this movement provides an interesting set of answers to the question posed at the beginning of this chapter: if the state of democracy is a universal solvent capable even of dissolving the state, what container can hold it? In the first place, unlike

Athens and Rome, Great Britain, the United States, or the USSR, transborder democracy cannot have a tendency to become imperialistic, because it does not aspire to form the political entity capable of imperialism: the state. On the contrary it is continuously seeking to cross and reduce the boundaries among people that imperialism establishes. Moreover, unlike democratic movements contained within the boundaries of imperial states, it has no tendency to be corrupted into a movement for the "fair" and "democratic" distribution of the imperial spoils, the "justice among thieves" of the Roman Republic. The proletarian movement, as a movement of the despoiled, was supposed to be incorruptible for the same reason. But when imperialism created another yet-more-despoiled group of people on the other side of the border, it became possible for a labor movement to degenerate into a movement demanding its cut of the imperial loot. The whole point of the transborder movement is to cross all boundaries so as to include within itself the most despoiled. If it pursues this path faithfully, it will be immune to this form of corruption. (Of course it will not be immune to any form of corruption; no politics is perfectly immune to corruption.)

The transborder political movement need not base itself on the assumption that people are inherently virtuous, but it contains within itself a tendency to promote political virtue. Appeals across borders are convincing only if they are cast in the universal language of justice rather than in the particular language of interest. The practical need to recast interest as justice is a characteristic any politics may have, but this need is stronger in a transborder movement. In this situation the people have no state as a possible "enforcer" of their interests, and so their demands are powerful only insofar as they are formulated as appeals for justice. This link between justice and power has been known since Aristotle, but it tends toward *universal* justice only as more people are included.

The transborder movement, being a movement outside of and against the state, has a tendency toward organizational forms both larger and smaller than the state. "Think globally, act locally" is a good slogan, but sometimes is better reversed. I have participated as an observer to two international conferences of indigenous peoples in Asia; at both, indigenous peoples' representatives from all over the world argued fiercely for the value of their traditional communities and appealed for international support in protecting them from destruction by dam projects, logging, resort building, and other forms of "development." "Think locally, act globally." And in both their local and global actions, participants in this kind of movement tend to form face-to-face groups. Not only "tends," the movement exists—and has power—*only* if it organizes in this form. It has no state or party, no institution, within which people could be simply "contained" as a faceless mass. The movement exists as a network of autonomously interconnected groups, or it does not exist at all.

If the state of democracy is a universal solvent capable even of dissolving the state, what container can hold it? The answer suggested by the transborder democratic movement is: the world.

I know, of course, the risk taken by one writing political theory in attaching one's writing to any specific movement. Clever theorists tend to avoid this risk, so as not to have to eat crow later. On the other hand, why engage in political theory if theory cannot engage with real politics? But let me emphasize that what I have described above are not predictions but possibilities. Whether they come about depends on what people do. There are no iron laws.

Democracy in All Bodies

The state of democracy quickly self-destructs when it exists only outside of the real system of rule, or as an extraordinary interim period that is only a suspension of that system of rule. When it takes the form, so to speak, of leaving the city and sitting down on the Sacred Mount, it can be only temporary. The city is where the people's life is; their homes are there, their families are there, and their work is there. All they can hope to do from the Sacred Mount is to extract some demands from the power structure before their determination gives out. Often such a movement can bring important successes. A strike can win higher wages or better working conditions. A mass movement can bring down a government (South Korea in 1960, the Philippines in 1987, Poland in 1989). A sustained mass movement can contribute to the stopping of a war (Vietnam). But where the state controls a military organization unaffected by the democratic movement and is ready to use it, the result may be a massacre (Thailand 1976; Kwangju, South Korea, 1981; China 1989).

Moreover, where the main system of rule in a society is the economy—the control of the citizenry by the managerial control of their work—and where the democratic movement operates only outside this system of rule, then of course the success of that movement can be only an ephemeral and temporary phenomenon. If the state is organized as an antidemocratic military body, an antidemocratic economic body, and a "democratic" political body to which working citizens are able to devote only a small part of their leisure time, it is easy to see that attempts to radicalize democracy only within that third limited sphere must be short-lived. If democracy is to mean that the people rule, they must rule in all bodies into which society is organized. Democracy will continue to have very little staying power until the democratic movement has succeeded in establishing a democratic civil society and, in particular, in democratizing the world of work.

The possibility of the genuine democratization of work suggests yet another answer to the question, How can a state of democracy create order? If democracy is the universal solvent of orders of unequal power, it does not, as I argued above in Chapter 3, dissolve the order of work. Where workers control their work, they do not necessarily work in any way they choose. Workers who know what they are doing will still plant crops in rows and in the proper seasons, sweep stairs from the top down, and sharpen saws one tooth at a time. Cooperative work will still display its tendency to order communities. Only when democracy is expelled from the workplace and forced to make its presence felt exclusively in the streets does it contain the danger of turning into a mob or an arbitrary collective tyrant, or of suddenly evaporating. The Parliament of the Streets (as they called it in the Philippines) would be less fragile if the people in the streets had democratic workplaces to return to.

The democratization of work entails more than just some formal arrangement—the nationalization of industry, the owning of stock by workers, or the like. It entails all of the changes in management, scale, machinery, speed, and kinds of work implied in Chapters 2 and 3 above. I recognize that to say this is to go directly against what seems to be the wave of our time, when the alleged triumph of the free market has liberated the corporation to organize the world and the people in it according to its own principles. I recognize that the distance between a world of democratized work and what we have now is immense. But in a time when the ideologists of liberalism are saying that with the demise of socialism we have come to the End of History, isn't it bracing to realize that we still have plenty to do?

5

the democratic
virtues

Public Trust

Democratic order finds a congenial ally in the natural order of nonoppressive work, but in itself it is a political order, not an economic one. It is distinguished from other forms of order by the nature of the bond which holds it together. It is not founded on such "guarantees" as state violence, indoctrination, fear of God, or bureaucratic management. It is also not founded on a set of "essential" first principles from which its necessity can be infallibly deduced. In a democratic situation, people are bound together into a state of order not by necessity but by trust. The possibility of a social order grounded in trust depends on the peculiar human ability to make promises, "the only alternative," Arendt wrote, "to a mastery which relies on domination of one's self and rule over others."[1]

The possibility of order created by trust is often expressed in political philosophy through the myth of the social contract. When Rousseau asked his famous question, How is it possible for people to live in an orderly community and still be "free as before," his answer was the social contract. A contract is of course a promise. And promises do establish order without violating freedom. That is, a promise is not a promise unless it is made freely. Keeping a promise means doing the thing we said we would because we said we would: standing by our words. Of course promises or contracts may be strengthened by added guarantees: rewards if they are kept, punishments or vengeance if they are not. But these guarantees are the beginning of an evolution from promises to something else. We rely on rewards and punishments when we do not trust one another.

Trusting that a promise will be kept is different from believing a fact or a theory to be true or predicting that something will happen tomorrow. The appropriate object of trust is not a thing, fact, theory, or event, but a person. Trust means expecting that a person will do something or refrain from doing something. But it is trust only when the person has the freedom to do otherwise. Trust presupposes the freedom of the other. It is not trust if I expect you to digest your dinner. It is not trust if I lock you in an iron cage and expect that you will still be there tomorrow. It is not trust if, putting a knife to your throat and saying, "Your money or your life!" I expect that you will hand me your wallet. It is not trust if I brainwash you and expect you to act accordingly. It is trust if I expect that you will not betray me when you could.

The phenomenon of trust in human relations is not fully captured by the image of the contract, nor is it limited to the keeping of actual promises. Most of the things we trust each other about are never articulated in specific contracts or promises. When we say a person is trustworthy, we mean that the person can be expected not to betray others even in matters that no one has thought to put into words. The greater part of the "contract" that holds societies together is tacit, embedded in common sense; only a small part is disembedded and put into specific words.

Still, the contract, in addition to being a useful form of promise making, is a good metaphor that can help us to see the nature of all trust relations. The negation of trust is not sin but betrayal. We consider trustworthiness a virtue, but it is different in character from moral goodness. If, for example, we were confronted with a perfect saint, that is, a person all of whose actions are governed by an absolute principle of goodness, we would not trust this person in the ordinary sense, though we would be able to predict his or her behavior if we knew the principle. And it is doubtful that a true saint would be capable of making promises in the ordinary sense. A promise with another saint would not be necessary, and a promise with one of us ordinary people would risk the saint's saintly status. In the real world it often turns out that not all of the things we need to do to keep promises are in accord with perfect morality. On the other hand, ordinary humans with spouses and children who make promises with the Absolute can find themselves involved in bloody horrors, as Abraham learned.

Consider the figure of the totally just monad proposed by Glaucon in Book I of Plato's *Republic*. In that story, Glaucon demands that Socrates show that justice is good not for its reputation but in itself, and he refuses to accept anything less than a demonstration that justice would be good for a person even if that person suffered under the reputation of being totally unjust.[2] The peculiarity, not mentioned by Plato, of the totally-just-person-with-the-reputation-of-being-totally-unjust is that such a person would be incapable of making promises. No one would trust you, and no one would expect anything good of you. With no promises you could neither keep nor break them; with no trust relations you could neither betray people nor be faithful to their expectations. Socrates' argument may be correct that his justice, in the sense that it is the state of health of the soul, is good-in-itself. But deprived of its capacity to generate trust in others it is, socially, good-for-nothing.

Trust relations are not arrived at by deduction from moral first principles. They are established in the web of human relations by thousands of promises and contracts, some explicit but most not, which people make in their daily dealings with one another over the years and over generations. Trust is not morality, but it produces virtuous behavior and virtuous persons. True, we sometimes say things like, "You can trust that man to stab you in the back every time he gets a chance," but this is only turning the word upside-down for the purpose of sarcasm. It is also true that people sometimes make promises to do evil together, the paradox we call "honor among thieves." As I mentioned earlier, Augustine considered this paradox the essence of the secular state, providing justice to its citizens and pillage to its neighbors. As I argued in Chapter 4, this dual consciousness is not stable, and there is the continual danger that, to borrow Burke's phrase again, the breakers of law in India will return to become the makers of law in England; that the thief part will overpower the justice part. And to be sure, there are times when breaking promises and deserting comrades may be the best thing to do, as for a person in an army on the wrong side of an imperialist war, or in a government that tortures prisoners, or in a company that poisons the sea. Be that as it may, the only point in this context is that, other things being equal, keeping promises is on itself good behavior; if it were not, "honor among thieves" would not be a paradox.

Nietzsche writes, "To breed an animal with the right to make promises—is not this the paradoxical problem nature has set itself with regard to man?"[3] Promises produce order through time. You promise to do something tomorrow, and you do it; you have to that degree put order into your action. Making promises and keeping them is the direct opposite to doing what you feel like. Keeping a promise means exactly doing what you said you would do whether you still feel like it or not. Does this mean that keeping promises is self-repressive, the action of the dictatorial superego crushing the free play of human emotions? Not according to Nietzsche. The very man who saw "bad conscience" as a sickness of the soul, a weakness produced by the self attacking the self, saw the making and keeping of promises as acts of power, freedom, and health:

> I do not mean a purely passive succumbing to past impressions, the indigestion of being unable to be done with a pledge once made, but rather an active not wishing to be done with it, a continuing to will what has been willed, a veritable "memory of the will"; so that, between the original determination and the actual performance of the thing willed, a whole world

of new things, conditions, even volitional acts, can be interposed without snapping the long chain of the will.[4]

The act of making and keeping a promise is a conquest of the chaos that would come if each of us followed our individual passions from moment to moment wherever they lead. It is a conquest that establishes order without placing humankind under a punishing God, a punishing leviathan, a punishing conscience, or a punishing order of exploitative work. In Rousseau's words, it leaves us "free as before." There is no need to ask why making a promise is an act of freedom: we make promises only where there is freedom. Where there is no freedom there is no need for a promise. True, we sometimes say things like, "I promise to be hungry by dinner time"; the point, again, is that this is a joke. Through promises, people faced with more than one choice can create order by collectively willing one. (Of course order can also be created when one person with power issues an order, which is why an "order" is called that.) The specific content of a promise need not, as mentioned above, be moral or honorable. But even when it is indifferent ("I will meet you at 7:00 P.M. in front of the post office"), keeping it takes on moral weight. This weight does not come from some metaphysical source: god, transcendent law, absolute reason, the form of the good. It comes from the people themselves, and their act of promising.

Trust in a Brutal World

Trust is different from all metaphysical sources of morality in that no one would think of grounding it in proof. Again, where the behavior of the other can be predicted with certainty, there is no need for trust. When we trust a person, however, we usually do so on the basis of evidence: the person's actions up to now. We hope that people who have proved trustworthy thus far will continue so. But when we say that democracy is an order based on trust, do we mean that we must somehow be willing to trust people we have never met? This might not be a problem if we lived in some kind of democratic utopia, where for generations there had been none but trustworthy people. But where we do live the idea sounds like plain foolishness. We have no experience suggesting that we can safely trust people we don't know, or people in general. On the contrary, experience teaches us that people are sometimes trustworthy and sometimes not, that we should be selective in whom we trust, and that we should not trust people without guarantees.

One must begin with the world as it is. We dream of trust; we live in a world where, in the words of Bob Marley's song, "everywhere is war"—

a world in which unwillingness to drop atomic bombs on people would disqualify a person for the office of head of state of any of the major powers, unwillingness to exploit people would disqualify a person for work in the business world, and unwillingness to shoot people or beat them with clubs would disqualify a person from work in the police force of any country. There is no call for a lengthy argument demonstrating the brutal gap between the dream of a world of trust and the world we actually live in. Rather, let us take this gap as the starting point. From this starting point, what are the moves we might make?

One move is sentimentalism, a flight from reality into the fantasy world of well-meaning politicians, charitable capitalists, kindly soldiers and policemen. The particular advantage of wearing rose-colored glasses is that you can't see the blood. Another move is despair. Despair has the advantage over sentimentalism that it is realistic; from despairing writers we can sometimes get a picture of the world which has an almost scientific clarity. Anyone who knows despair, however, knows that it is to be avoided if possible. From the position of despair we cannot *do* anything, which means we cannot live.

A third move is cynicism. Cynicism shares with despair the advantage of being realistic. As with despairing writers, cynical writers can teach us much truth about the world and provide a good antidote to sentimentalism. Moreover, cynicism has the advantage over despair that it allows us to act. It also allows for humor, which matters much. But it has the very great disadvantage that it includes oneself among the things it is cynical about. Cynicism is a complex arrangement by which our condemnation of the evils of the world is somehow used to justify our participation in those evils. No matter how convoluted its evasions may become it can never escape its beginning, which is self-contempt. The cynic maintains a divided self: the critic and the actor. The critical cynic through his contempt for the corruption of the world maintains the power of criticism and the values on which it is based. The acting cynic is liberated by the very same cynicism from the necessity to act on the basis of these values. In his wonderful analysis of modern cynicism Peter Sloterdijk writes, "This is the essential point in modern cynicism: the ability of its bearers to work—in spite of everything that might happen, and especially, after anything that might happen."[5] This is the state of consciousness of the great majority of the people working in managerial and bureaucratic positions in the rich industrial countries. Cynicism keeps them at this work: when I said the cynic can act, I meant only that. The cynic can continue to work in the system that he or she condemns as meaningless or worse, and will do nothing to change it. A person who has fallen into cynicism can rarely be talked out of it: the cynical consciousness has heard everything and has a place within itself to file away any new fact or argument. I shall attempt no such refutation of cynicism here but limit myself to the comment that a consciousness grounded in self-contempt is not a happy one.

A fourth move is religious faith. This takes many forms, but if I understand Sören Kierkegaard and other commentators correctly, its essence is positing that there is a transcendent good that justifies the horrors of this world and believing in it without understanding it. In the Jewish and Christian traditions, faith is presented as the highest form of trust. In the Old Testament God takes the form of a person—that is, a being capable of making a promise—and the origin of faith is expressed through the image of a promise—a covenant—between him and Abraham. As God is omnipotent and his purposes are unknown to Abraham and his descendants, they have no way of enforcing the covenant or of checking to see if God's side of it has been fulfilled. So their belief in the promise and in the good faith of the other party becomes a new form of trust, trust raised to a higher power. I shall not attempt here an analysis of the phenomenon of faith; all I wish to do is to point out some of the advantages and disadvantages of this move in the context of this discussion. The first of its advantages is that it permits a realistic view of this world. There are of course pseudofaiths based on sentimentalism, but there is no trace of sentimentalism in the great heroes of faith, Abraham and Job, or in the great theologians such as Augustine and Aquinas. On the contrary, faith in the Absolute gives one a chillingly clear picture of how far humankind has Fallen. At the same time, faith prevents one from falling into the agony of despair. Like cynicism, it permits one to go on living and acting; unlike cynicism it allows one to live in hope. Moreover, unlike the cynic, the faithful person will seek to be better. The faithful, however, will never be able to be as good as the Absolute demands; this inevitable gap is the origin of bad conscience. The self-criticism of bad conscience is different from the self-contempt of the cynic. It is based on something living and active: a conscience. In the case of the cynic, it is one's own atrophied conscience that is the chief object of contempt. The conscience is the great achievement of faith. This list of advantages is impressive: realism about the world, combined with a reason to keep on living and acting and even to try to act well and in hope. The great disadvantage is that while it offers some degree (the degree depends on the theologist) of hope in this world, its ultimate hope is not for this world.

After Ludwig Feuerbach—and after Marx, after Kierkegaard, after Nietzsche—we know that faith is, indeed, a "move." We know, that is, that if we want to understand faith we must look at it as an act taken in this world, not as something provided us from outside this world. This view includes understanding that the object of faith is also a human construction and a human choice. If religious readers object to this formulation, I am ready to rephrase it and to say only that at least this essay proceeds from that position, to say with Feuerbach (*The Fiery Brook*[6]) that "religion is the dream of the human mind" (p. 258). In the case of the Jewish religion, as well as of its two major offshoots Christianity and Islam, this dream has contained a large element of nightmare for both the believers and their victims. But without judging whether on the whole it was worth the cost (a judgment surely no human being is qualified to make) we can say that the invention of faith, in that it gave people a power to be "better, braver, and more active" was a great achievement.

Feuerbach argues that the attributes people have given to God are actually their own: "You believe in love as a divine attribute because you yourself love, and believe that God is a wise and benevolent being because you know nothing better in yourself than wisdom and benevolence" (p. 115). But though God is created in man's image, he is also clearly different: he is perfect and man is not. On the other hand, this difference can be stood on its head with the observation that there is one virtue of which human beings are capable and God is not: faith itself. Faith requires imperfect knowledge, but God is omniscient; besides, what could God have faith *in*? According to Feuerbach, this difference leads human beings into self-contempt: "In order to enrich God, man must become poor; that God may be all, man must be nothing" (p. 124). His project is to redirect this religious impulse, to shift its gaze from an imagined object to a real one: from God to humankind: "What I . . . do to religion—and to speculative philosophy and theology as well—is nothing else than to *open its eyes* or rather to turn *outward* its *inwardly directed eyes*; in other words, I only lead the object from its existence in the imagination to its existence in reality" (p. 258).

Feuerbach's project is noble but filled with dangers. As an object for the religious impulse God has great advantages over human beings. He is a safe place in which to put our faith, for the simple reason that he is posited as such. The affair is arranged so that no matter what happens to us on earth we can never say that God has betrayed us or that our faith has been misplaced. Presumably the Book of Job was included in the Old Testament to hammer this lesson home. God's nature is ineffable and his purposes are beyond our understanding, so there can never be a reason for us to follow the advice of Job's wife, to "curse God, and die."

But what of human beings? Feuerbach's celebration ("The Divine Being is nothing other than the being of man himself"; p. 111) is marvelous and brave, but is it wise? God is defined so as never to betray us, but can we say the same of human beings? We do not know what God does or thinks, but we do know something of what human beings do and think, including ourselves. Is Feuerbach asking us to place our faith *there*? Does he not realize that placing our full trust in human beings would require a faith even beyond the imagination of Abraham? Wasn't it the untrustworthiness of human beings which led to the positing of "God" in the first place?

Replacing God with man as the object of faith is a dangerous move; it can cause one to pass rapidly through the stages of sentimental humanism to disillusion and despair and finally to cynicism. This transition is no mere speculation; who would deny the relationship between the massive secularization of Western culture since Feuerbach and the deep cynicism by which it is characterized today?

There is a position halfway between religious faith and cynicism which can stop, or at least delay, the slide from the former to the latter: belief in "progress." This move has the advantage that it follows Feuerbach's program of secularization while avoiding the worst dangers of that program. The believer may dispense with the metaphysical entity "God" while retaining one of his alleged effects on the world: providence. It is easier to live without the hypothesis of a divine being if we can convince ourselves that the world is anyway constructed *as if* it were the creation of a divine intelligence and that history progresses *as if* it were the unfolding of a divine plan. This belief permits us to put our faith in human beings without that faith's being threatened by anything human beings actually do. We put our faith in the human beings of the future, and "the human beings of the future" will never let us down because they are, like God, the products of our imagination. They are an abstraction, and we can construct them any way we like. Again our faith is deposited in a safe place, where none of the crimes, stupidities, or failures of the people living in our own Dark Times can get at it. This safety gives us hope, and a reason to act. These are great advantages.

But there are disadvantages. If faith in progress, and in the human of the future, is immune to betrayal by the actual human beings living in the present, at the same time it gives us no particular reason to be loyal to them either. If the human of the future is the goal, it is perfectly consistent to treat the human of the present with sublime contempt, as steppingstones, building blocks, "human resources," or cannon fodder, that is, as *means* to the future. Faith in progress allows us to maintain two very different attitudes side by side. With regard to the human of the future we can be idealists, dreamers. With regard to the humans of the present we are able to behave just like the cynics. The believer in progress can have it both ways, being Abel later and Cain now. Of course ordinary people do not usually carry this form of faith to such as extreme, but in this century we have witnessed some of the chilling forms this position can take. Just as the deep faith of the Middle Ages could produce, with no logical inconsistency, the faithful inquisitor and the *auto-da-fé* (Portuguese for "act of faith"), so the historical faith of the twentieth century could produce, with equal consistency, progressive idealists such as Stalin, Truman, Robert McNamara, and Pol Pot.

The peculiar brutality that faith in progress has brought to our era grows from the fact that it is faith placed both in the wrong time and in the wrong sort of object. Faith is trust raised to a higher power, and the proper object for both is human beings. Faith in the humans of the future is faith in an abstraction; it is trust that cannot be reciprocated or grounded in any real promise. It is an evasion of the real task, the one thing needful, which is to work for a world founded on real trust among real humans, now. Just as its object is an abstraction, so its enactment becomes an abstraction; it is fulfilled not by the keeping of promises but by the operation of "laws of motion" and "historical forces." In short, in being transferred from God to Progress, faith is transformed from religion to superstition.

Democratic Faith: Choosing Isaac

The reintroduction of real persons as the original and only proper object of faith is the starting point for democratic thinking. As I have said, this step is not easy—its difficulty is the very reason we have invented so many ways of escaping it. Faith, the decision to continue to believe despite the evidence, has the power to raise us out of despair and to cure cynicism. At the same time faith in the wrong object has the power to make us into stupid, intolerant, and brutal "true believers." The only faith that can make us "better, braver, and more active" without the danger of also making us stupid and intolerant is faith in real human beings: democratic faith.

Faith in human beings is the hardest faith, yet we all have it in some degree. We have to, to live. It is the very stuff out of which our personal lives are shaped; it is so common we barely notice it. When people die or sacrifice their personal happiness for a Cause we are dazzled; when they do the same for their family or friends we admire them but are not so surprised. We do not reward them with fame and glory or establish national holidays in their honor. To do so would be embarrassing. Still, this faith is a tremendous power in history, far more powerful than all the force that has so far been held by states, armies, and other violence-wielding organizations. The proof of this power is that, despite these organizations, civilization still exists.

This view returns us to the point made earlier, that radical democracy does not require the introduction of some heroic new ethic into the world: it requires only that we put to better use some of the common-sense virtues we already have. To do so we need to gain new confidence in these common-sense virtues. We have a political mythology that denigrates them. Political order, we are taught, was established by men (meaning males) who were ready to sacrifice personal loyalty to do so. Cain killed Abel and built a city; Romulus killed Remus and founded Rome; Brutus killed his sons and founded the Roman Republic; Abraham held the knife over his son and founded the Hebrew people and became the Father of Faith. Democratic faith, common-sense faith, is founded differently, by the people who do *not* kill their brothers and children. It is founded by the people who will say calmly, with E. M. Forster, "If I had to choose between betraying my country and betraying my friend, I hope that I should have the guts to betray my country."[7]

One may push the point further and say that from the standpoint of democratic faith Abraham's act was a failure of faith. Had he the true faith of a *father*, he would have had perfect confidence that God would not punish him for refusing to kill the boy. Any *mother* would have understood that. If he had a covenant with his God he had another with his son, the tacit covenant one enters into by bringing a child into this world. From the standpoint of common-sense faith, he should have kept that covenant, the one with the weaker party, whom it was his duty to protect. Think of the horror and despair of Isaac when he saw his father raise the knife over his bound body—could anything that came after ever make things all right again? Are we to say that faith is the belief in a God who would hate Abraham for refusing to submit his son to that? Should we not reinterpret the entire myth and say that actually Abraham failed the test, that an amazed and horrified God mercifully stopped him from carrying out the despicable act and then punished Abraham and all his descendants by laying on them the Curse of Abraham's Faith, under the yoke of which we have been sacrificing our parents, children, brothers, sisters, and comrades to the State, the Party, the True Religion, and other Higher Causes ever since?

For a new beginning, we need an Abraham who would not kill the boy. But we need not look far to find him: most fathers in the world, I believe, would not, and neither would most mothers. Most would think, I do not believe that God will really punish me for refusing; If he does he is not really God; Even if he is God and he punishes me I will take the punishment before I will kill the boy. Or they would think nothing at all, but simply be unable to raise their arms to do the deed. It is because the world is mainly made up of people like these that there is hope.

The common-sense democrat will find this big talk embarrassing. Faith is a heavy word. We need it to give the argument here sufficient weight. Later we can substitute some more modest term like "tenacity" or "decency." But here let us call it faith and make the argument straight out: democratic faith is the true faith of which all other faiths are evasions; it is the faith of which all other faiths are imitations or indirect expressions or distorted forms; it is *radical* faith, at once the most natural and the most difficult.

The naturalness and the difficulty of democratic faith are rooted in the essential paradox of trust. The only proper object of trust is people, *because* people are capable of untrustworthiness; only people are capable of untrustworthiness, *because* they are trusted. We do not trust a rock to be hard, or a hen to lay eggs, or a falling object to accelerate at 32 ft./sec.^{2}. Trust—and trustworthiness—was invented as a way of dealing with the uncertainties of human beings, who are free. It does not change the uncertainties into certainties. Trust is not a proof but a judgment and a choice.

Democratic faith is not simply trusting everybody equally; it is not sentimental foolishness. It is grounded on a lucid understanding of the weaknesses, follies, and horrors people are capable of. It is precisely because of those weaknesses, follies, and horrors that something so weighty as faith is called for. Democratic faith is the decision to believe that a world of democratic trust is possible because we can see it in each person sometimes. It is the decision to believe in what people can be on the basis of what they sometimes are. It is the decision to believe that each polity and each person contains the possibility of a democratic version of itself. It is the belief that as people are free, they are free to become that, too. None of this has been proved, but neither can it be disproved. One is free to believe either way. The move to embrace democratic faith gives one hope and the ability to act, without self-deception about the actual state of things. The gap between the possibility in which the democrat believes and the reality that we have is a wide one; among leaps of faith, this is a long one. That is why, of all faiths, it needs to be the strongest.

So the democrat is not impressed with the Abraham who puts his faith in God the Omnipotent, the Omniscient, the Unchangeable, the Eternal, as against the little boy who, for all we know, sometimes steals cakes from the kitchen, dreams forbidden dreams, and is now wishing he had any other father in the world but this one. Obeying the omnipotent is no great feat compared with gambling on the boy.

The business turns another shade darker if we think of it from the standpoint of Feuerbach. For then we must see the God of Abraham as created by Abraham, for the purpose of giving himself and posterity an unshakable basis for faith, which he is unable to find in human beings. Abraham has created this homunculus and taught it to command him to sacrifice the boy, in order to raise himself above the uncertainties of mere human trust. The democrat does not join the theologians in applauding this attempt to evade the complexities of seeking to establish an honest order among human beings, using only human strength and wit. It is the worst possible beginning for a quest for the promised land. Feuerbach argues that human beings created God out of the best human qualities. But this God has another, inhuman quality: moral certainty. Human beings cannot arrive at moral certainty on their own. The story of Abraham and Isaac is a parable of this idea as well: it teaches how a person possessed of moral certainty passes outside the realm of the human and becomes a terrifying and incomprehensible force. There is no way we can think our way to that degree of certainty with merely human thoughts. Faith only among human beings, none of whom is "absolute," can never yield so mighty a consequence. The voice of the people is not the voice of God; democracy has no need of that hypothesis. It is only the voice of the people.

The State of Public Hope and the Art of the Possible

In the spring of 1985, in the last months of the Marcos dictatorship, I visited the Philippines on what they call there an "exposure tour," sponsored by a loose alliance of anti-Marcos movement organizations. The nine-day visit put me in a state of shock. It was not culture shock, or poverty shock. The only name I could think of for it was hope shock.

In Japan, where I live, most people have private hope. They believe that privately their lives will go well—that they will find work, earn adequate money, and live in comfort. Few of them fear that they or their children will fall into poverty, suffer malnutrition, be forced to turn to crime, or die violent deaths.

Most, however, have no public hope. Their attitude about the future of their country, or the future of the world, is typically one of bland despair. They talk easily and vaguely about the probable continuation of the destruction of nature, of the unlikelihood that they will ever achieve popular control over the entrenched political cliques that run their government, about the inevitable death of freedom in the technomanagerial society of the future. The belief that none of these things can be avoided by the action of mere human beings (which is to say, the belief that democracy is impossible) has become common sense.

In the Philippines in 1985 there were few objective reasons for hope. Under the Marcos development dictatorship, the economy was starving the people and the government was murdering them. Privately most young people, except those from very rich families, faced bleak futures. But everybody I talked to was filled with hope. Of course we will win, they told us. We will drive out this dictator. We will drive out the predatory foreign capitalists. We will drive out the U.S. bases. We will make the Philippines into a just and prosperous country. By the actions of ordinary people, they told us, these things will be done.

There was an atmosphere of freedom everywhere. We heard people sing forbidden anti-Marcos songs in public restaurants. We attended rallies and participated in marches. We walked with ten thousand people, mostly workers from the Battaan Export Processing Zone, where only a few years before union activity had been unthinkable, in a march from Mariveles to Batanga which took two days. Only once I saw government soldiers: three army jeeps whizzed by looking like hedgehogs with rifles sticking out all around, and the marchers hooted at them. We all camped in a public schoolyard. I remember thinking, What kind of dictatorship is this? If ten thousand antigovernment demonstrators set up camp in a public schoolyard in Japan or the United States or any other of the "democratic" countries, the riot police would drive them out in less than half an hour.

This was the shock: to be transferred suddenly from a society in a state of public despair into a society in a state of public hope. The "Miracle of EDSA" was not a sudden phenomenon; the process leading up to it had been well under way a year earlier. The tragedy of that "miracle" was that it turned into a ritual for transferring the people's public faith from People's Power to state power. Has there ever been a clearer illustration of the antidemocratic potential of "democratic elections"? The election of Corazon Aquino to the presidency marked not the beginning but the end of People's Power in the Philippines—at least for the time being. The country was freer in the last days of the Marcos regime than it is today. (I suppose the same could be said of Poland in the days when Solidarity had all the power except state power, compared to later with Lech Wałęsa in the presidency.) Today, the Philippines is a country struggling with despair.

Nevertheless, in their moment of public hope the Philippine people accomplished a deed that will be remembered throughout that country's history. And the possibility remains that it can be repeated.

The state of public hope is difficult to analyze or account for in the technical language of ordinary political science, and major people's movements and revolutions always catch the experts by surprise. Political science searches for causes. But the state of public hope is in a sense self-causing. The same is true for the state of public despair. When people will not join together in public action because they believe it is doomed to failure, then it is doomed to failure. The subjective belief creates the objective fact that proves the belief to be "correct." This state of things we commonly call "political realism."

In the state of public hope this vicious cycle is reversed. People begin to believe that public action can succeed. It doesn't matter why they believe—it could be for the wrong reason. When hope is shared by many, it becomes its own reason. Public hope is itself grounds for hope. When many people, filled with hope, take part in public action, hope is transformed from near-groundless faith (which it was in the state of public despair) to plain common sense. It is this capacity seemingly to defy the law of cause and effect, to create something out of nothing, which leads people to use the expression "miracle" to describe public action. It is also the reason movements sometimes unexpectedly turn into revolutions, going beyond their original goals: as the movement grows it becomes realistic to make demands that were unthinkable at the beginning. (Even something so unpolitical as the spontaneous growth of mutual-aid organizations out of people's efforts to survive the effects of an earthquake can be the catalyst for a new democratic movement, as happened in Mexico.)

In the Philippines, it is true, many people believed that success in throwing out Marcos was possible because of the power of the New People's Army (NPA). This belief was not groundless; the NPA was crucial in the delegitimization of the Marcos dictatorship and in the alteration of the balance of power in the country. But the self-generating dynamic of public hope soon developed into a tornado of power which far surpassed, albeit briefly, the military power of the guerrilla army and achieved something that army could not do, the overthrow of the dictator. The NPA is still there and still has military power, but public hope and people's power are not.

The expression "Politics is the art of the possible" is attributed to Otto von Bismarck. It is usually understood in a Bismarckian fashion: politics should be limited to *realpolitik*; it should rid itself of its utopian and idealistic elements and stick to a possible agenda. To enter politics is to give up being a dreamer, to abandon one's highest hopes, and to resign oneself to the realities of power. In this sense, "Politics is the art of the possible" has been the slogan of cynical politics.

The democrat, however, will take it in a different sense. In democratic politics, the art of the possible means the art of extending the possible, the art of creating the possible out of the impossible. It is true that the logic of *realpolitik* is the only logic that is effective in the context of the state of public despair. Democratic politics has the power to bring about a political change of state and make possible what was impossible before. This is not sentimental idealism but plain realism: it can happen and it does happen. If all the soldiers refuse to fight, the war is over; if all the citizens take to the streets, the dictatorship is out of power; if all the unions strike on the same day, they are in control of industry; if all the indebted nations simultaneously abrogate their debts, the International Monetary Fund and the World Bank are abolished. This is the *realpolitik* of democratic politics.

We have been taught by Hobbes to fear the state of nature. In this state where each wars against all in an endless agony of despair, public hope has vanished altogether. The state of nature is not a time in the far past; it is an ever-present possibility, a specter that follows us all through history and is always just a hairsbreadth away, ready to spring into reality any time we make the mistake of challenging the power of Leviathan. This miserable image, always just on the other side of the looking glass from political reality, operates as the constant killer of hope on this side too.

Against this image the democrat posits the image of the state of public hope, the state of democracy. This state, we say, is also an ever-present possibility, also just a hairsbreadth away. Knowing this gives us a reason not to lose hope even in the worst of political situations, even now.

Public Happiness

Arendt has eloquently described how, when political action succeeds in generating real power, the participants experience a kind of happiness different from the kinds of happinesses one finds in private life.[8] Public happiness is different also from the sweetness of revenge, the satisfaction of triumphing over a competitor, the pride of holding power over others or of being a member of a privileged elite. These are isolating joys and are rooted in their opposites; they depend on one's being released from rage, fear, or humiliation and on being in a position to impose those feelings on others. They are the joys promised us in the world of Thomas Hobbes.

Public happiness is not isolating but shared. It is the happiness of being free among other free people, of having one's public faith redeemed and returned, of seeing public hope becoming public power, becoming reality itself. It is the happiness of experiencing the moment when history is no longer an alien force by which one is squeezed and buffeted about, but is what one is doing now.

Public movements often arise from pity or self-pity, but neither of these emotions has staying power because when a movement begins to generate real public hope the people will no longer genuinely feel them. Moralists in political movements sometimes criticize people who admit the pleasure they feel in political action. To oppose this pleasure is dangerous, because only in a movement that is bound to fail can pity and self-pity be sustained throughout.

The experience of public happiness is an exceptional one in the politics of our time, but not such a rare exception. It has been known in many countries in this century, on every continent, in societies of every kind of political, economic, and cultural configuration. It has been felt, if sometimes only momentarily, everywhere, and therefore it is possible everywhere.

conclusion:
persephone's return

At the beginning of this book I wrote that I would not propose institutional solutions, a promise I hope has been mainly kept. Perhaps by now the reason for this eccentricity has become somewhat more clear. I have sought to argue that democracy is better described not as a "system" or a set of institutions but as a state of being and that the transition to it is not an institutional founding but a "change of state."

Does this argument mean that democracy cannot be institutionalized? If one reasons strictly from the above distinction, the answer is that it cannot. Once again I must hastily add: this reply does not at all denigrate the importance of what are commonly called democratic institutions. Many of the experiences most precious to human life cannot be institutionalized. Laughter cannot be institutionalized—which does not mean that we should abolish institutions such as comic theater. Love cannot be institutionalized—which does not mean that the institutions of courtship and marriage are useless. Wisdom cannot be institutionalized—which does not mean that educational institutions are a waste. Health cannot be institutionalized—which is no argument against hospitals and doctors. We design institutions, hoping that they will help to bring about, or preserve, a certain state of being. Often they do, and sometimes they don't. And sometimes the state of being may appear without the support of any institutions. People may fall in love watching a comedy, or laugh out loud during a wedding.

The same uncertainty of cause and effect is true of democracy: virtually all the institutions alleged to bring it about may be assembled, and still the state does not come about (think of the apathetic and/or corrupt "representative democracies"); yet all the institutions designed to suppress it may be assembled and it will break out before your very eyes (think of revolution).

Democracy is essential politics: the art of the possible. As an art, democracy is a performance art, like music, dance, and theater. Societies can build theaters, can organize orchestras and troupes of dancers and players, but the art itself exists only while it is being performed. Possible (from the Latin *posse*: to be able) means *merely* possible; we call a thing possible only when it is also possibly *not*. (Consider that no technology can make the experience of a recorded performance the same as that of a live performance. A recorded performance is already over. In a live performance you witness something that at each instant contains the possibility of failing to happen, happening.)

We call democracy the power of the people. Power (this word also from the Latin *posse*) is what takes the possible out of the hands of random fortune and transforms it into an art: a creative enterprise. Power brings into existence what would never come into existence in the process of the blind, automatic "development" of history. Power transforms dream and fantasy into possibility, and possibility into actuality. But the actuality of democracy itself—the people's power—exists while the performance is taking place. As Arendt taught us, it is not "making" but "acting." It is not something that can *be*, but only something that can *be done*.

But if democracy cannot directly become an institution, still when it appears it tends—as I argued in Chapter 1—to take on certain typical forms. People develop a desire to act together, and to talk to one another about their common life. They tend to gather in groups small enough to make this talk possible—in what have been called committees of correspondence, councils, soviets, affinity groups, sectoral groups, and so on. These become the form of "civil society." These groupings typically evolve into institutions, but this fact does not mean that democracy itself has been institutionalized; on the contrary, the formalization of these groupings may be the beginning of their petrification, as spontaneity evolves into ritual.

As democracy may evolve institutions, it also may consciously found them. That is, democratic movements have typically sought to invent, establish, alter, or abolish the institutions of the state in such a way as to make the democratic condition easier to bring about or harder to suppress. Democratic movements overthrow monarchies; establish constitutions; set up election systems; pass laws that limit state power and guarantee people's rights; found labor unions; seek to redistribute wealth by reforming land ownership, by changing inheritance laws, by taxing the rich, by setting up welfare systems—to give a complete list one would have to retell the history of the last three centuries, at least. The institutions founded through these struggles are of vital importance to us, but again it is incorrect to say that democracy itself has been institutionalized in them. Some have even been self-defeating, as when a democratic movement seeks to force changes in society through the violence of an all-powerful state, or places all its trust in a leader who turns out to be a demagogue, or confuses freedom with the free market.

Does the fact that democracy cannot be institutionalized mean that there is no way to make it last? The answer depends on whether "last" means "forever" or "for a while." If it means "forever," then the answer is clear: despite the illusions that have been spun by various theorists of progress since Condorcet, history knows nothing of "forever" (except, of course, "forever gone"). Since the French Revolution, people have wanted to believe that someday we would hear an earth-shaking "click," the great ratchet of history would move to a new position from which it could not go back, and democracy would change from something we have to struggle for into something that is just there, like the air. I would not like to abandon the belief that this permanence may be possible for some states, for example the state of peace. Peace, after all, does not mean doing something but rather means not doing something, that is, not murdering one another. It is possible to conceive that the state of peace could exist without effort. But if the state of democracy means a state of public action, then there is no conceivable stage of history at which it can be had without effort. To suggest that there is would be like suggesting that there could be a time when human consciousness has become so elevated that it is no longer necessary to educate the young. No matter what the future may bring, what in principle can be had only by effort will still be had only by effort. And when people's efforts flag, those things may again be lost.

On the other hand, if "last" means "for a while," the answer is also clear. The only remaining question is, How long is "a while"? Sheldon S. Wolin has suggested that democracy should be reconceived as a "fugitive" in history, "a political moment, perhaps the political moment, when the political is remembered and created," and "a mode of being which is conditioned by bitter experience, doomed to succeed only temporarily, but a recurrent possibility as long as the memory of the political survives."[1] I agree, with the provisions that we should be cautious about the deterministic overtones of the word "doomed" and that we should remember that in history "temporarily" can be a long time.

Does this temporariness mean that the labors of the democrat are the labors of Sisyphus, that we must heave the stone up the mountain with the certain knowledge that the work is futile, that the stone will roll back down again, bringing all our efforts to nothing? A generation ago, when Albert Camus used the image of Sisyphus as a symbol of action in the face of absurdity, action devoid of hope, he was speaking to a world that still longed to believe in one or another version of progress theory—to believe that history was moving irreversibly through stages of the human spirit, or stages of the relations of production, or stages of economic growth. To say that the stone would roll back down again sounded like a message of despair.

Before the modern age, however, virtually all people everywhere saw human affairs as moving in recurrent cycles, just as nature does. And today even those of us who have been taught to believe in unilinear progress still unconsciously, or instinctively, use cyclical images to describe political phenomena. When oppression eases we call it a "thaw"; when a new democratic movement arises we call it "spring" or a "dawning"; if the movement is strong enough to affect the shape of society we call it a "birth." Interestingly, while Camus was never able to explain convincingly why his Sisyphus, locked in his cycles of futile labor, was (as Camus claimed) happy, it is not at all absurd to feel glad at the coming of spring, or rejoice at a new birth, even though we know it is the beginning of a cycle that will come to an end.

Let's change the image, then. To symbolize recurrence, let's replace the myth of Sisyphus with the myth of Demeter and Persephone. You will remember the story. Hades, king of the Underworld, fell wildly in "love" with Persephone and dragged her screaming down to his kingdom, overstepping his kingly powers. Persephone's mother, the corn goddess Demeter, searched the world frantically for her daughter and, having located her, called a general strike of the plant kingdom until Persephone would be restored to her. The earth was cast into winter. To avert catastrophe Zeus arranged for Persephone's return, on condition that she had not eaten any of the food of the dead. Persephone, however—being, like all the Greek gods and goddesses, human—had fallen prey to temptation and eaten seven pomegranate seeds. Her transgression was discovered, and she was sent back to Hades. Finally, a compromise was worked out whereby Persephone would remain in the Underworld for three months of the year and be with her mother for the remaining nine (in some versions it is six and six). And so the world began to move in cycles of spring, summer, fall, and winter.[2]

What can we extract from this tale? Spring is a wonder and a miracle every time it comes; the wonder of it is not compromised by the fact that summer and fall and winter will come again. It is a new beginning every time, without needing to be different from the springs that came before. When it comes, it comes with overwhelming power; the gloom of winter is swept away. At the same time as we move into summer we must choose what to be: grasshopper or ant, hippy or politico? Do we make music or prepare for winter? The wise will prepare for winter: build and stock storehouses, gather firewood, repair leaky roofs, add extra insulation, arrange so that the summer heat, in the form of food and fuel, can somehow carry them through the coming winter. Shall we call these efforts the attempt to institutionalize summer?

There is no question about it: the ant is the wise one in the story, the grasshopper the fool, for it is essential to survive the winter somehow. But there is a danger here. If our preparations for winter are too thorough, we may forget that it is winter. Eating preserved food, we may forget the taste of fresh; standing by the heater, we may forget the warmth of the summer sun. And here is where the analogy begins to break down. For the democratic spring does not roll around by itself, at a regular time. It comes only when people make it come. Without a great collective effort to bring it about, it might not come at all. And if we deceive ourselves into believing that it is summer when it is not, we are less likely to make that effort or even to grasp that it is necessary.

What we mostly have in the "actually existing representative democracies" is winter, with a lot of elaborate equipment designed to help us to survive it: "democratic institutions." We are right to cherish those institutions; flawed as they are, we should never allow ourselves to be forced to face winter without them (my argument for a recognition of political cycles should not be taken as meaning that we must accept cycles of democracy and dictatorship). But we must not start thinking of the cave, which we originally entered to get out of the wind, as if it were the whole world, or confuse the stove with the sun. This is the error we fall into when we define democracy as identical to the institutions of the "actually existing democracies." And this error is surely one of the reasons that, even in this age when virtually everybody claims to be a democrat, democracy itself has still no more than a fugitive existence. If eternal democracy is too much to ask, fugitive democracy is too little. Demeter forced the King of the Underworld to return her daughter for nine months out of the twelve. That's not a bad bargain, and maybe we can do as well. It would be something to hope for.

notes

Introduction

1. I was able to locate two: Tsurumi, who contributed "Japanese Democracy and the American Occupation" (*democracy* 2 [January 1982]: 75–88), and Kato Shuichi, who wrote "The Japanese Myth Reconsidered" (*democracy* 1 [July 1981]: 98–108).

2. My first attempt to express this view was also published in *democracy*: "The Radicalism of Democracy" in vol. 2 (Fall 1982): 9–16.

3. Of particular interest in recent democratic writing are the attempts to rediscover or reestablish links between democracy and socialism. It is as if a team of American positivist political scientists and a team of European dialectical materialists began tunneling toward each other but miscalculated and, instead of meeting halfway as planned, dug past each other, each popping up in the other's country to find the other no longer there. Thus we have a positivist democratic socialism—for example Samuel Bowles and Herbert Gintis, *Democracy and Capitalism: Property, Community, and the Contradictions of Modern Social Thought* (New York: Basic Books, 1986); Robert A. Dahl, *A Preface to Economic Democracy* (Berkeley: University of California Press, 1985)—and a dialectical materialist pluralism—for example Ernest Laclau and Chantal Mouffe, *Hegemony and Socialist Strategy: Towards a Radical Democratic Politics* (London: Verso, 1985)—engaging in uneasy search for a common language that would make dialogue possible—for example Chantal Mouffe, ed., *Dimensions of Radical Democracy: Pluralism, Citizenship, Community* (London, Verso, 1992). Laclau and Mouffe's book has the reputation of being next to unreadable, but it is easier to grasp if one reads it as if it were an Umberto Eco novel. Think of two brave enemy agents entering the hitherto impenetrable fortress of Dialectical Materialism disguised as members of the Cabal. They have memorized all the secret passwords and are adept at the entire body of ritual; thus the iron and oaken doors, locked for others, spring open for them one after another until they arrive at the inner sanctum at the very center of the fortress. There they cry out the forbidden words: "The One is not one: it is Many!" The spell is broken, the walls crack, and the fortress crumbles. Benjamin Barber's *Strong Democracy: Participatory Politics for a New Age* (Berkeley: University of California Press, 1984) contains a vigorous and thought-provoking critique of liberalism from the democratic position. Unfortunately it seems to conceive the boundaries of the democratic imagination as coterminous with the U.S. border. Carol C. Gould's *Rethinking Democracy: Freedom and Social Cooperation in Politics, Economy, and Society* (Cambridge: Cambridge University Press, 1988) contains a bold attempt to overcome this limitation (see chap. 12: "Geopolitical Democracy: Moral Principles

among Nations"), and Gould's main argument, that the democratic principle needs to be extended to the economy and the society, is welcome. But her philosophical argument, that rights exist prior to politics, seems to me rather similar to arguing that words exist before language.

Of course, the new wave of democratic theory is older than the last decade. The important work of C. B. Macpherson is well known. I myself am particularly influenced by the critiques of liberalism—overlapping, but not identical—developed by the political theorists who were at U.C. Berkeley when I studied there in the 1960s. Norman Jacobsen's "Political Science and Political Education," *American Political Science Review* (September 1963): 561–69, is, I believe, seminal, if one may use that expression about a work so short and so ignored. In John H. Schaar's *Legitimacy and the Modern State* (New Brunswick, N.J.: Transaction Books, 1981) the subject of democracy itself is mainly avoided (e.g., "It is not the primary task of this essay to set forth a genuinely democratic conception of equality: that is a work for another time," p. 203), but it is the main position from which Schaar launches his fierce critique of the liberal ideology. Sheldon S. Wolin's critique of liberalism dates back to his *Politics and Vision* (Boston: Little, Brown, 1960) but does not become a positive search for a theory of radical democracy until the launching under his editorship of the journal *democracy*. See especially his "The People's Two Bodies," *democracy* 1 (January 1981): 9–24. For a wonderfully provocative work by a scholar influenced by (among others) the latter two, see Joshua Miller's *The Rise and Fall of Democracy in Early America, 1630–1789: The Legacy for Contemporary Politics* (University Park: Pennsylvania State University Press, 1991).

4. For this stance there is at least one honorable precedent. In the prologue to *The Human Condition* Hannah Arendt writes, "To these preoccupations and perplexities, this book does not offer an answer. Such answers are given every day, and they are matters of practical politics, subject to the agreement of many; they can never lie in theoretical considerations or the opinion of one person, as though we dealt with problems for which only one solution is possible." Arendt, *The Human Condition* (New York: Anchor, 1958), pp. 5–6.

Chapter 1   Radical Democracy

1. See Herbert S. Storing, *The Anti-Federalist* (Chicago: University of Chicago Press, 1981).

2. In the Putney Debates of 1647 Henry Ireton asked why, if men without property were given the vote, "those men may not vote against all property." Colonel Nathaniel Rich, on the other hand, pointed out how in ancient Rome "the people's voices were bought and sold . . . and thence it came that he that was the richest man, and of some considerable power among the soldiers, made himself a perpetual dictator." Of course for Ireton and Rich these were arguments against democracy, but they identified the two main principles whose mutual struggle has been the history of liberal politics throughout the capitalist era. "The Putney Debates," *Divine Right and Democracy*, ed. David Wootton (Harmondsworth: Penguin, 1986), pp. 296, 297.

3. In this sense, radical democracy itself is immune to the method of deconstruction as practiced by Jacques Derrida and other postmodern theorists. Or, rather, it is the end point of such deconstruction. Similarly, a follower of Michel Foucault would be adding no new information in revealing that radical democracy is "really" about power: of course it is about power. On the contrary, the Foucaultian critique of soci-

ety as a system of reified power over the people is a critique (rather than simply the observations of a sociophysicist) only from the standpoint of radical democracy.

4. Here I am disagreeing squarely with those theorists who define democracy as a "method," beginning with Joseph Schumpeter's famous redefinition of democracy in 1942: "The democratic method is that institutional arrangement for arriving at political decisions in which individuals acquire the power to decide by means of a competitive struggle for the people's vote." Schumpeter, *Capitalism, Socialism and Democracy* (1942; rpt. New York: Harper, 1975), p. 269.

5. Benjamin Barber, in his critique of liberal theory, opposes the notion (espoused from Thomas Hobbes to John Rawls) that "a sturdy house of politics can only arise on an unexpungable and infallible foundation, set deep in prepolitical granite." Barber, *Strong Democracy: Participatory Politics for a New Age* (Berkeley: University of California Press, 1984), p. 51. But despite the coincidence of the metaphor (granite), the radical base I am discussing here is not the same as "the fallacy of the independent ground" (p. 65) which Barber says is destructive of democratic theory. Nor is it another form of the "essentialism" criticized by Ernesto Laclau and Chantal Mouffe in *Hegemony and Socialist Strategy: Toward a Radical Democratic Politics* (London: Verso, 1985), e.g. pp. 10–11. As described here, radical democracy is not "independent" ground; it is not prepolitical but the essence of politics itself. In this sense, perhaps "radical humidity" is a more apt figure than "radical rock."

6. Henry B. Mayo, *An Introduction to Democratic Theory* (New York: Oxford University Press, 1960), p. 58.

7. Ibid., p. 59.

8. This restatement of Schumpeter's definition (see n. 4) is from Robert M. MacIver, *The Web of Government*, rev. ed. (New York: The Free Press, 1965), p. 198.

9. The closest work I know of to a manifesto for radical democracy is Karl Marx's chapter "On Democracy" in his "Critique of Hegel's Philosophy of Right." Marx, *Selected Writings*, ed. David McLellan (Oxford: Oxford University Press, 1977), pp. 27–30. But after he became a communist, Marx never returned again to address the question of democracy at any length, at least in the same way. According to Maximilian Rubel, "Far from breaking with his first conception of democracy when he became a communist, Marx sublimated it. In communism as he understood it, democracy was not only maintained, but acquired even greater significance." Rubel, "Marx's Concept of Democracy," *democracy* 3 (Fall 1983): 103. Be that as it may, the chapter in the "Critique" stands alone in his writings as a sustained discussion of democracy itself.

10. "Democracy is the solution to the riddle of all constitutions. Here the constitution is constantly, not only in itself and essentially, but also in its existence and reality, brought back to its real basis, the real man, the real people, and set up as its own work." Marx, *Selected Writings*, p. 28.

11. It will be seen that the position taken here is different from that of Robert Nozick, who argues in his *Anarchy, State, and Utopia* (New York: Basic Books, 1974) that the fundamental question that political philosophy must answer is "Why not have anarchy?" (p. 4). For Nozick, anarchy means (as it did not for Pëtr Kropotkin, for example) a nonpolitical or prepolitical state (p. 6); for the term "anarchy" he quickly substitutes "state of nature" (p. 4). Nozick is able to write calmly, comfortably, and wittily about the disadvantages of this state because it poses no danger: it is defined from the start in such a way as to be untenable. By so structuring the argument (state

of nature or state power, take your choice) Nozick succeeds in keeping the genuinely subversive (because the choice is possible) question—"Why not have radical democracy?"—out of sight.

12. Thomas Hobbes, *Leviathan*, ed. Michael Oakeshott with an introd. by Richard S. Peters (New York: Collier, 1962).

13. John Locke, *Two Treatises of Government*, rev. ed., with an introd. by Peter Laslett (New York: New American Library, 1963), p. 454.

14. See Hannah Arendt, *Crises of the Republic* (New York: Harcourt, Brace, Jovanovich, 1969), p. 86.

15. Though Nozick bases his entire argument on a revised version of Locke's notion of the state of nature, nowhere does he mention the state of nature in its revolutionary second phase. For that matter, he never mentions that Locke was a revolutionary theorist: the word "revolution" does not appear in the index to *Anarchy, State, and Utopia*.

16. For a lengthy discussion (which, however, does not mention Mexico) of the origins of the concept of civil society, see Jean L. Cohen and Andrew Arato, *Civil Society and Political Theory* (Cambridge, Mass.: MIT Press, 1992). On civil society in Mexico,Carlos Monsiváis writes, "The earthquake raised the term to the height of its glory. And on the 22nd of September [the day of the earthquake] it starts to be commonly used, at first as a synonym for 'society' without any additional organizational emphasis or meaning. But by the beginning of October practice dominates: civil society is self-generated community power and solidarity, the space independent of the government, the actual antagonistic zone." Monsiváis, *Entrada libre: Crónicas de la sociedad que se organiza* [Admission free: Chronicles of a society organizing itself] (Mexico City: Biblioteca Era, 1987), p. 78; quotation trans. by Frank Bardacke.

17. Adam Ferguson, *An Essay on the History of Civil Society*, 4th ed. (1773; Farnsborough: Gregg International Publishers, 1969), p. 47.

18. Subcomandante Marcos, *Shadows of Tender Fury: The Letters and Communiqués of Subcomandante Marcos and the Zapatista Army of National Liberation*, trans. Frank Bardacke, Leslie Lopez, and the Watsonville, California, Human Rights Collective, introd. by John Ross, afterword by Frank Bardacke (New York: Monthly Review Press, 1995), p. 231.

19. Robert A. Dahl, *Who Governs? Democracy and Power in an American City* (New Haven: Yale University Press, 1961), p. 311; Seymour Martin Lipset, *Political Man: The Social Bases of Politics* (Garden City, N.Y.: Anchor Books, 1960), p. 439; Daniel Bell, *The End of Ideology: On the Exhaustion of Political Ideas in the Fifties*, rev. ed. (New York: The Free Press, 1962); Bell, "American Exceptionalism Revisited: The Role of Civil Society," *Public Interest*, no. 95 (September 1989): 56, 48.

20. Edward Shils, "The End of Ideology?" *Encounter* 5 (November 1955): 52–58.

21. Edward Shils, "The Virtue of Civil Society," *Government and Opposition* 26, no. 2 (1991): 3.

22. Shils even finds a place to plug his venerable elitism into the civil-society argument: a high degree of civility, it turns out, is only really required of elites, though a "spark of civility exists in the breast of most individuals" even at the bottom of the "pyramid of civility" (p. 18).

23. "All societies . . . are sites of conflicting interests in the sense that, when one part obtains more of anything, there is less for the other part" (p. 15). In short, all games are zero-sum. In fairness to Shils, it must be mentioned that he also writes that

there is, in addition to "politeness," a "substantive civility," meaning "to give precedence to the common good" (p. 16). But if every good in the society is subject to the "more for me, less for you" rule, then the notion of common good is untenable. In any case, the only concrete example I can find in the essay of what Shils might mean by concern for the common good is keeping an eye out for criminals and juvenile delinquents.

24. Moreover, there is an ambiguity surrounding the relation between the civil society and women. As Susan Moller Okin remarks, " 'Public/private' is used to refer both to the distinction between state and society (as in public and private ownership), and to the distinction between non-domestic and domestic life. . . . The crucial difference between the two is that the intermediate socio-economic realm (what Hegel called the 'civil society') is in the first dichotomy included in the category of 'private' but is in the second dichotomy 'public.' " Okin, "Gender, the Public and the Private," in *Political Theory Today*, ed. David Held (Stanford: Stanford University Press, 1991), pp. 68–69.

25. David Held, *Political Theory and the Modern State* (Stanford: Stanford University Press, 1989), p. 182.

26. Václav Havel, "The Power of the Powerless," in Havel et al., *The Power of the Powerless: Citizens against the State in Eastern Europe*, ed. John Keane, introd. by Steven Lukes (Armonk, N.Y.: M. E. Sharpe, 1985), p. 27.

27. Italics in original. Some readers may be put off by the appearance here of the troublesome word "truth." Perhaps the expression could be made more persuasive (to some at least) by noting that as Havel says that the greengrocer "begins to say what he really thinks," we could say that he has begun striving to establish an "ideal speech situation."

28. Carl Schmitt argues that true sovereignty can be found in the "decision that interrupts the process of development or discussion." Schmitt, *The Crisis of Parliamentary Democracy*, trans. Ellen Kennedy (Cambridge, Mass.: MIT Press, 1985), p. 56. But Schmitt can imagine such a decision being made only by a person at the head of the government—at least at the moment the decision is made, by a dictator. In times of normal routine the state bureaucracy and/or the law seem to be sovereign, but true sovereignty reveals itself in the exceptional situation—the situation that the law has not anticipated: "Sovereign is he who decides on the exception." Schmitt, *Political Theology: Four Chapters on the Concept of Sovereignty*, trans. George Schwab (Cambridge, Mass.: MIT Press, 1988), p. 5. But the greengrocer's decision has the characteristics Schmitt suggests, without being dictatorial. With his decision he interrupts the process of development as it unfolds under the rules of the state bureaucracy. He decides to become an exception. In deciding to do what his conscience "commands" he has regained sovereign power over his own actions. If he is joined by enough other people, the decision by the dictator at the head of state will be a decision no longer, but only empty words.

29. Havel, "The Power of the Powerless," p. 71.

30. Cohen and Arato, *Civil Society*, pp. 19–20.

31. Havel, "The Power of the Powerless," p. 68.

32. Cohen and Arato, *Civil Society*, p. 16.

33. For an interesting and remarkably persuasive proposal that the U.S. House of Representatives be chosen by lot see Ernest Callenbach and Michael Phillips, *A Citizen Legislature* (Berkeley, Calif.: Banyan Tree Books and Clear Glass, 1985). Barber, *Strong Democracy*, has also proposed a more limited introduction of choice by lot.

34. The key to the operation of the U.S. Constitution, Madison argues, is that it is constructed on the "policy of supplying, by opposite and rival interests, the defect of better motives." James Madison, "No. 51," in Alexander Hamilton, James Madison, John Jay, *The Federalist Papers*, introd. by Clinton Rossiter (New York: New American Library, 1961), p. 322.

35. "Where the whole community is assembled on any alarming occasion, we may venture to say, that we have found the origin of the senate, the executive power, and the assembly of the people; institutions for which ancient legislators have been so much renowned." Ferguson, *Essay*, p. 141–42.

36. To repeat the point made in note 28 above, the same may be said for the "dictator" of the authoritarian political theorist Carl Schmitt. Schmitt's dictum "Sovereign is he who decides on the exception" could use a little deconstructive criticism. For the radical democrat the dictum will read, "Sovereign are they who decide whether the 'dictator's' decision really is a decision and not the pronouncements of a usurper or a crackpot Hyde Park orator." Particularly important are the people who decide whether or not to carry the decision out. To illustrate "the exception" Schmitt asks, "Who assumes the authority concerning those matters for which there are no positive stipulations, for example, a capitulation?" *Political Theology*, p. 10. The answer is that generally the soldiers do, by voting with their feet.

37. Plato, *Republic* 1.331. The translations below are those of Francis Macdonald Cornford in *The Republic of Plato* (London: Oxford University Press, 1941).

38. Jacques Derrida suggests that the original "aggression of rationalism" against madness, the moment at which it established its supremacy by "*constituting* its contrary as an object in order to be protected from it and be rid of it," may not have been in the seventeenth century as Foucault has argued but in the work of Socrates. Derrida, "Cogito and the History of Madness," in *Writing and Difference*, trans. Alan Bass (Chicago: University of Chicago Press, 1978), pp. 34, 40; emphasis in original. He writes, "If dissension [between reason and madness] dates from Socrates, then the situation of the madman in the Socratic and post-Socratic worlds—assuming that there is, then, something that can be called mad—perhaps deserves to be examined first" (p. 42). If so, one might be tempted to locate this "original sin" of logos in the *Republic*, beginning precisely with Socrates' response to Cephalus. The question posed in the *Republic*, however, is not whether madness should be locked out of sight but whether it should be given the sword of power. The issue is not, as it is for Derrida, madness as the pure principle of unreason, but madness in its political form, madness empowered. And to take a political form, that is, to become a power, madness must mix with rationality. To take command, it must follow Ahab: "All my means are sane, my motive and my object mad." The sword symbolizes both power and the instrumental rationality that is the necessary condition for power: the sword is no power if held from the wrong end. It is this rationally empowered madness—i.e., tyranny—that Socrates condemns as the worst possible form of rule.

39. For a discussion of the *Republic* as "the most magnificent cure ever devised for every form of political ambition," see John Bremer, *On Plato's Polity* (Houston, Tex.: Institute of Philosophy, 1984); quotation is from p. 8.

40. Postmodern theorists point out that as we now know that there is no "master narrative" behind our discourse (Derrida, "Force and Signification") democratic theory must free itself from the myth of "essentialism" (Laclau and Mouffe) or the belief in an "independent ground" for political theory (Barber) (see n. 5 above). Socrates is

sometimes identified as the historical villain who introduced these hoaxes into our philosophy. Perhaps. But simultaneously, through his philosophical praxis, he left us also a different message: though we may dream about the Book, talk about the Book, believe in the Book, what we have here and now in daily life is never-ending, ever-changing dialogue (discourse). Socrates wrote no book.

41. Meno, 86b, W. K. C. Guthrie translation, in Edith Hamilton and Huntington Cairns, eds., *Collected Dialogues of Plato* (New York: Pantheon, 1961), p. 371.

Chapter 2   Antidemocratic Development

1. See Gustavo Esteva, "Development," in Wolfgang Sachs, ed., *The Development Dictionary: A Guide to Knowledge and Power* (London: Zed Books, 1992), pp. 6–25.

2. Cf. Sheldon S. Wolin's description of the U.S. political system as a "political economy, in which the state [is] grounded in economic relationships and act[s] mainly through its administrative branch." Wolin, "The People's Two Bodies" *democracy* 1, (January 1981): 15. Compare also Robert S. Lynd, over fifty years ago: "Power is no less 'political' for being labeled 'economic' power." Lynd, foreword to Robert A. Brady, *Business as a System of Power* (New York: Columbia University Press, 1943), p. viii.

3. "In most tropical areas the white man is unable or unwilling to perform manual labor, and in order to carry on its activities outside enterprise must rely either upon the local population or upon imported coolie labor. Since the material wants of primitive peoples are few and they are unfamiliar with a money economy and unaccustomed to arduous and continuous toil, they are usually unwilling to-work for European entrepreneurs. Out of the conflict between native indifference and the desires of outside governments and industrialists forced labor has arisen in many areas. Many of the chief tropical railways and roads have been constructed by forced labor. Indeed, it is doubtful whether the tropics could have been held and developed to their present extent by outside forces had not this practise been employed." "Forced Labor," *Encyclopedia of the Social Sciences* (New York: Macmillan, 1933). In the 1968 edition of the *Encyclopedia*, which was entirely revised under the modernization/development paradigm, this very informative entry has been dropped. The index shows that forced labor is mentioned twice in the *Encyclopedia*'s seventeen volumes, once in reference to medieval serfs, the other a one-line reference to forced labor in Nazi Germany and in the USSR. I have never seen the subject mentioned in any post–World War II work on economic development.

4. Karl Polanyi, *The Great Transformation* (New York: Octagon Books, 1975).

5. See C. Douglas Lummis, "Equality" in Wolfgang Sachs, ed., *The Development Dictionary: A Guide to Knowledge as Power* (London: Zed Books, 1992), pp. 38–52.

6. And returning to the nineteenth century gives us the opportunity to take a new look at the nineteenth-century socialist William Morris. Morris saw capitalism and industrialism as virtually identical: the industrialization of work *was* the system for oppressing the worker. For Morris, under a socialism of truly free labor, industrialism itself would fade away. See especially his beautiful *News from Nowhere*, in Morris, *Selected Writings*, ed. G. D. H. Cole (New York, London: Nonesuch Press, 1934), pp. 3–197.

7. Still the best discussion I know of the relation of management science to democracy is Sheldon S. Wolin, *Politics and Vision* (Boston: Little, Brown, 1960), chapter 5.

8. Alexander R. Magno, "Development and the 'New Society': The Repressive Ideology of Underdevelopment," *Third World Studies Papers*, series no. 35, Third World Studies Center, University of the Philippines, August 1983.

9. See for example Ferdinand E. Marcos, *Notes on the New Society of the Philippines* (Manila: Marcos Foundation, 1973).

10. Republic of the Philippines, Constitutional Commission of 1986, *The Constitution of the Republic of the Philippines* (Quezon City: National Bookstore, 1986). Reference to the 1935 and 1973 constitutions are also from this National Bookstore edition.

11. See for example Third World Studies, ed., *Marxism in the Philippines* (Quezon City: Third World Studies Center, 1984).

12. Ricardo D. Ferrer, "Theoretic and Programmatic Framework for the Development of Underdeveloped Countries," typed manuscript.

13. "The essence of the spirit, its supreme imperative, is that it should recognise, know, and realize itself for what it is. It accomplishes this end in the history of the world; it produces itself in a series of determinate forms and these forms are the nations of world history. Each of them represents a particular stage of development, so that they correspond to epochs in the history of the world." G. W. F. Hegel, *Lectures in the Philosophy of World History, Introduction: Reason in History*, trans. H. B. Nisbit, with an introd. by Duncan Forbes (Cambridge: Cambridge University Press, 1975), p. 64. For Hegel's association of this notion with the mystical idea of Providence, see pp. 35–43.

14. Karl Marx, "Preface to the First Edition," *Capital* (Harmondsworth: Penguin Books, 1976), 1: 91.

15. Karl Marx and Friedrich Engels, "Manifesto of the Communist Party," in Robert C. Tucker, ed., *The Marx-Engels Reader* (New York and London: Norton, 1978), p. 476.

16. Ibid., p. 475.

17. I do not mean to imply that the government under Lenin was the first to launch a program of intentional national industrialization. Surely Japan's Meiji government was the first to do so. The point here, however, is not to locate the historical "first" but to trace the history of the notion of development in Western thought. Japan's economic development was not taken seriously as an object of study in the West until after World War II.

18. V. I. Lenin, *The Development of Capitalism in Russia: The Process of the Formation of a Home Market for Large-Scale Industry* (Moscow: Progress Publishers, 1956).

19. V. I. Lenin, "The Chief Task of Our Day," in *Collected Works* (Moscow: Progress Publishers, 1965), 27: 163; 1st pub. in *Izvestia*, VTs1K no. 46 (March 12, 1918).

20. Lenin, "The Immediate Tasks of the Soviet Government," *Collected Works*, 27: 238, 241; 1st pub. in *Pravda*, no. 83 (April 28, 1918).

21. Lenin, "On Co-operation," in *Collected Works*, 33: 475; 1st pub. in *Pravda*, nos. 115, 116 (May 26, 27, 1923).

22. Lenin, "Economics and Politics in the Era of the Dictatorship of the Proletariat," in *Collected Works*, 30: 112; 1st pub. in *Pravda*, no. 250 (November 7, 1919).

23. Lenin, "The Immediate Tasks," p. 244.

24. Lenin, "Economics and Politics," p. 115; emphasis in original.

25. Lenin, "Once Again on the Trade Unions," in *Collected Works*, 32: 84; orig. a pamphlet of the same title dated January 1921.

26. Lenin, "The Immediate Tasks," p. 271; emphasis in original.

27. Lenin, "Report on the Immediate Tasks of the Soviet Government," in *Collected Works*, 27: 300; 1st pub. as "Minutes of the Sessions of All Russia C.E.C., 4th Convention," held April 29, 1918 ("Verbatim Report," Moscow, 1920).

28. Lenin, "The Immediate Tasks," p. 259.

29. "Resolution of All-Russian Central Executive Committee," February 2–7, 1920, quoted by Lenin in "Integrated Economic Plan," in *Collected Works*, 32: 138; the latter 1st pub. in *Pravda*, no. 32 (February 22, 1921).

30. "Resolution on Electrification Adopted by the Eighth All-Russian Congress of Soviets," December 29, 1920, quoted by Lenin in "Integrated Economic Plan," p. 141. The editors of the *Collected Works* note, "The draft resolution was written by Lenin" (p. 539n.38; emphasis in original). In May 1921 Lenin asked in a list of questions for investigation, "Have the gubernia and uyezd libraries copies of the Plan for Electrification of the R.S.F.S.R., which was submitted as a report to the Eighth Congress of Soviets? If so, how many copies? If not, it shows that the local delegates to the Eighth Congress of Soviets are dishonest and ought to be expelled from the Party and dismissed from their responsible posts, or else they are idlers who should be taught to do their duty by a term of imprisonment." Instructions of the Council of Labor and Defense to Local Soviet Bodies," in *Collected Works*, 32: 396; 1st pub. as a pamphlet in 1921.

31. Marx, *Capital*, 1:557. Marx is here referring specifically to the "extinction of the English hand-loom weavers."

32. Lenin, "Speech Delivered at the Third All-Russia Congress of Economic Councils," January 27, 1920, in *Collected Works*, 30: 132; 1st pub. in *Pravda*, no. 19 (January 29, 1920).

33. Karl W. Deutsch, "Social Mobilization and Political Development," *American Political Science Review* 4 (September 1961): 494.

34. "In some relatively nonmodernized societies the armed force organization may be the major precedent for a bureaucratic or semibureaucratic experience." Marion J. Levy, *Modernization and the Structure of Societies* (Princeton, N.J.: Princeton University Press, 1966), 2:588–89. "The problems of creating coherent political organizations are more difficult but not fundamentally different from those involved in the creation of coherent military organizations." Samuel Huntington. "Political Development and Political Decay," *World Politics* 17 (April 1965): 403–4.

35. "Totalitarian lawfulness, defying legality and pretending to establish the direct reign of justice on earth, executes the law of History or of Nature without translating it into standards of right and wrong for individual behaviour. It applies the law directly to mankind without bothering with the behavior of men. . . . Totalitarian policy claims to transform the human species into an active unfailing carrier of a law to which human beings otherwise would only passively and reluctantly be subjected." Hannah Arendt, *The Origins of Totalitarianism*, 2d ed. (New York: Meridian, 1959), p. 462.

36. Lenin, "The Immediate Tasks," p. 241.

37. H. W. Arndt, "Economic Development: A Semantic History," *Economic Development and Cultural Exchange* 29 (April 1981): 463.

38. "Noncapitalist Path of Development," *The Great Soviet Encyclopedia* (New York and London: Macmillan, 1978); translation of the 3d ed. of *Bol'shaia Sovetskaia Entsiklopediia* (Moscow, 1974), 17: 584.

39. Christopher Hill, *Lenin and the Russian Revolution* (1947; Harmondsworth: Penguin, 1971), p. 167. Twenty years later, in a description of the violence that ac-

companied the industrial revolution in England, Hill permits himself the jibe: "It would be nice if it had been otherwise; but even the most liberal historians cannot have their cake without breaking eggs." One wonders how Lenin would have taken the use of the word "even" in this application of his famous remark. Hill, *Reformation to Industrial Revolution (The Pelican Economic History of Britain*, vol. 2: *1530–1780*), (1967; Harmondsworth: Penguin, 1969), p. 232.

40. Harry S Truman, "Inaugural Address" [1949], *A Decade of American Foreign Policy* (Washington: U.S. Government Printing Office, 1950), p. 1366.

41. Harry S Truman, *Memoirs*, vol. 2: *Years of Trial and Hope* (New York, Doubleday, 1956), pp. 232, 230.

42. Ibid., p. 230.

43. See Charles Douglas Lummis, "American Modernization Theory as Ideology," *Kokusai Kankeigaku Kenyu*, 7 [Research in international relations] (Tsuda College, Japan, March, 1981), pp. 113–29.

44. Lyle W. Shannon, "Preface," in *Underdeveloped Areas*, ed. Shannon (New York: Harper and Row, 1957), p. x.

45. David Apter, *The Politics of Modernization* (Chicago: University of Chicago Press, 1965), p. 460; emphasis in original.

46. Paul A. Baran, *The Political Economy of Growth* (New York: Monthly Review Press, 1957). "Although many of its notions are present in earlier Marxist debates on colonialism and imperialism, Underdevelopment Theory first emerged in the 1950s as a critique of Keynesian and neo-classical approaches to the problems of economic development of post-colonial societies. . . . Its major concepts, formulated by Paul Baran, were later extended by a number of authors, notably Celso Furtado and Andre Gunder Frank." Tom Bottomore, ed. *A Dictionary of Marxist Thought,* 2d ed. (Cambridge, Mass.: Basil Blackwell, Inc., 1991), pp. 554–55.

47. Andre Gunder Frank, *Latin America: Underdevelopment or Revolution* (New York: Monthly Review Press, 1969).

48. Gustavo Esteva, "The Archaeology of Development: Metaphor, Myth, Threat," proposal presented before the 18th Conference of the Society for International Development (SID), Rome, July 1–4, 1985, p. 1; typed manuscript.

49. Ibid., p. 7.

50. Gustavo Esteva, "Cease Aid and Stop Development: An Answer to Hunger," paper presented to the International Seminar of Food Self-sufficiency, CESTEM-UNESCO, August 6–9, 1985, p. 11; typed manuscript.

51. Alexander R. Magno, "Authoritarianism and Underdevelopment: Notes on the Political Order of a Dependent-Capitalist Filipino Mode," in *Feudalism and Capitalism in the Philippines* (Quezon City: Foundation for Nationalist Studies, 1982), pp. 101–2.

52. In *Unequal Development: An Essay on the Social Formations of Peripheral Capitalism*, trans. Brian Pearce (New York: Monthly Review Press, 1977), Samir Amin writes, "Whereas at the center growth means development . . . in the periphery growth does not mean development" (p. 292). On a different page he writes that the underdeveloped economy is characterized by "the impossibility, whatever the level of production per head that may be attained, of going over to autocentric and autodynamic growth" (p. 202). In one formulation growth is unsatisfactory when it does not bring "development"; in the other development is unsatisfactory when it does not bring "growth." That is, one or the other term is held in reserve to symbolize an imag-

inary condition in which economic development does not somewhere generate mass poverty. Must we conclude that even Amin has stopped short of accepting the full implications of world-systems theory?

53. Robert S. McNamara, "Address to the Board of Governors," Nairobi, Kenya, September 24, 1973.

54. John Ruskin, *Unto This Last* (1860; Lincoln: University of Nebraska Press, 1967), p. 30.

55. Thorstein Veblen, *The Theory of the Leisure Class* (1899; New York: Mentor, 1953), p. 39.

56. Ivan Illich, *Tools for Conviviality* (New York: Harper, 1973), pp. 54–61.

Chapter 3   Antidemocratic Machines

1. Lewis Mumford, *The Myth of the Machine*, 2 vols. (New York: Harcourt Brace Jovanovich, 1964, 1970).

2. Siegfried Giedion, *Mechanization Takes Command* (New York: Norton, 1948), pp. 51–76.

3. Thomas Hobbes, *Leviathan*, ed. Michael Oakeshott, introd. by Richard S. Peters. (New York: Collier, 1962), pp. 100–101.

4. Karl Marx. *Capital*, vol. 1, introd. by Ernest Mandel, trans. by Ben Fowkes (Harmondsworth: Penguin, 1976), p. 563.

5. Evidence presented before the Commission on Trades Unions by Jack Nasmyth (identified by Marx as "the inventor of the steam hammer") in *Tenth Report of the Commissioners Appointed to Inquire into the Organization and Rules of Trades Unions and Other Associations: Together with Minutes of Evidence* (London, 1868), pp. 63–64; quoted in ibid., p. 563.

6. Andrew Ure, *The Philosophy of Manufacturers* (London, 1835), pp. 367–70; quoted in ibid., pp. 563–64.

7. Karl Marx and Friederich Engels, "The German Ideology," in Karl Marx and Friederich Engels, *Collected Works*, vol. 5 (Moscow: Progress Publishers, 1976), p. 47.

8. I am aware that a powerful argument can be made, at a more metaphysical level than the discussion here, that the sources of modern domination can be located in our system of knowledge itself. For two recent examples see Benjamin Barber, *Strong Democracy: Participatory Politics for a New Age* (Berkeley: University of California Press, 1984), pt. 1, and Frederique Apffell Marglin and Stephen A. Marglin, eds., *Dominating Knowledge* (Oxford: Clarendon Press, 1990).

9. Frederick Engels, "On Authority," in Karl Marx and Frederick Engels, *Collected Works*, vol. 23 (Moscow: Progress Publishers, 1988), p. 423; first pub. in *Almanacco Repubblicano per l'anno 1874*, December 1873; trans. from Italian.

10. Quoted in E. P. Thompson, *William Morris: Romantic to Revolutionary* (Stanford: Stanford University Press, 1955), p. 471.

11. These notions on Morris owe much to conversations with Sakamoto Rumi, then a Tsuda College master's degree candidate. See Sakamoto, "Political Ecology and William Morris' Utopian Thought" (M.A. thesis in Political Theory, Essex University, 1991).

12. William Morris, "A Factory as It Might Be," in G. D. H. Cole, ed., *William Morris: Studies in Prose, Studies in Verse: Shorter Poems, Lectures and Essays* (London: Nonesuch Press, 1948), p. 650.

13. Marx, *Capital*, 1:492.

14. William Morris, *News from Nowhere*, in Cole, *William Morris*, p. 168.

15. Niccolo Machiavelli, *"The Prince" and "The Discourses"* (New York: Modern Library, 1950), p. 27.

16. Marx, *Capital*, 1:499.

17. Hannah Arendt, *The Human Condition* (New York: Anchor, 1958), p. 238.

18. Ailton Krenack, ". . . Where the Mountains Are Not Only Mountains, Where the Rivers Are Relatives," interview in *AMPO: Japan-Asia Quarterly Review* 21 (Fall 1989): 47.

19. Jacques Ellul, *The Political Illusion*, trans. Konrad Dellen (1965; New York: Vintage, 1967).

20. Gerrard Winstanley, *The Law of Freedom in a Platform; or, True Magistracy Restored*, ed. Robert W. Kenney (New York: Schocken Books, 1973), p. 75. The following insights were developed in the context of conversations with then–Tsuda College master's degree candidate Urano Mariko. See Urano, "Gerrard Winstanley—Was He a Conservative?" *The Study of International Relations* (Tsuda College, Tokyo), no. 19, supplement (1992): 1–16 (in Japanese).

21. For this and other reasons George Schulman judges *The Law of Freedom* as an expression of Winstanley's disillusion. Schulman, *Radicalism and Reverence: The Political Thought of Gerrard Winstanley* (Berkeley: University of California Press, 1989), p. 216.

22. "His education was only tolerable; years later he was able to adorn his writing with a few Latin phrases, but some English usages, such as agreement in plurality between subject and verb, remained more mysterious to him than to many of his contemporaries." Robert W. Kenny, "Introduction," to Winstanley, *The Law of Freedom*, p. 10.

23. It may be that what I describe here as "the order of work" is no more than a different way of looking at what Kropotkin calls "mutual aid." Petr Kropotkin, *Mutual Aid: A Factor in Evolution*, foreword by Ashley Montagu (1902; Boston: Porter Sargent, n.d.).

24. Nakao Hajime, "Three Mile Island: The Language of Science and the People's Reality," trans. Sara Acherman and Rebecca Jennison, *Kyoto Review*, no. 12 (Spring 1980): 1–21, and no. 13 (Spring 1981): 36–53. Nakao, "Kagaku ni Azamukareta Juumintachi" ["Residents deceived by science"], in *Hoshano no Nagareta Machi* [The radiated city], ed. Hironaka Natsuko and Ogura Mieko (Tokyo: Aun Press, 1989), pp. 74–79.

25. Roger Posadas, "Leapfrogging the Scientific-Technological Gap," *Diliman Review* 34 (January–February 1986).

26. Ivan Illich, *Tools for Conviviality* (New York: Harper, 1973), p. ix.

27. See Douglas Lummis, "Starving in Sugarland," *AMPO: Japan-Asia Quarterly Review* 18, no. 1 (1986): 43–48.

Chapter 4   Democracy's Flawed Tradition

1. Baron de Montesquieu, *The Spirit of the Laws*, trans. Thomas Nugent, introd. by Franz Neumann (New York: Hafner, 1949), p. 20.

2. Ibid., p. 22.

3. Hannah Arendt, *On Revolution* (New York: Viking, 1963), chap. 6 passim. "Each time they [councils] appeared they sprang up as the spontaneous organs of the people, not only outside of all revolutionary parties but entirely unexpected by their leaders" (p. 252). Arendt saw the council system in the American, French, Russian,

and 1956 Hungarian revolutions. Surely she would have seen it in the eastern European revolutions since then, as well as in the "sectoral organizations" of the Philippine people's movement that lay behind the People's Power uprising of 1987.

4. See for example W. Robert Conner, *Thucydides* (Princeton: Princeton University Press, 1984). On the other hand the more recently published *The Democracy Reader*, which in standard fashion places Pericles' Funeral Oration at the head of its canon of democratic readings, describes the situation as "a democracy's struggle against an authoritarian enemy" and calls the speech "in a sense . . . the first Cold War document" (p. 2). Does this signal the end of the "Vietnam Syndrome" in Thucydides scholarship? Diane Ravitch and Abigail Thernstrom, eds., *The Democracy Reader* (New York: Harper Collins, 1992).

5. All quotations cited below are from *The Complete Writings of Thucydides: The Peloponesian Wars* (New York: Modern Library, 1951).

6. See the discussion of this point in Conner, *Thucydides*, pp. 63–75.

7. A similar argument is made by a Corinthian speaker before the war begins (1.40) and also in Thucydides' discussion of the revolt in Corcyra (3.84).

8. Conner, *Thucydides*, discusses the textual connection between Melos and the invasion of Sicily on pp. 147–68.

9. The quotations below are from Livy, *The Early History of Rome*, trans. Aubrey De Selincourt, introd. by R. M. Ogilvie (Harmondsworth: Penguin, 1960), pp. 129–42.

10. The quotations here and below are from Polybius, *The Rise of the Roman Empire*, trans. Ian Scott-Kilvert, introd. by F. W. Walbank (Harmondsworth: Penguin, 1979).

11. Karl Marx, "The Eighteenth Brumaire of Louis Napoleon," in Karl Marx and Frederick Engels, *Selected Works* (Moscow: Progress Publishers, 1969), 1:398.

12. J. G. A. Pocock, *The Machiavellian Movement: Florentine Political Theory and the Atlantic Republican Tradition* (Princeton: Princeton University Press, 1975).

13. "For what are thieves' purchases but little kingdoms, for in thefts the hands of the underlings are directed by the commander, the confederacy of them is sworn together, and the pillage is shared by the law amongst them?" St. Augustine, *The City of God*, ed. R. V. G Tasker, trans. John Healy, introd. by Sir Ernest Barker (London: Everyman, 1945), 1:115.

14. "[Machiavelli] was, then, both a republican and something like a protofascist." Hanna Pitkin, *Fortune Is a Woman: Gender and Politics in the Thought of Niccolo Machiavelli* (Berkeley: University of California Press, 1984), p. 4.

15. See Chapter 2n1.

16. The rape of the Sabine Women was "done in Rome's most ancient and honourable times." St. Augustine, *The City of God*, p. 55.

17. Xenophon, *Hiero* 4.3. The translation used is from Xenophon, *Scripta Minora*, trans. E. C. Marchant and G. W. Bowerstock (Cambridge: Harvard University Press [Loeb Classical Library], 1925).

18. Muto Ichiyo, "Keynote Speech: For an Alliance of Hope," keynote address delivered at the Minamata Conference of the People's Plan for the 21st Century, Minamata, Japan, August 1989, in *AMPO: Japan-Asia Quarterly Review* 21 (1989): 123. See also *The Minamata Declaration*, based largely on Muto's speech, in the same issue.

19. Samuel P. Huntington, "The Clash of Civilizations?" *Foreign Affairs* 72 (Summer 1993): 22–49.

Chapter 5   The Democratic Virtues

1. Hannah Arendt, *The Human Condition* (New York: Anchor, 1959), p. 220.

2. Plato, *Republic* 2.360e–61d.

3. Friedrich Nietzsche, "The Genealogy of Morals," *"The Birth of Tragedy" and "The Genealogy of Morals,"* trans. Francis Golffing (New York: Anchor, 1956), p. 189.

4. Ibid., p. 196.

5. Peter Sloterdijk, *Critique of Cynical Reason*, trans. Michael Eldred, foreword by Andreas Huyssen (Minneapolis: University of Minnesota Press, 1987), p. 5.

6. Ludwig Feuerbach, *The Fiery Brook: Selected Writings of Ludwig Feuerbach*, trans. and introd. by Zawar Hanfi (New York: Anchor, 1972).

7. E. M. Forster, *Two Cheers for Democracy* (London: Edward Arnold, 1951), p. 78.

8. Hannah Arendt, *On Revolution* (New York: Viking, 1963), pp. 111–37.

Conclusion   Persephone's Return

1. Sheldon S. Wolin, "Fugitive Democracy," in *Constellations: An International Journal of Critical and Democratic Theory* 1 (April 1994): 23.

2. I offer my apologies to people in the tropical and subtropical regions for the temperate-zone chauvinism built into this image. I am sure the same point could be made in tropical-zone imagery.

index